PÉTAIN'S CRIME

Paul Webster was born in Coventry and writes for the *Guardian*. Most of his career in journalism has been spent abroad, principally in Africa, Asia and Australia. He is a regular contributor to the BBC, RTÉ and French radio and television news and documentaries. One of France's most popular non-fiction writers, he has written several best-selling books on history, literature and politics, which have been translated into a dozen languages. His work includes a biography of Antoine de Saint-Exupéry, published by Pan. In 1999 he was awarded an honorary doctorate by Oxford Brookes University in recognition of his research on *Pétain's Crime*. He lives in Paris with his wife and three children.

PETAIN'S CRIME

THE FULL STORY OF FRENCH COLLABORATION IN THE HOLOCAUST

PAUL WEBSTER

PAN BOOKS

First published 1990 by Macmillan

This updated edition published 2001 by Pan Books
an imprint of Macmillan Publishers Ltd
25 Eccleston Place, London SW1W 9NF,
Basingstoke and Oxford

Associated companies throughout the world
www.macmillan.com

ISBN 0 330 48785 X

1 3 5 7 9 10 8 6 4 2

A CIP catalogue record for this book is available from
the British Library.

Typeset by SX Composing DTP, Rayleigh, Essex.
Printed and bound in Great Britain by
Mackays of Chatham plc, Chatham, Kent

December 1789
Bear in mind that, whatever one thinks, it can never be politic to condemn to debasement and oppression a multitude of men who live in the middle of us.

Maxmilien Robespierre, in support of
emancipation of French Jews

February 1942
The French Government would be happy to get rid of the Jews in any way whatsoever, without too much fuss.

German Embassy assessment of
Vichy anti-Semitic measures

July 1995
These dark hours have sullied our history for ever and are an insult to our past and traditions.

Jacques Chirac, President of the Republic, admitting
France's 'criminal' complicity in the deportations.

CONTENTS

ACKNOWLEDGEMENTS

I was given considerable help and guidance in writing this book and would particularly like to thank the librarian and staff at the Centre de Documentation Juive Contemporaine in Paris. Invaluable assistance in research was given by Patricia Dawson and Marc Uzan. Preparation was helped by a generous grant from The Authors' Foundation.

I have also drawn on the report of the Mission d'étude sur la spoliation des Juifs de France headed by Jean Mattéoli which released its three-year study of the confiscation of Jewish property in 2000. The commission, which included lawyers, historians and leaders of the Jewish community, also drew up the first complete repertory of all anti-Semitic legislation published by French and German official journals. The final accounts of Jewish property still being held by public and private institutions, which provides the basis for outstanding compensation claims, can be consulted on www.ladocfrancaise.gouv.fr.

The printed version of the legislation and commission findings can be obtained from La Documentation française, 29–31 quai Voltaire, 75344 Paris Cedex 07. A CD-ROM, published by the same government organisation, contains the facsimile of all laws of confiscation and restitution. Intended for libraries and researchers, the disk also contains guidance on thematic and chronological research material.

La Douce France

Thirty miles south of Toulouse on the road to the Spanish frontier, the bare Garonne plateau is suddenly broken by low hills of pastureland and vine above the small town of Noé. A byroad siphons off traffic from the Route Nationale into a main square surrounded by Roman-tiled houses shaded by tall plane trees. There is an air of permanent calm and unending sunshine among the stone buildings and narrow streets that lead past the fountain to a wide stretch of the Garonne river. Like so much of the Midi, the pace of life has not changed over the centuries. Noé illustrates the lasting traditions of contented French provincialism, a gentle image evoked in a popular song by Charles Trenet called 'La Douce France'.

He wrote the song about the 'dear country of my childhood' during the war, its nostalgia for village churches and rural peace doing much to raise morale. Nearly fifty years later, in 1988, it was again a popular hit after being chosen as the theme song for the presidential campaign of François Mitterrand, whose election posters also recalled a France of untroubled rural backwaters set among the harmony of rolling hills.

On that beautiful spring morning when I drove to Noé, 'La Douce France' might have been inspired by the tranquillity of the small town and its 1200 inhabitants, who had resisted the pull of time. But if the song was heard there in 1942 at the peak of its popularity, it could only have been received as a terrible hymn to hypocrisy. Although Noé had never been at the centre of military action, the small town at the heart of 'Gentle France' served as an assembly point for Jews before the long and fatal journey to Auschwitz.

In August 1942, the sick and old, who made up most of the internees in a concentration camp beside the river, were forced into cattle wagons by French gendarmes as their contribution to the Final Solution. The camp chaplain, Rabbi René Kapel, watched in tears as armed police in their familiar képis and dark blue tunics stood guard over a train whose only cargo was the helpless and the dying. 'Until the end of my life, I will see in front of me these old people, men and women, lying on the straw in cattle wagons, silent and resigned, having accepted their fate with staggering serenity,' he said.

Noé was part of a well-established system for the control, detention and eventual deportation of Jews. As early as the summer of 1940, after the collapse of the French Army, there were several big, permanent concentration camps and a string of forced-labour centres, transit areas and temporary prisons scattered about the Unoccupied Zone of the South of France, a region administered by the French Government at Vichy, a spa town in the central Auvergne, near Clermont-Ferrand.

By July 1942, more than twenty camps held thousands of Jews, and the number would be sharply increased by widespread arrests in areas of French administration. Conditions in some of the centres under French police guard were even worse than those of Noé, which caught my attention when I came across photographs taken in January 1942 of Jewish detainees, stripped naked and showing the familiar emaciated images of survivors of Belsen. The town, named after Noah, whose Ark saved humanity, had turned out to be a bitter refuge for Jews who had put their faith in France's 1789 Declaration of the Rights of Man.

Since visiting Noé, I have seen many other wartime photographs underlining French complicity in the Holocaust. Contemporary documents have also revealed a relentless bureaucratic process that isolated and ground down Jews into a form of human detritus before being handed over to the Germans for the dumps of Auschwitz. In all, 75,721 French, foreign and stateless Jews passed through this ruthless machine and nearly all disappeared for ever into the night and fog of Nazi extermination.

Thousands died of starvation, disease and neglect in French camps even before they could be packed into death trains where many deportees were killed by suffocation, thirst and police violence. Others spent years in hiding, not from the Gestapo, but from French policemen hunting them with the aid of detailed racial censuses justified by anti-Jewish laws introduced within weeks of the Fall of France in June 1940. Treatment in the camps was often barbaric and was compared by survivors to the cruelty of the German SS.

For all the horrifying aspects of a system put into place without pressure from the Germans, the most striking lesson to be drawn from France's racial insanity was the ordinariness and constitutional legality of the logic of persecution. Post-war attempts to discredit the Vichy Government and its leader, Maréchal Philippe Pétain, could not disguise the fact that his was a legitimate administration put in place by the elected members of both the National Assembly and Senate. The control of foreigners and displaced persons, which later particularly concerned Jews, had been set in motion before the war started. The hundreds of decrees that authorised racial persecution were discussed at Cabinet meetings attended by eminent pre-war politicians and officials, who encouraged hysterical outpourings from the anti-Semitic press by removing penalties for racial invective.

French initiatives which led to the wilful destruction of families, including at least 11,600 children and babies, started with apparently innocuous measures to review naturalisations in July 1940 and a government-led propaganda campaign in favour of a quota system for Jews in the professions. Relentlessly, after German political refugees were handed over to the Nazis following the Fall of France, discrimination was increased step by step without causing a popular outcry. By the summer of 1942, French police forced children of three or four years of age into cattle trucks to send them to their deaths; hitting their mothers with rifle butts to make them abandon their infant sons and daughters in French detention centres where there was little food and even less medical care.

The settings for this inhuman crusade were often even more ordinary than that in quiet villages like Noé. The main transit block in the Paris suburbs was at Drancy, near Le Bourget airport, where gendarmes robbed and tormented their unhappy prisoners. Most Jews who finished in German hands passed through Drancy, an uncompleted group of council flats occupied today by poor immigrant families in surroundings that have barely changed since they were developed before the war. From Drancy, Jews were taken by local public transport to Le Bourget railway station before being loaded into cattle trucks from a platform normally used to assemble sheep for the slaughterhouse.

French police, who carried out most arrests without German supervision, also had the honour of guarding deportees on the way to the station or of riding with them to the German frontier to ensure that no outsider gave water or food to human freight often made up of tiny children. The use of familiar green and white Paris buses, with their regular uniformed drivers, to transport Jews towards extermination was one of the many ways that genocide was given a mundane, reassuring look. The state railway system, the SNCF, regularly supplied and operated chartered passenger trains to carry Jews to detention centres inside France or to the German frontier. Among the deportees was the future European Parliament President, Simone Veil, who was sent to Drancy when sixteen years old in a third-class carriage attached to the Nice–Paris express before being taken to Auschwitz.

In numbers, the French contribution to the Holocaust may seem marginal but it provides a unique opportunity to study the politics of racism on a comprehensible scale as well as the guilty aftermath that divided the nation for more than half a century when Governments on left and right refused to face up to the past. The men, women and children sent to die in Germany from Vichy-controlled areas were the only Jews to be deported from a European territory that was not occupied by the Germans. This truth was so unpalatable that for decades there was a deliberate attempt to hide the facts and encourage a form of national amnesia. Until 1983, official school textbooks censored the fundamental information that the mass murder of Jews would have been impossible without French complicity, encouraged by the most influential areas of domestic life, including the Catholic Church, the civil service and the judiciary. Arrests and anti-Jewish legislation were attributed to German policies and the impression was given that Vichy resisted racial pressure. Successive Governments during the Fourth and Fifth Republics supported this cover-up with the result that generations of French men and women grew up unaware of Vichy's anti-Semitic statutes approved personally by the Head of State, Maréchal Pétain, and carried into practice by French officialdom.

Post-war historians and politicians were reluctant to face up to a reassessment of Vichy's betrayal of the Jews until a long and painful process of awakening national awareness began with the election of a Socialist President and Government in 1981. The most significant turning point was the rewriting of the school history manuals, an educational revolution that was not completed until 2000 when schools introduced compulsory lessons on the Holocaust that included uncompromising accounts of French treachery. And it was not until the last years of the twentieth century that President Jacques Chirac officially declared Vichy a criminal regime, inducing a fundamental change in national thinking. The country that had spent half a century trying to bury the issue rapidly introduced a national day of mourning, opened up secret archives and started compensating Jews for their suffering and for property confiscated by Pétain's Government – worth £800 million in modern currency. The Catholic Church publicly begged forgiveness 'for its sins' and decades of objections to judging ageing Vichy officials for Crimes against Humanity were swept away, leaving France to face the new millennium with an almost-clear conscience.

None of these changes was achieved without controversy, notably caused by the ambiguous attitude of François Mitterrand, President between 1981 and 1995, who obstructed trials of wartime collaborators such as the national police chief, René Bousquet, murdered in 1993 while awaiting trial for Crimes against Humanity. Mitterrand's role as a former Vichy civil servant and the extent of his friendship with Bousquet will be re-examined in the later chapters of this book on the post-war years and the damage caused to the national fabric by a reluctance to recognise Vichy's guilt until the rush of repentance in the dying years of the millennium.

When this book was first published in 1990, the evolution of France's re-interpretation of the Vichy years was impossible to predict. At that time, indifference was still general, access to archives was difficult and pressure for re-evaluation of Pétain's leadership was led almost entirely by the country's Jewish population, the biggest in Europe outside the former Soviet Union. The community, which now numbers more than 600,000, had doubled with the influx of North African Sephardi settlers after the collapse of French colonialism in Morocco, Algeria and Tunisia in the 1960s. The North African Jews quickly became the most active political and economic group in France, contributing to an era of Jewish influence that united them with established families going back 400 years and pre-war Eastern European Ashkenazi immigrants who had suffered most from wartime discrimination. The drawing together of these strands was already striking by the end of the 1980s. Mitterrand's closest personal adviser came from a Jewish family, as did the Speaker of the

National Assembly. Several Jews held Cabinet posts while two men of Polish-Jewish parentage, Cardinal Jean-Marie Lustiger and Henri Krasucki, headed the Catholic Church and the Communist-led Confédération Générale du Travail, the biggest trade union.

Helped by an impressive echelon of Jews in the top ranks of the legal profession and press, this assimilation was crucial to a campaign conducted mainly by sons and daughters of deported Jews and a handful of survivors. Their memories of wartime suffering and a sense of culpability at neglecting the search for the reasons why their relatives and friends were treated like enemies of the state became a powerful emotional motive for analysing the Vichy years. Serge Klarsfeld, the son of a Roumanian immigrant, abandoned a job in television to study law and became the recognised leader of a movement intended both to honour the memory of deported Jews and to bring Nazi and Vichy leaders to justice.

Other survivors felt shamed by the lack of recognition given to Jewish Resistance workers, particularly by the Communist Party, whose most effective urban guerrilla units were made up of newly arrived Eastern Europeans. Non-Communist movements have also been criticised for obscuring the fact that Jews were the first to rally to de Gaulle's Free French and, proportionately, provided the biggest single contribution of any religious community to the Resistance as a whole.

As a result of belated research by historians and journalists, an abundance of evidence has come to light in the past few years. Rare French and Nazi documents as well as eyewitness accounts have rectified formerly equivocal or misleading analyses of official records, political memoirs and testimony at war crime hearings in the immediate post-war years. Of even more significance is the evidence given at the much-delayed trials of Paul Touvier, an officer in Vichy's anti-Semitic militia, and Maurice Papon, a senior civil servant in wartime Bordeaux, which revealed more than fifty years of high-level protection. Their court cases in 1994 and 1997 for Crimes against Humanity confirmed that Vichy, backed by a large section of the French population, believed that anti-Semitism was a matter of urgent national interest and that Jews had to be eliminated from public life despite Papon's admission that the administration knew that deportees faced 'a cruel fate' and would probably be killed.

Tracing the relentless progress of persecution revealed little or no opposition to the principle of racial laws excluding Jews from all except menial jobs even when families had lived in France for generations. The Catholic Church, one of Vichy's most important allies along with the defence forces, big business, the judiciary and the civil service, approved measures drawn up by Pétain's personal entourage whose number included fanatical anti-Semitics. Exclusion of Jews from the civil service, professions, teaching and the entertainment industry caused little recorded reaction among Christians. Academics were among establishment figures who voluntarily declared they had no Jewish blood in order to keep their jobs or ensure promotion, a declaration often verified by official inspections of family tombstones.

Institutional anti-Semitism was made easier by general indifference and self-serving denunciation of Jewish colleagues to benefit from aryanisation procedures in which businesses, private property and artworks were confiscated and the management ceded to the informers. Cinema and theatre stars not only denounced their Jewish colleagues to take their place, but willingly worked for a Nazi-run production company that sponsored the most popular wartime films. Many of France's best-known writers supported anti-Semitism, among them the pacifist playwright Jean Giraudoux who campaigned for a Ministry of Race and said that Hitler was right to think that policy did not reach 'its superior form' until it was racial.

Protests by a few Jewish and Christian welfare organisations against the enforced internment in appalling conditions of about 40,000 foreign and stateless Jews in the so-called Zone Libre, the

Vichy-administered area, were ignored. Nor was there any public outrage when at least 3000 internees died of starvation, disease and maltreatment during the first two winters. It was only when the quiet of small provincial towns like Noé was disturbed after mass deportation began in earnest in the summer of 1942 that some of the population reacted.

While there is little evidence of a rejection in principle of isolating the Jewish population, stripping them of jobs or confiscating their goods, the purely humane response of ordinary French people to Pétain's crime is the other side of the story. Of an estimated 330,000 Jews in France at the beginning of the war, about 250,000 survived. They escaped by many means, among them emigration, living in hiding, joining the Resistance, using Jewish-run escape routes or through the protection of non-Jews inspired by personal courage or profit. Many were saved by the bureaucracy and police forces that were supposed to arrest them and thousands owed their lives to protection provided by Italian forces in south-eastern France before Rome's surrender to the Allies in 1943. Others survived openly, wearing a yellow star in the Occupied Zone in the North or with identity cards stamped 'Juif' or 'Juive' in the South, remaining free from arrest only because the liberation of France in the summer of 1944 brought the deportation programme to a halt. There were thousands of unknown heroes who defied death to save one or two Jews, while others owed their lives to a brave campaign waged in 1942 by churchmen who had approved anti-Semitic laws in silence and then were horrified by the results. Pressure from a handful of Catholic leaders, supported by Jewish and Protestant spokesmen, helped to bring the round-ups to a temporary halt in 1942 when Vichy, fearing popular reaction, broke deportation agreements with the Nazis.

Although the Germans publicly declared that Adolf Hitler had given priority to the deportation of Jews, the Vichy Government decision was accepted by Berlin without reprisals in order to maintain good economic relations with France, by then an indispensable industrial component of the Nazi war machine. Germany's complacency at what might have been seen as an act of defiance in suspending the transfer of Jews across the frontier provided striking proof that Vichy had the power to act independently of German orders on the Jewish issue.

Once Pétain had been reassured that most of the population, led by the Catholic Church, still trusted him, the deportations were resumed, but the Head of State had been right to fear a change in popular opinion when the French people were recovering from the humiliation of 1940. Protests over Pétain's failure to protect a vulnerable minority was the first positive sign of disillusionment with his regime, encouraging recruitment for the pro-Jewish underground operating escape routes and undermining the Head of State's claims to being the shield of a broken nation.

Unhappily, the laws and administrative instructions which enabled the French to carry out racial persecution were left in place, or even reinforced, after German troops moved into the Unoccupied Zone in November 1942, following the Allied invasion of North Africa. The event accelerated opposition to Jewish arrests among the French but the Germans fully exploited the domestic legal infrastructure to justify repression. Zealous French administrators, like Maurice Papon, and armed auxiliaries, such as Paul Touvier, were able to claim at their trials that they had acted within a legitimate framework of more than 1700 pieces of anti-Jewish legislation justifying French police co-operation at varying levels and covering the recruitment of thousands of French staff to aid the Gestapo. Despite the reaction to the 1942 arrests, no evidence has emerged that Vichy gave any secret instructions to obstruct deportations, which continued until the regime fell in September 1944. Instead, Pétain's administration was actively drawn into the Nazi racial murder policy on its own soil with the development of a Milice, dedicated to 'eradicating the Jewish leprosy' by summary executions, and which became a force more feared than the SS.

In the summer of 1987, the show trial of Klaus Barbie, the Lyons Gestapo chief, took place in the south-eastern city that was the capital of both collaboration and Resistance in the Free Zone. Although the hearing revived public condemnation of collaboration and maltreatment of Jews, the trial had a serious failing: it treated the story only from 1943, when the German Army had taken control of the whole territory, confiscating meaningful political independence from Pétain. Much of the evidence submitted before Barbie was given a life sentence for Crimes against Humanity – he died in prison in 1991 – underlined high-level French collaboration. Among the often-mentioned names of living wartime functionaries who had helped the Nazis were René Bousquet; Jean Leguay, his deputy as national police chief; Paul Touvier of the Lyons Milice; and Maurice Papon, responsible for Jewish Affairs in wartime Bordeaux.

Private moves to prosecute all four had been struggling against official obstructions since the first initiatives were made as early as 1979. Although Touvier and Papon were eventually brought to court, the two most important figures, Bousquet and Leguay, died before the conclusion of multiple delaying actions by the judiciary, encouraged by Mitterrand's public statements that exhuming the Vichy period threatened civil order. At the time, a significant measure of public opinion was on his side. The trial of any leading Vichy official was, by implication, an attack on the reputation of Philippe Pétain, who died in jail in 1951 at the age of ninety-five. Mitterrand was among those who felt the wartime leader had been wrongly treated.

Despite the fact that Pétain had been sentenced to death and then reprieved in 1945 for high treason (the Jewish question was only briefly raised), post-war historians had reinforced Charles de Gaulle's view that the First World War hero had been manipulated and was too old to be responsible for his acts. Blame was shifted to his Prime Minister, Pierre Laval, who died in front of a firing squad after an expeditious trial for treachery. By focusing on Laval as the primary villain, a relentless campaign to rehabilitate the Maréchal made considerable progress during the Mitterrand era. The Vichy leader's original supporters were mainly soldiers from the Great War and, as those died, their places were taken by the many ordinary people who saw the Maréchal as a national saviour after the 1940 collapse. On a more extreme level, adulation of Pétain concentrated in the neo-Fascist National Front created by Jean-Marie Le Pen, which used Vichy legislation as a blueprint for its own anti-immigrant programme.

Evidence given at the Touvier and Papon hearings, as well as the opening of national archives and Chirac's condemnation of Vichy as a criminal regime, cut across the indulgent image of a misguided and befuddled leader. Pétain was at the heart of anti-Semitic legislation from the beginning, appointing an entourage that had campaigned for Jewish statutes well before the war. He had more power than any French leader since Napoleon and had total control over his ministers, even sacking Laval in a showdown in 1940. During the most intense period of voluntary collaboration, between July 1940 and April 1942 when Laval returned, Pétain's regime was based on a military hierarchy in which his chief executive, Admiral François Darlan, a partisan of racial laws, accepted orders in conformity with his lesser rank.

Pétain also claimed personal responsibility for all policies, saying that he alone should be judged by history, a request that all leaders of the Fifth Republic declined. Even Jacques Chirac, who damned Vichy as criminal, avoided mentioning Pétain by name, although trying to dissociate the wartime Head of State from the consequences of his abuse of power is a position now defended only by an obstinate and dwindling rearguard.

In the decade before the war, Pétain had considered taking up a political career and took as his adviser a constitutional lawyer,

Raphaël Alibert, who drew up the first Jewish Statute in October 1940. Anti-Semitism was Alibert's obsession and he had campaigned all his life against the legacy of the Revolution, whose leaders made France the first European nation to emancipate Jews in 1791. Ideological right-wing anti-Semitism, subscribed to by Pétain, developed well before the end of the nineteenth century and became an act of faith during the Dreyfus affair, when a Jewish army officer was falsely imprisoned on Devil's Island on a trumped-up charge of spying.

The Army was a stronghold of the anti-Dreyfus camp, which remained active throughout the pre-war years during the anti-Jewish crusades which depended on cold reason or induced xenophobia. They reached a new pitch with the arrival of Austrian and German Jews after Hitler came to power and by the election of a Jewish Prime Minister, Léon Blum, in 1936. Many Vichy leaders were associated with these campaigns, openly calling for discriminatory legislation long before Pétain came to power, accusing Jews of conspiracy against the state and of associating with enemy Governments. Strong links between immigrant Jews and the Communist Party reinforced this conviction and were used to justify deportation.

Crude ethnic arguments and political opportunism were everpresent but French anti-Semitism was distinguished from simplistic xenophobia by the intellectual brilliance of some of the most influential writers and politicians of the day. They pretended that Nazi-style insistence on racial factors was not a motivation, arguing that France operated only what was called 'state anti-Semitism' inspired by a belief that Jews were incapable of national solidarity and were intent on destroying national values. Eventually, this semantic justification merged with the Nazis' simple answer to the Jewish problem – mass murder.

Because this is not a book about German policy, it contains little detail about atrocities committed outside France except to show the inevitable outcome of anti-Semitic legislation. It is also more pertinent to demonstrate the long-term damage of racial policies and the difficulties of reopening a debate. Official post-war apathy, which included delay in commemorating memorials until the last decade of the twentieth century, was not entirely to blame for belated reassessment. After the purge of collaborationists during the liberation of France, the country went from crisis to crisis. Feeble Governments wrecked the coherence of the post-war Fourth Republic while de Gaulle's Fifth Republic was created in an atmosphere of civil war. Defeats in Indo-China and Algeria removed a national will to dwell on the past.

Jewish families, themselves, could not face up to the trauma of Vichy treachery, an attitude recalled by the Archbishop of Paris, Cardinal Lustiger, who converted to Catholicism while on the run from the French police. In his family the subject was taboo. 'The suffering was too great,' he said. 'No one was able to talk about it. Even I couldn't speak about it. I don't believe there was a single Jewish father of that generation who talked of this to his children or even wanted to.'

Like many of his contemporaries, the cardinal still avoids talking about the issue, although he has more cause for personal anger than many. His predecessor as Archbishop of Paris, Cardinal Emmanuel Suhard, gave enthusiastic support to Pétain's sanctimonious National Revolution dedicated to a moral revival, but remained silent over racial laws in 1940. Without these discriminatory measures, Lustiger's mother would not have been arrested by French police and sent to Drancy before being gassed in Auschwitz.

This is only one of many personal stories quoted in this book to show how Pétain failed to carry out a promise to protect Jews from Nazi reprisals. I was continually reminded that, whatever historical and social lessons can be drawn from French complicity in the Holocaust, it was first of all a sequence of individual family tragedies further darkened by France's treacherous claim to being 'une terre d'asile' – a land of refuge. Nearly every Jew I spoke to had lost a father, mother or child during the Vichy years and would continue to suffer for the rest of their lives. Each seemed to be haunted by a desire to comprehend the betrayal. Some were desperate to lay blame, others were determined to forgive.

Among the many people I saw was Robert Badinter, then president of the Constitutional Council, a form of supreme court. He had just written a book about the Jewish emancipation in 1791, a campaign led by a Catholic parish priest, Abbé Henri Grégoire, whose remains were transferred to the Panthéon in 1989. Badinter was a former Justice Minister who successfully campaigned for the abolition of capital punishment in 1981 and has always criticised the execution of collaborators. The interview in Badinter's office was particularly moving because his book was dedicated to his father, Simon, who went to France from Russia in 1917 and was sent to his death in Germany in 1943.

'He was passionately attached to France long before he came here,' his son told me. 'He read everything French and refused to let us speak any other language. He came to France for a special reason: he saw the country as a shrine of human rights. He believed that the 1789 Declaration des droits de l'homme meant all it promised – that all men were born equal.'

Like thousands of other Jews, Simon Badinter took refuge in the Vichy-controlled area of France after being forced to quit his business as a fur trader because of aryanisation policies. Although he had to scrape a living through menial work, he still spent much of his time helping refugees at the Lyons headquarters of the official Vichy welfare institution, the Union Générale des Israélites de France, UGIF. While there he was arrested during a raid led by Klaus Barbie.

After a lifetime arguing in court or defending Government legal policies, Robert Badinter is a man who weighs his words with the utmost care but when we discussed the appropriate historical judgement of the man who led France during the anti-Semitic persecution, he made this assessment of Pétain: 'Un salaud, un vrai salaud' – a swine, a real swine.

In 1945, the Maréchal was brought to trial in a hearing that passed rapidly over the Jewish question. 'J'ai toujours, et de la façon la plus véhémente, defendu les Juifs,' he said, pushing aside the fact that his most active ministers, with equal vehemence, set up an anti-Semitic legal apparatus in an atmosphere of refined cruelty and hysterical cynicism. At Noé, at the heart of La Douce France, there was no need to go far for evidence that Pétain had lied. In 1942, Noé's cruel conditions were cited by a courageous clergyman, Archbishop Jules-Géraud Saliège of Toulouse, when he publicly condemned Vichy for treating Jews 'like a foul herd'. At the Liberation, the comfortless 125 barrack huts where the sick and old were housed before deportation were used as prisons for collaborationist camp guards, policemen, civil servants and profiteers who had all been well served by Pétain's Crime.

CHAPTER ONE

The Origins of Hate

A T DAWN ON 16 July 1942, the Rajsfus family was awakened by a knock on the door at their two-room flat in Vincennes, a suburb on the eastern limits of Paris. They recognised the uniformed policeman outside as their former neighbour on the third storey of the recent but grim block of apartments built incongruously on top of an old mansion. The policeman was accompanied by another Frenchman in civilian clothes. They told the parents and their two adolescent children to pack bags with blankets, sheets, working clothes, pullovers and their ration cards.

A detailed list of basic needs had been suggested by the Gestapo during weeks of negotiation with the French police on a proposed mass arrest of Jews. The policeman neighbour, Marcel Mulot, was not aware of this. His instructions that morning were taken from a long briefing prepared by the Paris municipal force chief, Emile Hennequin, a German-born former Tsarist police officer. Mulot, who had never sought much contact with the Polish émigré family when living next door, carried out the Rajsfus arrests without any attempt at friendliness. Orders sent to the Vincennes station three days before had insisted on the operation being completed 'quickly, without any useless words or commentary'. Even if he had felt like giving an explanation, Mulot would have been stopped by the plainclothes inspector who accompanied him.

The two men carried out the next part of their written orders, turning off the gas and electricity, before escorting the family to an assembly point in the garage of a private house in a nearby road. Vincennes police force had been told to arrest 153 Jews that morning, all of them officially registered in a massive filing system kept by a special French squad charged with keeping records of French and foreign Jews. About 100 men, women and children were eventually hustled into the garage to wait for Paris city buses that would take them either to a transit centre in the Paris indoor bicycle stadium, the Vélodrome d'Hiver, or straight to the suburban concentration camp in council flats at Drancy. By then, police guards had told the arrested Jews that they were being sent to work camps in Silesia in German-occupied Poland.

The anxious families were not yet aware that they represented only a tiny group caught in the biggest anti-Jewish operation since the Fall of France, a French police swoop which became known as 'La Grande Rafle' or Black Thursday. The youngest member of the Rajsfus family, Maurice, was fourteen years old at the time and, for much of the day, he waited without food and water in the crowded garage watched by the occupants of flats opposite. When it was decided that the children should go home because transport arrangements were chaotic, most parents could not face separation and clung to their sons and daughters. Maurice's mother, an active member of the Polish Socialist Bund movement, told her two children to return home.

They arrived to find the concierge already looting the sparsely furnished flat where the family had lived on the father's earnings as a market hawker, selling socks from a barrow because he was unable to find a job meriting his qualifications as a language teacher. Like so many of his Jewish friends, Maurice's father had left anti-Semitic Poland soon after the First World War expecting to be safe in France, a country that prided itself on being 'une terre d'asile', a land of refuge. Instead, he and his wife were sent to be murdered in Germany and their two children never saw them again.

During the rest of the war, Maurice and his sister continued to live in the flat, sharing the anxiety of pariahs forced to wear a yellow star, subject to an 8 p.m. curfew and restricted to shopping between 3 p.m. and 4 p.m. They survived because new deportation programmes intended to empty France of all its Jews could not be completed before the Liberation.

Their story has elements typical of thousands of family tragedies, among them the fact that the original scene of the arrest has not changed since 1942. The block of cheap thirties' flats, built to accommodate Parisian workers or immigrant labour, remains exactly as it was. On any hot summer day, like the one during La Grande Rafle, the atmosphere of Black Thursday remains alive among the long shadows in the concrete courtyard where Maurice's father kept his hawker's barrow.

The policeman, Marcel Mulot, still lived nearby in retirement and, like most of his colleagues who arrested Jews, could not see why he should be called to account for obeying routine orders. Few of the 9000 men mobilised for the arrests have had to justify the help they gave to the Nazis, although the chief, Emile Hennequin, was sentenced to eight years' forced labour for collaboration.

At Vincennes town hall no official record was kept of the raid and no memorial was proposed for the Jews who disappeared. At the time, no press reports were published and no photographs were released. Precise details of the events before and during La Grande Rafle only came to light much later in captured Gestapo documents describing the two-day operation involving every *arrondissement,* or local district, in the capital and every local commissariat.

An exact count of arrests was sent to Berlin on 18 July 1942 by SS-Lieutenant Heinz Röthke, the newly appointed Gestapo officer responsible for Jewish affairs in Paris. In all, 12,884 people, including 4051 children and 5802 women, were taken either to Drancy or to concentration camps near Orleans in the Occupied Zone south of the capital. Nearly all died in Germany, where some were transported within a week of being caught.

The sequel to the Paris operation was even more cynical. Because police failed to reach a promised quota, about 10,000 Jews held in Free Zone concentration camps like Noé were forced into trains and handed over to the Germans. The eleven weeks between 16 July and 30 September 1942 were the blackest period of the war when 33,000 Jews were sent to their deaths as a result of policies decided by a legitimate French government, technically at peace and recognised by democratic nations like the United States.

Legal persecution of Jews began with the appointment of Maréchal Philippe Pétain in July 1940, but it would be wrong to interpret the anti-Semitism that led to the nationwide arrests as an aberration linked to Nazi pressure. Racial intolerance was so deeply instilled into conservative ideology that discrimination would probably have been put into effect by a Pétainist-style government even in peacetime.

For 150 years there had been resentment at the Revolution's decision to emancipate Jews, the first community in Europe to be given equal rights. Calls to eliminate them during the nineteenth and twentieth centuries swung between intellectually subtle arguments over their inability to integrate and crude rallying cries for their isolation or expulsion as the enemy within. By the time the Vichy Government began its racial purity campaign, the theory that Jews were one of the main causes of national disgrace was a popularly held assumption.

Vichy based its action on what was called 'state anti-Semitism' to distinguish it from 'anti-Semitism of the skin'. Jews were excluded from most professions on the grounds that they were incapable of fulfilling their duties as citizens because of divided patriotic and religious loyalties. One of the simplest examples was the incompatibility between the obligations of compulsory military service and recognition of the Sabbath.

Unfortunately, the fundamental debate on whether a community with so many religious differences could be absorbed into a rigid, lay society was not satisfactorily concluded when Maximilien Robespierre and a progressive Catholic priest, Henri Grégoire, persuaded the National Assembly to grant Jews equal treatment under the Declaration of the Rights of Man. Grégoire preached in the Jewish areas of eastern France and was shocked by the degradation, humiliation and persecution of Jews, comparing their treatment to the black slaves in French colonies.

Generations of anti-Semitic campaigners, republican and royalist, exploited the Revolution's failure to clarify the duties of citizenship to call for a reversal of emancipation. Much of the debate was hypocritical, disguising an irrational hatred of Jews. By 1940, anti-Semitism had been reinforced by a more easily recognisable form of xenophobic racism because of immigration from eastern Europe.

In the end, the established Jewish community, whose patriotism had been tested by the Great War, and the detested eastern European immigrants shared a common fate. Essentially, both were betrayed by a naive belief in France's proclaimed role as the founder of human rights and the land of asylum. Foreign Jews were to die in much greater numbers, but French Jews could be forgiven for feeling that they were the real victims of political treachery and bad faith.

Only three or four generations separated established families from memories of the pre-Revolution period when Jews lived in abject poverty subject to special taxes and allowed to do only menial jobs. During centuries of royalist rule, family survival depended on a rigorous respect for the law and a humble acceptance of the most extreme forms of intolerance, periodically marked by massacres and expulsion.

Comparison made by some modern historians between persecution of the Jews and campaigns against Christian groups like the Cathares in the Medieval period and Protestants later is irrelevant because Jews never posed a political threat and were too few in number to be an economic force. At the Revolution, they numbered barely 40,000 in a country of 25 million Christians. Defenceless and despised as outcasts, they became public scape-goats, irrationally blamed and punished even for natural disasters like crop failures.

Emancipation came in two phases. The first Jews to be made citizens in 1790 were an exceptional case: rich Sephardis from Bordeaux, descendants of families exiled during the Inquisition. Many claimed to be Christians while practising their religion in secret. They had achieved a form of assimilation long before their community was given full rights.

This was followed a year later by citizenship for the dominant but scattered Ashkenazi sects in Lorraine and German-speaking Alsace. The peasant community traced its origins to Ashkenazi settlements in Poland where one out of three people was Jewish. Those in France conversed in their own form of Yiddish, maintaining links with other poor exiles in Germany and Austria.

The garrison and farming area on the eastern border covered cities like Nancy, Strasbourg and Mulhouse where anti-Semitism was traditional. Many Jews in the region were involved in textile, grain and horse-trading. While most lived from hand to mouth, usually from petty usury, a few built up fortunes as suppliers to the Army.

Official integration, even at a religious level, was reasonably quick, despite a revival of anti-Semitism in the late Napoleonic era. By then, Bonaparte had encouraged the grouping together of tiny religious communities, known as Shtetls, into a centralised Consistory system in which the administrators were made equal to Catholic and Protestant hierarchies in 1831. The state took over payment of rabbis and, in 1846, all vestiges of separate treatment disappeared.

Behind the policy was a belief that Jews would be assimilated into a conformist, secular society as they abandoned strict religious observance and took advantage of educational and political institutions. Attempts to disturb this process by attacking Jews as racially incompatible had only limited impact in the first half of the nineteenth century, although spurious ethnic studies like Arthur de Gobineau's *Essai sur l'inégalité des races humaines* in 1855 was later to become part of Nazi propaganda.

By the end of the nineteenth century, Jews could look back on a remarkable period of material success. Many had achieved fame in politics, law, literature or the arts. Some personalities with Jewish backgrounds like the actress Sarah Bernhardt, the writer Marcel Proust and the painter Camille Pissarro had become international figures.

The intellectual, academic and political influence of Jews continued to flourish until Vichy's anti-Semitic laws of 1940, but the warnings that they would have to pay a blood price for emancipation had been sounded seventy years before.

Anti-Semitic doctrines that influenced Vichy officials can be traced directly to the aftermath of France's defeat by Bismarck's Prussia in 1870. Before the national collapse in Napoleon III's reckless war, anti-Jewish feeling was mainly a reaction to usury and left-wing condemnation of capitalism, considered to be a Jewish invention. Jew-hating as an emotional right-wing cause developed rapidly after 1870. One of the first to suffer was the composer Jacques Offenbach whose music had been the heart and soul of the gay Second Empire. Offenbach, a naturalised German Jew, was blamed for undermining French martial spirit and ostracised.

In 1873, Maréchal Patrice MacMahon, a monarchist like Pétain and one of the defeated 1870 generals, was appointed President by Parliament. He had restored his prestige by ruthlessly destroying the Paris left-wing Commune in 1871 when his troops killed 20,000 Parisians. The Communards had set up a popular administration that became the inspiration of the Communist movement.

The morally repressive atmosphere that followed the Commune's destruction and the mass deportation of Communards to forced labour colonies foreshadowed Pétain's National Revolution. As in 1940, there was a revival of strict bourgeois Catholicism, narrow-minded nationalism and nostalgia for the pre-Revolutionary *ancien régime* of the Capetian kings. Anti-Semitism was stimulated by the search for a hidden enemy to explain the French collapse in the Prussian war. Jews were an obvious target because most were from border areas and had kept links with German communities. Despite a deliberate policy of integration, in which rabbis preached in French and wore a form of *soutane,* the Jewish religion was still seen as an impediment to loyalty.

Virulent anti-Semitic campaigns started again with the arrival in Paris of thousands of fleeing patriotic French Jews following the seizure of Alsace and parts of Lorraine by the Germans. There was a flood of what were to become familiar caricatures of hook-nosed, repulsively ugly, rapacious Jews barely able to make themselves understood through thick German accents – images that would be copied by Pétain's propaganda services.

By the end of the nineteenth century, the Jewish community had grown to 80,000. About three-quarters, including most Bordeaux Jews, settled in Paris where they were accused of scurrilous trading practices. New arrivals concentrated in the 9th, 10th, 11th and 12th *arrondissements* where they dominated the clothes business, increasing the impact of their relatively small numbers.

Jews either ignored the hostility or treated it as a passing phenomenon in a naive attitude that was sustained during the more intense anti-Semitism of the thirties. The nineteenth-century Jewish sociologist, Emile Durkheim, the son of an Alsatian rabbi, wrote that assimilation had already been achieved by 1890. This was the dominant feeling in a community known for its often unctuous respect for established order and its care in avoiding political provocation.

Rabbis projected a sycophantic form of patriotism. One prayer included the line: 'France, of all countries, is the one which You prefer because it is most like You.' The Consistory spoke of the similarities between Judaism and French civilisation, describing the French as the new Chosen People.

To the anger of a small group of politically aware politicians like the future Prime Minister Léon Blum, the Consistory, dominated by the De Rothschild banking family, refused to grasp the significance of vengeful intolerance that developed around the Church, the Army, big business and the civil service. Community leaders seemed unaware that Jewish emancipation was at the centre of a fundamental political argument over the merits of a republic or monarchy.

Anti-Semitic campaigns were dominated by royalists who wanted a return to pre-Revolution values. They argued that both democracy and Bonapartism had brought France nothing except internal upheaval and defeat by foreign armies. A permanent hierarchy was needed with the highest places reserved for those of pure French descent cherishing conservative ideals. By inference, Jews were excluded on three grounds – their race, their religion and their attachment to the republican system which had liberated them.

Under MacMahon, the Third Republic constitution was finally established in 1875 as a holding operation to prepare for the return of a king. The initiative broke down because of divisions inside the right which continued into the next century. Only the campaign for racial purity remained as a joint priority for right-wing factions even when divided by personality battles or quarrels over the best system of authoritarian government.

In another foretaste of Vichy, nineteenth-century anti-Semitism intensified to fill the gap caused by dissension on the right. Specious racial theories increased when laws forbidding religious insults were lifted in 1881. The most striking example of a rising anti-Jewish current was provided by a journalist Edouard

Drumont in his 1886 book, *La France Juive.* His condemnation of racial mixing went into more than one hundred editions and enabled him to found the Anti-Semitic League and the anti-Jewish newspaper, *La Libre Parole.*

Drumont's book and newspaper stirred up hatred that led to a national crisis with the Dreyfus Affair when the Jewish officer Captain Alfred Dreyfus was arrested on false spying charges. The controversy split the country from the day he was stripped of rank in the courtyard of the Ecole Militaire in Paris in January 1895 until his rehabilitation ten years later.

If Dreyfus had not been a Jew, the Affair would have been no more than a minor controversy in which jealous and incompetent rivals tried to destroy the career of a fellow officer by forging evidence of spying for Germany. The accusation against Dreyfus, the first Jewish staff officer, was revealed in *La Libre Parole* newspaper, quickly followed by *La Croix,* an equally anti-Semitic publication belonging to a fanatical Catholic order, the Assumptionists.

The most important right-wing figures in the army, politics, civil service, judiciary and journalism, backed by the petite bourgeoisie, recklessly seized on the accusation as proof that Jews were incapable of loyalty to their adopted country. The right was further exasperated by Dreyfus' stoical acceptance of banishment to Devil's Island penal colony, since his attitude was seen as an attempt to prove Jewish readiness to put the country's interests first.[1]

When the lies and cheating were exposed and Dreyfus' opponents disgraced, a whole generation had been marked by the long-running struggle that led to the fall of a right-wing government. The right never admitted its defeat, nor that the real culprit was a degenerate aristocrat, and instead reinforced its anti-Semitism. A desire for revenge was still evident in the Vichy years, during which the dominating influences were men who had been in their early twenties at the height of the Affair or whose fathers had been politicians or officials at the time.

A policy of smearing Jews, powerful defenders of the democracy that had emancipated them, had already proved a seductive theme for conservatives on at least two occasions. The Drumont book revealed the solidarity of the petit bourgeois, shopkeeper electorate with the Catholic Church, aristocracy, big industry and the Army. They were joined together by a lust for power, greed, opportunism, belligerent nationalism and distorted spirituality in addition to well-intentioned attempts to find a more stable system of government.

The same sentiments were exploited by the fanatical Assumptionists, an order founded in 1847 to revive French Catholic faith by pilgrimages to Rome and, later, Lourdes. Its three enemies were Freemasons, Protestants and Jews, whom it tried to combat with big-business methods linked to a bank, the Union Générale.

When the bank collapsed in 1882, ruining thousands of small savers, the Assumptionist newspaper *La Croix* invented a Jewish conspiracy to explain the disaster. The accusation persisted for decades, finding echoes in Vichy. The Archbishop of Lyons, Cardinal Pierre-Marie Gerlier, justified his original lack of reaction to Pétain's anti-Jewish laws by recalling that his father had been ruined in the bankruptcy.

In the years leading up to the hysteria of the Dreyfus Affair, *La Croix* or its sister weekly, *Le Pèlerin,* repeatedly exploited the anti-Semitic theme. They joined campaigns that blamed Jews for other financial scandals, and a useful precedent for slandering Jews was confirmed in 1892 when the French Panama Canal operation collapsed, impoverishing thousands of small investors.

The anti-Semitic campaign which began after the 1870 war received its symbolic defeat when Alfred Dreyfus was fully rehabilitated in 1906 and awarded the Légion d'Honneur in the military school courtyard where he had been disgraced a decade before. During the Great War, he rose to the rank of lieutenant-colonel, but the scandal left lasting political divisions. Anti-Semitism and philo-Semitism had become passwords for right and left.

The Republic emerged triumphant from a confrontation in which the defence of a Jew was at its core. Contempt for Jews was proof of belonging to right-wing movements which wanted to revive the monarchy, detested Parliament, opposed the ideal of universal equality or wanted to create a form of Fascism in which Catholic values, including isolation of Jews, was dominant. Anti-Semitism was to become an act of faith demanded from left-wing deserters like Pierre Laval and Jacques Doriot, who respectively quit the Socialist and Communist movements in the thirties and became leading Vichy personalities.

On the other hand, it was impossible to hate Jews and remain a progressive, anti-clerical republican dedicated to democracy and social justice. Defence of these principles had been at the centre of pro-Dreyfus campaigns led by giant figures of the left like Emile Zola and the future Premier, Georges Clemenceau. The same principles were the guiding force of the new Radical Party, founded in 1901, a centre–left group that became the dominant political movement until the war. It was particularly attractive to an emergent political lobby of young, rich Jews.

If Jews felt more secure after Dreyfus' vindication and by a left-wing landslide parliamentary victory that followed, they were further comforted on the road to assimilation by the appointment in 1914 of the first Jew to the Académie Française, a temple of the French establishment. The philosopher Henri Bergson added to this honour by being awarded the Nobel Prize for Literature in 1927. The esteem in which Bergson was held added to the illusion that anti-Semitism was a discredited rallying cry. But, only fourteen years later, Bergson's death was accelerated by racial laws administered by French police that killed many other leading academics, scientists, teachers, writers and poets.

Bergson had to register as a Jew at his local commissariat in Paris' 16th *arrondissement* in autumn 1940, although he was eighty-one years old and seriously ill. He went in his dressing-gown and slippers, barely able to walk, as an act of solidarity with the Jewish community despite a late secret conversion to Catholicism. The ordeal added to the humiliation of the most eminent philosopher of his generation. A few weeks later, in January 1941, he died.

If the anti-Semitic campaigns sometimes appeared to lose their impact after the Dreyfus Affair, the right never abandoned its virulence. One of the most ominous events during the Affair was the foundation of the royalist Action Française movement in 1899 by the Provençal poet Charles Maurras. He was thirty-one at the time. As he aged, his white beard and hair gave a patriarchal look to a man who, despite being narrow-minded, misanthropic, mean and stone deaf, became the emotional inspiration of all right-wing elements embittered after their defeat by the pro-Dreyfus lobby. It was Maurras who invented the intellectual formula of state anti-Semitism, that allowed Vichy supporters to deny charges of irrational racism. However it was his friend, the Duke of Orleans, pretender to the French throne, who promoted another argument called economic anti-Semitism which gave spurious credibility to the seizure of Jewish property. This justified attacks on Jewish financial interests considered detrimental to France's 'natural genius'.

Inspiration for future Vichy legislation can be read in articles written by Maurras in the ultra-nationalist newspaper, *La Cocarde*, as early as 1896. Referring to Dreyfus as a German-Jewish spy, Maurras called for the expulsion of 'thousands of unbearable and dangerous métèques'. Implicitly identifying Jews from Alsace as non-French, he recalled Athenian laws in which foreigners paid special taxes, were given only menial jobs and were denied the right of property.

Like the Assumptionists, Maurras' main enemies were Protestants, Freemasons and Jews, and he felt that even naturalised families should be excluded from responsible jobs for at least three generations. Although he was a classical Graeco-Roman scholar, his use of the word 'métèques' to describe foreigners soon became a fashionable insult. Maurras became one of the most dangerous racist cranks of the century through his newspaper, *L'Action Française,* founded in 1908, three years after he set up the militant Ligue de l'Action Française. In the newspaper, Maurras expressed an endless series of hates including the Revolution, the Republic, democracy, parliament, the proletariat, free education and all forms of social justice; at the same time he yearned to turn back the clock to the eighteenth century.

He was an agnostic who once described the Gospels as having been written by 'four shabby Jews' and Christianity as the 'religion of the rabble', yet the Church was one of his greatest allies until the Vatican banned the organization in 1926. Thirteen years later, when Maurras was elected to the Académie Française, the movement was reinstated by Pius XII. At the time, Maurras' newspaper had reached the peak of hysterical calls for the destruction of Jews and he had recently been jailed for inciting murderous attacks on the Socialist leader, Léon Blum.

In his ambiguous relationship with the Catholic Church, Maurras was later outdone by Pétain, who was sycophantically honoured by Church leaders and advised by the Vatican on racial laws, although he was an agnostic who had put himself outside the Church by marrying a divorcée.

While Maurras played no direct political role, his personal influence was crucial to defining large areas of Vichy's programme. The Action Française movement, which repeatedly called for the extermination of those who opposed Maurras' extremism, provided the pre-war network of emotional and theoretical contacts for the most powerful figures of Pétain's administration, notably in respect of anti-Jewish legislation.

Maurras also gathered around him brilliantly provocative young writers, including Robert Brasillach, editor of the anti-Semitic newspaper *Je Suis Partout,* who was executed at the

Liberation. They were attracted by writing for an elite audience of soldiers, senior civil servants, lawyers, doctors, bishops, priests, writers, the nobility and right-wing students, whose influence was out of all proportion to the movement's membership, reflected by the circulation of *L'Action Française*, which sold only 50,000 copies a day.

Writers like Leon Daudet – whose father, the humorist Alphonse Daudet, opposed Dreyfus – and the historian Jacques Bainville wrote such vile and transparent propaganda that Maurras' ideas should have been destroyed by ridicule. That feeling was shared by the American foreign correspondent and author William L. Shirer, who, while reporting in Paris between the wars, felt that *L'Action Française* journalists were fairly harmless eccentrics saved by their witty invective. He was often astonished at the waste of talent on what he thought was a forlorn cause, but he usually began his day by turning to the front page of *L'Action Française* to read the 'outrageous outbursts of Daudet, Maurras and their frenzied collaborators'.

'That, at the beginning of the twentieth century, the well-born, right-thinking upper classes, and especially Army officers, priests, bishops, writers and intellectuals could take such drivel seriously reveals the sterility of the Right,' Shirer recalled in his book, *The Collapse of the Third Republic*. 'Maurras and his followers did succeed in inoculating an elite with burning contempt for the Third Republic. It convinced them that the regime was full of crooked swindlers and traitors destroying the country.'

L'Action Française fed the moral outrage of the defeated anti-Dreyfus faction throughout the twenties when anti-Semitism was still rabid but less effective. French Jews had proved their patriotism in the Great War. The arrival of 25,000 Russian Jews in the years up to 1914 had been absorbed without resentment by a population saturated by the Dreyfus Affair. When Edouard Drumont's *Libre Parole* newspaper collapsed in 1924 for lack of readers, Jewish claims that anti-Semitism was a passing fashion seemed justified.

There were repeated attempts to fan the flames through the twenties and thirties with a flood of scurrilous literature hoping to revive Drumont's success of forty years earlier. Publications like *L'Invasion Juive* in 1927 described Jews as 'oriental lepers and the real vermin of the world' and, in a warning that would be taken literally thirteen years later, the French were told to watch out for 'hooked noses, fleshy lips, crinkly hairstyles, the owners of which jargonise in their native Yiddish'.

Few writers could resist joining in a debate that was started at the end of the century by a Catholic novelist Maurice Barrès, whose hard-line anti-Semitic opinions were taken up venomously by novelists like Louis-Ferdinand Céline and Pierre Drieu La Rochelle, both of whom collaborated with the Nazis. Brasillach, Céline and Drieu La Rochelle were all elegant writers from middle-class backgrounds, but they used crude gutter language when referring to Jews. Brasillach claimed that he was only putting instinctive French hostility to Jews into words.

There were several newspapers aimed specifically at an Action Française readership and some of the most virulent, like *Gringoire,* transferred to the Free Zone in 1940 to support Vichy's crusade. Among the working classes, the damage was caused by the huge success of *L'Ami du Peuple,* which published a million copies daily in 1930 and claimed to reach 3 million people because it was cheaper than other papers. Its founder, an illiterate cosmetics millionaire, François Coty, who was also behind the Fascist Solidarité Française movement, led his own campaign against Jews and foreigners with a hatred that even Maurras found hard to match.

Coty's success with a traditionally left-wing urban electorate worried the Communist daily newspaper, *L'Humanité,* whose editor Paul Vaillant-Couturier said in a 1934 leader that *L'Ami du Peuple*'s influence had 'reached the tragic proportions of a popular epidemic' and that Coty was addressing 'shameful demagogy at the poorest'.

By then, the supposedly dying embers of Jew-hating had been revived with the arrival of 30,000 German Jews fleeing Hitler. Even though government restrictions meant that only 7000 settled in Paris, they added to a flood of Polish immigrants who had turned parts of the capital into ghettos. It was enough to reinvigorate an unstoppable campaign to rid the country of all Jews.

Two calumnies developed side by side. One was the fear that foreigners would take French jobs during the depression. The second was a revival of the basic accusation of the Dreyfus Affair that Jews were traitors by nature.

Often repeated arguments in the anti-Semitic press were summed up by two articles. In 1927, Henri-Robert Petit, in *L'Invasion Juive,* warned against Jews who had 'escaped from all the ghettos of Europe coming to take your jobs, your money, your future. The Jews are your masters today and they will govern France.' Six years later, Léon Daudet wrote in *L'Action Française:* 'It is quite clear that these Semite immigrants, in their desire to be accepted by the German authorities, will put themselves under German orders in case of war or invasion.'

The allegations were basically the same as those made during the Dreyfus Affair against the established Jewish population, who were still accused of suspect loyalty by anti-Semitic newspapers. The attacks became so vile that it was at last decided to gag the racial press by decree in April 1939. The decree gave anti-Semitic newspapers an opportunity to accuse the Government of trying to cover up warmongering by the Jewish banking families, de Rothschild and Lazard, 'who are counting on making enormous fortunes on the Bourse through this criminal operation'.

L'Action Française saw the decree only as proof of a new Jewish conspiracy and headlined its report of 26 April: 'Le Gouverne-ment au service des Juifs', adding that both Government and Jews were wrong to think they could bring an end to anti-Semitism by law. The sinister prophecy came true fifteen months later when the Republic which tried to protect Jews proved too weak even to save itself.

CHAPTER TWO

A Republic Dies

LONG BEFORE THE 1940 débâcle, the Third Republic was doomed. Alternate doses of right-wing incompetence and left-wing impotence acted like a slow poison. Apart from the brief experiment with Socialism during the 1936 Popular Front, the electorate shunned both the idea of social reform and agitation for more authoritarian government. They placed most faith in the biggest political movement, the Radical Party, a flexible force on the centre–left recruited largely from provincial notables whose indecisive leadership, unreliable coalitions and dubious compromises did much to discredit parliamentary democracy.

In the end, the German Army, which had played its part in the French national crisis at the turn of the century, returned to provide cover for right-wing revenge. It is doubtful whether conservatives could have come to a power-sharing agreement at Vichy without the collapse of the nation, with parliamentarians themselves administering the Republic's *coup de grâce*.

Although the French establishment were united by the emotional appeal of traditional Action Française crusades, to which Communism had been added, conservative movements were divided by conflicting solutions ranging from restoration of the monarchy to Fascist dictatorship. Whenever there was a brief truce between right-wing parties, it was wrecked by personal rivalry.

By 1940, one lesson was clear. Time and again since the Dreyfus Affair, campaigns against Jews had served to cover apparently unbridgeable differences. In one exemplary case during the pre-war years, extremists overcame their divisions for long enough to bring them within reach of power, forming political bonds that would re-emerge in Pétain's Government.

The suicide of a criminal, Serge Alexandre Stavisky, on 8 January 1934, brought together several favourite unifying themes, including xenophobia, anti-Semitism and parliamentary corruption. Stavisky was born in Kiev and came to Paris with his father, a dentist, at the turn of the century. By the time Serge was twenty-six, his immoral way of life had shocked his father into committing suicide. From small-time underworld activities in his youth, Stavisky built up a fortune by corrupt links with politicians until, hounded by police, he shot himself in a ski chalet in Chamonix.

A parliamentary commission later said that Stavisky had been left to die by the police, an allegation that implicitly supported the press view that the Jewish swindler knew too many dangerous political secrets to be allowed to live. This was the conclusion leaped to by *L'Action Française,* delighted by a scandal where moral responsibility was shared between an immigrant Jew and the detested representatives of democracy. On 9 January 1934, the newspaper called for a march on the National Assembly and campaigned for a 'more vigorous revolt against the robbers' the following day.

Respected conservative dailies like *Le Temps* inflamed the sense of moral outrage. The capital was engulfed by days of unrest which reached a peak on 6 February 1934 when 40,000 rioters forced MPs to flee Parliament near the Place de la Concorde. Sixteen marchers were shot dead and 655 seriously injured. A policeman also died in the worst clash on Paris streets since the 1871 Commune.

A *coup d'état* seemed imminent. The Radical Party Premier, Edouard Daladier, who was abandoned by all his allies except Léon Blum, was forced to resign. Anti-parliamentarian forces had the Republic at their mercy, but the threat suddenly faded for lack of determined leadership.

The attacks had been headed by the royalist Camelots du Roi – the king's street-hawkers – and by leagues representing other activist right-wing organisations dominated by war veterans. Maurras left the Action Française Camelots du Roi to their own devices, spending 6 February writing poetry and sleeping. The biggest Great War veterans' association, Croix de Feu, led by Colonel François de la Rocque, refused to take any part in over-throwing a legal government.

Other leaders could not be found for days. In the confused aftermath, a new coalition government was formed of all parties except Communists and Socialists. Its leader, Gaston Doumergue, represented many of the offensive images the right had fought against. He was a long-serving Third Republican and had been President. He was also a Protestant and a Freemason, while, at seventy-one, he was too ill to be a credible Premier.

His appointment was a typical Third Republic compromise. To reassure the right, Philippe Pétain was appointed War Minister at the age of seventy-six, both to exploit his 1914–18 glory and to ensure the loyalty of veterans' leagues. The Maréchal had been cautiously testing the possibility of a political career for some time through contacts with right-wing political clubs.

With his post in Doumergue's Cabinet, Pétain was confirmed as a focus for reactionaries who believed he was the only man who could unite the country. Among the first to try and persuade him to overcome natural caution and seize supreme power was Raphaël Alibert, a leader of Redressement Français. This move-ment was founded in 1927 to provide a bridge between Maurras' emotional crusades for monarchy and right-wing pressures for technocratic reforms.

Alibert, a jurist and unsuccessful businessman, campaigned behind the scenes during the 1934 crisis. He contacted one of the Maréchal's military aides and members of a terrorist group, the Cagoulards, the hooded ones, who wanted to set up a Nazi-style regime.

Alibert's Pétainist campaign had strong support on the right, not least from Maurras, and there was even some sympathy for Pétain on the left, where he was considered a humane general. Over the next few months, Pétain must have seriously considered himself for high office as he took elocution lessons from a Comédie Française actress to correct his weak and shaky delivery. However, during his 1945 trial, charges of conspiring to seize power by illegal means were dropped when it was recalled that Pétain's behaviour during his Army career supported his claims that he had risen to the supreme military rank by strict obedience to orders and rigid respect for legality.

Doumergue's short-lived administration ensured Alibert an ally with the appointment of Pierre Laval as Minister for the Colonies. At the Fall of France, Alibert and Laval joined forces to destroy Parliament, drawing up a regime that suited them both and providing a legal framework which would overcome Pétain's scruples.

While the 1934 riots had brought the right within touching distance of supreme power, it was the left which profited first. Only two days after the worst rioting, Socialists and Communists set up a joint front against Fascism. In May the following year they were joined by the Radical Party, providing the basis for the Popular Front Government which, in May 1936, won 358 seats in Parliament against 222 for the right. Hardly two years after the country had been paralysed by political stagnation and conspiracy, the electorate had given an overwhelming vote of confidence in democracy through a general election which left Léon Blum as Prime Minister in the first Socialist-led administration.

More than thirty years before, André Gide, who won the Nobel Prize for Literature in 1947, said that Blum was 'too Jewish for his own good', a member of a superior race called on to dominate after being dominated for so long. 'He seems to think that the

time is coming which will be the time for the Jews.' Although
Gide, who knew Blum well, moderated his opinions much later,
saying he was referring to the Socialist leader's thirst for justice,
Blum really did prove too Jewish for his own good and that of the
community in general.

His origins were at the basis of Opposition campaigns that
made him the most insulted and misunderstood politician of his
generation. His promotion also further split French and foreign
Jews, who had strongly differing views on their political roles in
face of an increasingly aggressive right.

Léon Blum was sixty-four when he became the Third Republic's
100th Prime Minister after an early life that was typical of the new
Jewish bourgeoisie and a political career that alienated him from
most of it. Like nearly every rich Jewish family, the Blums came
from Alsace and owed their fortune to the clothes business. His
father set up a haberdashery shop in the rue Saint-Denis on the
edge of an area of the 2nd *arrondissement* known as Le Sentier
which became the centre of the textile trade, dominated by Jews.

The Blums' religious convictions were more dutiful than
devout, reflecting a general trend towards non-observance in the
community where only 6000 established families were registered
at the Consistory during the thirties. Many Jews had become
wealthy in the textile boom at the end of the century, particularly
those who had factories in the East before settling in Paris.
Although some still played dominant roles until the Second
World War, half the clothing industry was run by Polish and
Russian immigrants. Descendants of the Alsatian community
moved to other callings, not least the Bar.

Blum's own interest in law, which first took him to the state's
legal service, the Conseil d'Etat, was probably influenced by his
mother, who ran a shop specialising in legal literature. His first
ambition was to become a writer, a talent he used for much of his
life as a journalist and theatre critic, as well as for one of his most

enlightening books, *Souvenirs sur l'Affaire,* published in 1935. The book compared the apathy of French Jews during the Dreyfus Affair to their lack of reaction to anti-Semitism in the thirties.

While the condemnation of Captain Dreyfus was an essential part of Blum's political education, he pointed out that most Jews had refused to fight against the injustice of the case and resented attempts to clear the Army officer. It was the passionate combat of non-Jews like Jean Jaurès that brought Blum into the Socialist fold and he was again shocked at the lack of solidarity and political perception of the established Jewish community in the mid-thirties. French Jews, he said, 'imagined that anti-Semitic passion could be pushed away by their neutrality and faint-heartedness'.

'They secretly curse those who, in exposing it, put them in the hands of secular opponents,' he added, warning that Jews would be offered as victims to triumphant Fascism.

In his accusation of culpable smugness, he must have taken into account repeated pressure from leading French Jews who opposed left-wing political activity of any kind or openly associated with the right. The militancy of new immigrants – about 100,000 Jews arrived from Eastern Europe in the thirties – had created an air of panic in the Consistory. The chairman, Robert de Rothschild, accused politically active Poles and Roumanians of retarding assimilation, still the main motivation of the original community from Alsace and Lorraine, who insisted on being called Israélites to stress the religious, rather than racial, basis of Judaism. Referring to immigrants, the Consistory leader said: 'If they are not happy, they must go.' In a comment that must have delighted xenophobes, he added: 'They are guests whom we receive with pleasure but they must not break the china.'

The great fear of established families was that Judaism would be confused with Marxism or with moderate left-wing values represented by Blum, whose Socialism had been formed mainly by non-Jews. For most of the predominantly middle-class community, concentrated in big cities, there was no identification with working-class crusades or with Blum's insistence on social justice. A glance at the lifestyles of Jews who would become influential after the war shows how far removed they were from revolutionary ideas, let alone new causes like Zionism. Despite hysterical calls from the right, there was no hint of any official discrimination against established Jews, who felt that assimilation was just about complete.

François Jacob, who shared the Nobel Prize for Medicine with two other doctors in 1965, was brought up in one of the best districts of Paris near the Parc Monceau in the 17th *arrondissement*. His family's fortune came from a textile mill in eastern France and his father consolidated this wealth as a company administrator. Jacob's most important adult influence was his maternal grandfather, Albert Franck, who achieved the most senior general's rank in the French Army between the wars, commanding the Normandy region and proving that even the institution most harmed by the Dreyfus Affair was not blind to his community's claims to patriotism. Although François Jacob's parents observed Jewish feasts, he gave up religion as an adolescent and experienced no racism until he reached lycée, where an Action Française bully tried to force him to insult Léon Blum.

Raymond Aron, one of the best-known political commentators and philosophers of his generation, was also brought up in a bourgeois atmosphere in Montparnasse and Versailles. His father made a double break with his Ashkenazi Alsatian background by abandoning religion and the textile business to become a law professor. Aron attended the Ecole Normale Supérieure, an elite philosophy and teaching school split between opponents and supporters of Charles Maurras, but he took no leading role in debates on anti-Semitism and, after the war, had to defend himself against accusations that he had lacked interest in the Jewish question while working as a propagandist with Charles de Gaulle in London.

Blum obviously drew little support from any Jewishconsciousness movement, because French Jews had no strong idea of collective identity outside their French nationality once the religious hold had weakened. Simone Veil, who was appointed Health Minister in 1974, had to ask her father, an architect, what it meant to be a Jew. She was told it represented a superior attachment to culture, avoiding frivolous pursuits like the cinema. Her family did not observe Jewish rites and she asked whether she would be allowed to marry a non-Jew. Her father raised no objection except to say that, in his opinion, the only people who respected worthwhile values were 'other Jews and the aristocracy'.

Inside the French Jewish community, the most important areas of Blum's support came from the Ligue des Droits de l'Homme, an organisation founded during the Dreyfus Affair, which attracted many Jews fighting for human rights in general, and the Ligue Internationale contre l'anti-Sémitisme, LICA, founded in 1927. The first organisation brought him into contact with a young journalist, Daniel Mayer, who led the underground Socialist Party during the war and became President of the country's highest legal council, the Conseil Constitutionnel, in 1981. Mayer wrote for the Socialist daily, *Le Populaire,* to which Blum was a regular contributor. LICA, the League fighting anti-Semitism, had about 2000 followers, many of them young French Jews who agreed with Blum's view that the community would soon fall victim to Fascism if they did not become a political force.

As far as Blum was concerned, his prophecy came true even as he finished his *Souvenirs de l'Affaire.* He was unable to take part in the last phases of the 1936 election campaign after being all but murdered by Action Française fanatics on 13 February.

Charles Maurras and his journalists had kept up a front-page assault on Blum for weeks, calling him the son of a naturalised German Jew and a 'monster of the democratic republic'. From day to day, the insults hardened until Blum was written off as 'human detritus' who should either be shot in the back or have his throat cut with a kitchen knife, a repetition of an Action Française hate campaign which had led to the murder of Jean Jaurès in 1914.

The threats caught up with Blum when he was driving home from the National Assembly and his car became involved in the funeral cortège for the Action Française historian, Jacques Bainville, which was escorted by the Camelots du Roi. The Socialist leader was beaten and kicked as he lay in the road after being dragged from the car to cries of 'Death to the Jew!' He was rescued by workers from a nearby building site, his head covered in blood.

Three days later, 500,000 people marched through Paris in protest while Action Française claimed that the attack had been planned by Communists to discredit the movement. Even though Maurras was sent to prison for four months for incitement to murder and his militant movement banned, the violent message was not missed by the biggest section of the Jewish population, the immigrants who had fled Eastern Europe to escape the anti-Jewish bloodlust.

By the time war was declared, Paris sheltered the third biggest Jewish community outside Warsaw and New York. There were between 150,000 and 200,000 Jews in the capital, of whom about half were foreigners or stateless refugees; thousands more lived in working-class outer suburbs.[2] Many of those registered as French were immigrants' children or recently naturalised residents only barely tolerated by most Parisians. Much of this population spent the pre-war years, as Hitler's power increased, trying to find another home outside Europe, but other nations, like the United States, baulked at accepting more refugees.

Hope of permanent safety in France after the Popular Front's 1936 success was short-lived. The last vestige of this left-wing victory dissolved within two years. Ironically, it was the same Parliament which had promised so much in 1936 which handed over full powers to Pétain and his anti-Jewish legislators in July

1940. Léon Blum was one of the few opponents of this cowardly sell-out to a revengeful right – a right which would soon put him on trial, blaming him for the defeat.

The immigrant Jewish population had played a part in Blum's 1936 triumph, either through a strong attraction to Socialism or through an open attachment to the Jewish religion recalling Blum's origins. Robert de Rothschild's fears that immigrants were potentially dangerous militants as far as French Jews were concerned was justifiable. Few of the foreign community's leaders worried much about 'breaking the china', nor that Judaism would be assimilated to Marxism. Polish Jews, particularly, brought their politics with them and spread them through the closed worlds of the main immigrant areas in the capital.

Despite the fact that Jews represented only a tiny fraction of the 4-million-strong foreign population and were also dispersed in other big centres like Lyons and Marseilles, anti-Semitic newspapers such as *Gringoire* and *Candide* had no difficulty in giving the impression that at least a million Eastern European Jews had poured into France. There were predictions that in ten or fifteen years they would reach as many as 20 million.

The main community had concentrated in what was called the Pletzl, the Little Place, once an aristocratic area known as the Marais behind the Saint-Paul Métro station in the 3rd and 4th *arrondissements*. The damp, crumbling mansions in narrow streets developed into a ghetto where eight out of ten people were Jewish. They were also the poorest members of the community. Most of the 50,000 foreign Jews recruited as sweated labour for Jewish-owned clothes factories came from the Pletzl, where families lived under the constant threat of expulsion from the country.

In the last months before the war, when the Radical Edouard Daladier was Premier, foreign Jews were made as uncomfortable as possible. Instead of residence papers, they were given expulsion orders suspended in exchange for temporary permits that had to be renewed from week to week. To avoid police checks, thousands were forced to live a clandestine life long before Vichy legislation was introduced. Desperate, homeless and exploited, refugees would pay the heaviest toll during the war.

The Pletzl was also the area of the strongest religious observance, which tended to wane in more politically oriented centres like Belleville, a working-class quarter straddling the 19th and 20th *arrondissements* with a Jewish population of about 20,000. Polish Communists and Socialist Bundists did nothing to hide their political activity. Belleville produced many underground Jewish heroes during the war, among them the Communist Henri Krasucki, future leader of France's most powerful trade union whose father Isaac died in Auschwitz.

There were other Jewish quarters, notably a Russian settlement in the rue du Faubourg Saint-Antoine near the Bastille, where they ran the furniture-making trade, while the nearest equivalent to a petit-bourgeois immigrant population concentrated around Montmartre.

Most newly arrived Jews could speak only Yiddish and read Yiddish newspapers. They lived in isolation from the mainstream of French life with their political and religious existence organised by more than 130 Yiddish associations, which maintained the view that French Jews were embarrassed by their ethnic background. In 1935, Israël Jefroykin, President of the Fédération des Sociétés Juives, which grouped immigrant organisations, replied to Consistory criticism of newcomers by saying that the 'Jewish immigrant sees himself as the carrier of authentic Jewish culture while he sees his French co-religionist as neither here nor there.'

Even naturalised French Jews who were determined to accept the national way of life felt alienated. The future Cardinal Lustiger, whose maternal grandfather was a Polish rabbi, described the atmosphere in Montmartre where his parents kept a hosiery shop. His family were religious and felt that French Jews had lost their idealism: 'French Jews of old stock were looked down on because they were shameful Jews,' he said. 'Assimilation was a disparaging word. It meant a Jew who had lost pride in being Jewish.'

Right-wing suspicions that immigrant Jews also carried with them the germs of international revolution were fully justified. The Polish Bund had been active in Paris since 1900 and campaigned for a type of Socialist state far beyond anything considered by Léon Blum. Communists who came to France during the thirties often took refuge in Paris to continue a political struggle against Fascism that had become impossible in their own countries. During the Spanish Civil War, these exiled Communists provided big Republican contingents that some time later formed the basis of urban guerrilla units fighting against the Nazis.

Adam Rayski, who worked with the Communist underground press after the German invasion and helped to reveal the first news of the extermination camps, came to Paris as a student when he was seventeen and, by the age of twenty, was working full time for the Communist newspaper *L'Humanité*, as well as the Communist Yiddish daily, *Naïe Presse*. 'In Poland, Jews had to declare their nationality as Jewish, marking them out from the two other nations, Russian and Polish,' he said. 'Emigrant Jews arrived in France with a common identity and a common memory of family tragedies in the pogroms. It's not surprising that they were more aware of the political stakes than the French and began armed or passive resistance to the Germans before any other group.'

A logical result of this heightened awareness was evident even before the war and led a seventeen-year-old student, Herschel Grynszpan, to shoot dead a German diplomat, Ernst von Rath, in the Paris Embassy on 7 November 1938. Grynszpan, who was born of Polish parents in Germany, wanted to avenge the persecution of Austrian and German Jews by the Nazis. The shooting came only two months after the Munich agreement, when British and French leaders had been accused of appeasing Hitler.

Vengeful Germans reacted to the assassination by showing

their true violent face during Kristallnacht, when fanatics murdered at least forty Jews in German towns and cities, smashed their shops and burned down synagogues, before 25,000 German Jews were interned in concentration camps. Grynszpan was one of the first Jews to be handed over to the Germans at the Armistice and all trace of him was lost in 1942.

While the assassination inevitably increased the French community's mistrust of immigrants, Léon Blum's 1936 victory had built a bridge between the two populations as the Socialist Premier was admired by newcomers. The biggest and most conservative Yiddish newspaper, *Parizer Haint,* said on 12 May 1936 that Blum was 'not only a Jew with a Jewish heart and a Jewish mentality but a Jew who is even interested in a Jewish national homeland'.

Blum's standing with immigrants rose even further in 1938, after his Government had fallen, when the French Jewish establishment supported the Munich agreement and opposed giving refuge to 600,000 German Jews after Kristallnacht because, in the words of the Grand Rabbi Julien Weill, 'nothing appears to me more precious than maintenance of peace on earth'. A week later, on 26 November 1938, Blum told LICA that shutting the doors to German Jews was 'painful and dishonourable'. Criticising French Jews, he said he could not imagine how their attitude could preserve their tranquillity and security. 'There is not an example in history when safety has been attained by cowardice, neither for a people, for human groups nor mankind in general,' he added.

By then Blum had seen his Popular Front Government undermined by international events like the Spanish Civil War, and crumble under the repeated battering rams of anti-Semitism, internal quarrelling, economic failures and right-wing revenge. His ethnic origins had been at the centre of a vicious campaign not least in the National Assembly, where his first visit after the Popular Front victory was marked by an ominous confrontation with the anti-Semitic Xavier Vallat, who would be the first Vichy Commissioner-General for Jewish Affairs in 1941. 'Your arrival is unquestionably an historic event,' Vallat said. 'This ancient Gallo-Roman country will be governed for the first time by a Jew. I have said aloud what everyone is thinking silently that to govern this peasant nation which is France it is better to have someone whose origins, no matter how modest, spring from the womb of our soil, rather than a subtle Talmudist.'

With the collapse of the Popular Front, followed by Munich and Kristallnacht, the destinies of the most respected of French Jews and the most humble arrival from Eastern Europe were inextricably enmeshed in a web of hatred that would make France an ally in the Holocaust. Soon after the Fall of France, a law would be signed by Pétain, on 3 October 1940, which made every Jew of whatever nationality an enemy of the new Vichy state.

CHAPTER THREE

Pétain's Armistice

PHILIPPE PÉTAIN WAS hurriedly drafted into the Government as deputy Prime Minister in mid-May 1940 while serving as Ambassador in Madrid. His political career as War Minister in 1934 had been brief and he resisted pressure to seek election as President. Because he put few of his thoughts into writing, it was difficult to say whether this was a sign of natural caution or whether he was biding his time, certain that one day he would be called on as a national saviour without the indignity of an election campaign.

At the time, the country's main continental neighbours, Germany, Italy and Spain, were all dictatorships and many politicians felt that France could not survive without an authoritarian leader. Pétain had longer-standing reserves of personal prestige than Hitler, Mussolini or Franco. His victory against the Germans at Verdun in 1916, followed by the decisive way he had handled the 1917 mutiny, had made him a national hero with a reputation as a humane general. In addition to inspiring affection and loyalty from Great War veterans and a grateful nation, Pétain owed much of his wider popularity to his physical image. As he got older, his benign, grandfatherly appearance was exploited to reassure a population worried by the undercurrent of violence in an unstable Europe.

His posting to Madrid seemed to be the last step in his career as he was already eighty-three years old. It was also a political risk to accept credentials from Franco, the French left's most hated enemy after his victory over the Republicans. In fact, neither Pétain's advancing years nor his association with Fascist Spain harmed his prestige or his popularity.

On his recall from Spain on 16 May 1940, after the German invasion had begun, Pétain probably thought that he was being prepared for national leadership, but the Prime Minister, Paul Reynaud, had no intention of handing over power. Reynaud was struggling against defeatists in his Cabinet and needed Pétain's prestige to raise national morale and send a clear message to Germany that France was ready to stand and fight.

Reynaud's strongest support among his Ministers came from Georges Mandel, the Jewish Radical Party Interior Minister who had been brought into the Cabinet two months before as an earlier guarantee that France would stand firm. Mandel had been right-hand man to another Premier, Georges Clemenceau, during the 1917 crisis when France was pulled back from defeat. The Interior Minister had continually pressed for strong action against Germany before the war and was one of the first politicians to detect a crisis in French morale, telling a British delegate just before Pétain's return that 'there is no will to fight . . . there has been a collapse of the whole French nation'.

Mandel and Pétain would have been natural enemies even without the Maréchal's anti-Semitism. Mandel had no love for generals, while Pétain was contemptuous of politicians. They were constantly at odds inside the Cabinet, a factor which probably reinforced the Maréchal's petulance during the worst crisis in French history. Instead of rallying the nation during the rout of the French Army in May and June, Pétain sulked, talking only of giving up. He acted as if he had been brought back to France on false pretences, undermining Premier Reynaud's authority by associating with the defeatist faction inside the Cabinet. In contrast, Georges Mandel stood out as an implacable opponent of any talk of armistice, and supported Paul Reynaud – whom Pétain also despised.

The rivalry was settled when the Government hurriedly left Paris and took refuge in the Atlantic port of Bordeaux in the second week of June. The pessimistic Pétain was promoted to Prime Minister when Reynaud was forced to resign. The first man to be ousted from the new Cabinet was the belligerent Georges Mandel.

Even then, with the Germans already across the Loire river and bombing Bordeaux, the change was not intended to open the way to surrender. For the soldier in the field, the Maréchal's promotion must have seemed like a long overdue move to reinvigorate the demoralised defence forces. France had often been saved *in extremis* by near miracles, such as the 1914 Battle of the Maine when reinforcements were shuttled to the front line in taxis.

Even though the defiant Reynaud and Mandel had been removed from office, much of the Cabinet was still intact. Five Ministers were military men, including an Air Force general and an admiral. With France's most distinguished soldier as its leader, the Cabinet looked like a fighting force but, within hours, all illusions of new resolution had been destroyed. Pétain, who had never ceased campaigning for peace talks since his return from Madrid, outmanoeuvred supporters of the war and called for an armistice. Almost immediately, his new administration carried out its first anti-Semitic action by arresting Mandel.

Apart from being a Jew – he had once been ousted from the Radical movement in 1911 for supposed links with Jewish banking – Mandel was part of the detested parliamentary system and had made many enemies with his contempt for anyone who did not share his views, not least Pétain himself. The obvious contrast between Pétain and Mandel was a will to fight and Mandel was eventually to pay for his opposition to the Maréchal's defeatism with his life.

Mandel's resistance to Pétain coincided with Charles de Gaulle's flight to London, and they may well have become associates if the sacked Interior Minister had succeeded in escaping to join a government in exile, as he intended. He would have been a natural choice for anti-Pétainist forces in both France and Britain. The chairman of the National Assembly and Radical Party leader, Edouard Herriot, described Mandel as 'an admirable patriot, an inflexible patriot and an untameable patriot', while Winston Churchill, who greatly admired him, had written to congratulate the French Government on his appointment to Reynaud's Cabinet.

Mandel had many basic faults in the eyes of the anti-democratic faction. He was a veteran of the Third Republic, although only fifty-five at the time, and a member of the Radical movement whose compromises represented the weakness of Parliament. He was, however, an opponent and critic of Léon Blum, who later became his friend and confidant during a particularly cruel captivity.

While Blum would in due course be tried for failing to prepare for war, Mandel would be blamed, but never tried, for wanting to continue the battle. The fact that they were both Jews condemned them in advance. Mandel had long been a target for anti-Semitic propaganda. His real name was Rothschild and, although he was no relation of the banking family, he was often cited in hate campaigns in France and Germany which alleged that Jewish financiers deliberately provoked world disorder for their own profit.

Mandel, who used his mother's maiden name, had a traditional Alsatian Ashkenazi background, a family clothes business in Le Sentier. An agnostic since adolescence, his political career developed out of journalism in Clemenceau's newspapers, including *L'Aurore,* which had championed Dreyfus. What marked him out most from his French contemporaries was his personal campaign against Hitler. He also accused the French military of weakness in not facing up to the Germans when they occupied the Rhineland in 1936, and again during Munich and the Phoney War, the period between the declaration of war and the German invasion of France.

His arrogant habit of pointing out that he had been right made few friends for a man who claimed to be left-wing in foreign policy and right-wing in domestic affairs. Even Clemenceau was often irritated by Mandel's over-confident intellectual coldness and called him the 'Saint-Simon of the Ghetto', a reference to the nineteenth-century Comte de Saint-Simon, a precursor of technocratic Socialism. Mandel looked the part, with his grim square face, his expressionless eyes and his preference for impeccable black suits and wing collars.

On 17 June 1940, while eating in a Bordeaux restaurant with his mistress, a Comedie Française actress, Mandel was arrested and falsely accused of planning a *coup d'état*. He confronted Pétain and was given a written apology, only to be arrested again ten days later. He was never released and was murdered at the age of fifty-nine in July 1944 by Pétain's Milice. In his pocket was the Maréchal's letter of apology.

In a regime where much of the energy was provided by vengeance and spite, Mandel's outspoken criticism of Pétain had played into the hands of Raphaël Alibert, one of the key figures of the first months at Vichy. Alibert was brought into the government from Pétain's ministerial secretariat on 17 June 1940, as a junior minister responsible directly to the Maréchal. The post was reward for an association that went back to 1932 when Pétain had been impressed by an Alibert report on the threat of pan-Germanism issued through a right-wing club, Redressement Français. This group aimed to give coherence to the emotional demands of Action Française and to anti-parliamentary reforms, particularly for the economy. These had been outlined by a journalist, Gustave Hervé, a friend of Alibert, in a 1935 pamphlet called *C'est Pétain qu'il nous faut*.

Apart from flattering the old soldier, Hervé gave a remarkable insight into the Vichy of the future, even foreshadowing a meeting between Pétain and Hitler. All the main lines of Vichy policy, including the emphasis on renewed Christian morality, direct rule through a totalitarian state, the Milice and dependence on specialists or technocrats, were outlined, along with the prophecy: 'It is only in time of war and particularly in the case of defeat that we can carry out this operation.'

Contact with Redressement Français, which grouped businessmen and leading civil servants, was the first real experience of practical politics for Pétain when his Army career ended. In 1937, Alibert was introduced to the Maréchal by a reactionary senator, Henry Lémery, a Navy minister, who had appointed Alibert as his own ministerial secretary. Alibert's attempt at a political career had failed after he ran for a parliamentary seat at Pithiviers, near Orleans, a town he would not forget: it was chosen as the site for a notorious concentration camp for Jews. He had also failed in business. The role of backroom adviser suited him better. In the run-up to the war, he met Pétain on several occasions to talk over social problems, or rather to lecture him, for Alibert was recognised as an excellent teacher.

Pétain's passage as War Minister after the 1934 riots had rubbed in his ignorance of the political world, where he resisted pressure to play a greater public role, in particular from Pierre Laval, who proposed him for President of the Republic. In October 1939, Alibert went to Spain with Senator Lémery to talk with the Maréchal and warn him to be ready to lead a future government. The three men even drew up a Cabinet list that included Laval. This was the clearest evidence of plotting on Pétain's behalf that had begun with the 1934 riots. As a result, the main Ministries and staffs at Vichy were in place with remarkable speed. They were dominated by like-minded reformists whose planned changes had been prepared long before and had been refined through a network of right-wing clubs and Leagues, or through the columns of conservative newspapers.

Not the least of these new men was Alibert, then sixty-three years old, who was to be given the third-ranking post in the new administration as Minister of Justice in July 1940, only three weeks after his junior ministry in Bordeaux. Alibert's first important action on 17 June had been to lie and scheme to break Mandel, a man he referred to only as 'that Jew', seizing on unfounded rumours of a coup and ordering the Minister's arrest without consulting Pétain.

Anti-Semitism ran through Alibert's blood. His second manoeuvre, again only a few hours after taking office, was to trick anti-armistice MPs into leaving for North Africa and then to arrange the trial of two leading Jewish parliamentarians for desertion. His masterpiece was to be the 1940 Statut des Juifs, which revoked emancipation under the Revolution.

Despite his anonymity and mediocrity, Alibert's brief career fascinates because of the power he wielded for a few months before being ousted for his anti-German stance. At his trial in 1945, this attitude saved him from a death sentence. A charge of helping the enemy had to be dropped because he had never met any members of the invading Army, his hatred for Germany dating from long before Hitler. The Statut des Juifs was a purely French product, although he claimed to have had as little to do with its drafting as the typist who submitted the legislation to the *Journal Officiel*.

There is a photograph of the first Vichy Cabinet with Alibert's bald head visible in the second rank and enough of his face showing to give the impression of an austere and passionless man. As a jurist, he had once held the same senior rank in the Conseil d'Etat as Léon Blum, where both men were responsible for analysing projected reforms as *Maîtres des requêtes*. Blum's reports, with their emphasis on social justice, have been published, and their tone was probably contradicted by those of Alibert with his obsession for moral order.

At his trial, Alibert drew up a defence based on his pre-war ambition to see Pétain become the man who restored the energy and grandeur of France and 're-establish the notions of authority, order, respect and discipline'. His son, Jacques Alibert, confirmed his father's severe, monk-like image, saying he would have been happy in the thirteenth century as a legal adviser to St Louis, 500 years before Charles Maurras' ideal era under Louis XIV and XV. Eventually, Alibert retired to a Trappist monastery.

His influence over Pétain was that of a strict teacher, putting economic, moral and social flesh on to the instinctive sentiments felt by an old soldier already committed to the idea of unquestioning obedience. Although Alibert claimed at his own trial that he had met Pétain only seven or eight times before 1940 for what he described as 'technical discussions', he would also have given advice on reading matter that developed Pétain's priorities at leisure. In other words, claims that Pétain was a naive victim of his *éminence grise,* particularly over the persecution of Jews, have to be weighed against several years of reflection on what was at stake.

If Alibert was also the ideal adviser, little can be said of Pétain's scruples. The dry and unpleasant jurist, who slipped back into obscurity after devising laws that would help slaughter thousands of people, also engineered the *Massilia* Affair, an incident crucial to the political reputation of the post-war Jewish Prime Minister, Pierre Mendès France, and the event that completed the downfall of Georges Mandel.

The *Massilia* was a 16,000-ton liner requisitioned as a troopship after nearly twenty years on the South Atlantic run and berthed at Le Verdon, sixty miles from Bordeaux, after ferrying soldiers from North Africa. By 16 June 1940, the transfer of the whole Government to Algiers was almost a foregone conclusion and the *Massilia* was kept standing by. Three days later, after a vote by the Senate sitting in a cinema, it was agreed to embark on 20 June, backing up Pétain's Cabinet decision to send Ministers to Algiers by destroyer from a Mediterranean port.

When the *Massilia* finally sailed on 21 June after several agonising delays, only one Senator and 26 Deputies were aboard out of at least 200 who had kept up with the fleeing Government. Most of those on the ship were Socialists or Radicals who opposed the Armistice. They included Georges Mandel, Pierre Mendès France and the Popular Front Education Minister, Jean Zay. Unknown to them, the Government move had collapsed and the *Massilia* passengers would be labelled traitors and deserters. The Jewish backgrounds of Mandel, Mendès France and Zay would be exploited to make the charges stick.

By 16 June, France was already split into two political camps: those ready to follow Pétain and Laval into a deal with Germany and those like Mandel who believed resistance could be continued outside France. As the Germans approached Bordeaux after Pétain's promotion to Premier, the Maréchal decided to 'stay on French soil and assure by his prestigious presence the protection of its people and assets'.

This was the expression used by the new deputy Prime Minister, Camille Chautemps, to whom Pétain had promised to delegate his powers as Premier outside France. On the afternoon of 20 June, Chautemps met Pétain and the President of the Republic, Albert Lebrun, who had done little since the crisis except allow events to overwhelm him. Chautemps wanted to be sure that Lebrun would go to North Africa where his presence was crucial to head a legitimate exiled republic and 'pursue the war by any means possible from the Empire'. Official records of this meeting included Lebrun's reply when asked if he agreed to carry on the fight in North Africa: 'I am in complete agreement. My luggage is ready.'

At that instant, Pétain's hopes vanished of becoming head of state in a legal French administration on the mainland. A government in exile could call on 2.5 million armed men overseas, in addition to a fully intact Fleet and a powerful Air Force which had been kept in reserve. If Raphaël Alibert had not intervened with a lie, there might never have been a Vichy regime.

At Alibert's 1945 trial, an MP, Jean-Claude Fernand-Laurent, repeated a conversation he had held with an embittered Alibert in Clermont-Ferrand in February 1942 when the Maréchal's chief adviser had lost all his power. Alibert recalled how he had saved Pétain by making up a story on the spur of the moment that French troops were no longer on the run but were holding the German Army on the Loire.

Alibert suggested to President Lebrun that a decision on moving the Government should be put off until the following morning. Pétain must have guessed that his Minister was lying, but he nonetheless agreed. The hesitant Lebrun, who had been getting into his car to drive to the Mediterranean rendezvous just before the urgent meeting was arranged, backed down with the words: 'This is the last delay but I am ready to leave.'

Without informing Pétain, Alibert dictated letters to all Ministers telling them to stay in Bordeaux until further orders. He stamped the letters with the Maréchal's personal seal and signed them with Pétain's signature. They were taken on face value and the Government in exile disappeared in the confusion of the German advance and a campaign by Laval to stop more MPs joining the *Massilia*. 'Without this forgery, Pétain would never have become the head of state,' Alibert reportedly said.

The Maréchal's chief adviser rendered him another service on 20 June 1940, preventing a message getting to the anti-Armistice MPs who had hurriedly embarked on the *Massilia*. He pretended she had already sailed, although the ship was still at quay, held up by a mutinous crew.

Parliamentarians keen to carry on the war had been the first to arrive, led by Mandel, eager to meet British delegates in North Africa to discuss a new alliance. With him was his mistress, Béatrice Bretty, his ten-year-old daughter and a black bodyguard. Mandel's huge trunk caused considerable interest, which increased after his arrest in Casablanca when it was found to contain gold bars.

Among those who experienced the tense hours before the ship sailed after more delays and contradictory orders was a nineteen-year-old student social worker, Marie-Claire Schreiber. Thirty years later she married Pierre Mendès France, who boarded the ship in his Air Force officer's uniform with an order to join his unit in North Africa. Although he was an MP, he had come to Bordeaux looking for a squadron to which he had been attached as an observer and which had flown to Morocco.

Also aboard was Jean Zay with his three-year-old daughter and his wife, who was eight months pregnant. Zay, a second lieutenant, was covered by an official note appointing him as liaison officer in future negotiations between the North African military and the proposed government.

Marie-Claire Schreiber, whose father had founded the Paris financial newspaper *Les Echos,* and whose mother, Suzanne Crémieux, was Vice-President of the Radical Party, recalled the tension which prevailed up to the departure, with the crew on the edge of mutiny at the spectacle of what they believed was the flight of leading personalities. Among those aboard was the recently dismissed Navy Minister, César Campinchi, and the former Premier, Edouard Daladier, who had been part of the Popular Front Government as a Radical and had later signed the Munich agreement with Hitler. Insults from the crew, who even refused to handle baggage, were concentrated on the five Jewish politicians, who also included Georges Lévy-Alphandéry and Salomon Grumbach, another two of the fourteen Jewish Members of Parliament at the time.

Eventually, eighty Marines were sent to the *Massilia* to restore order and force the crew to sail. News of the Armistice was received while the ship was two days from the Moroccan landfall. Realising they had been tricked, the fleeing MPs unsuccessfully tried to send a cable asking to be recalled. By the time the ship arrived in Casablanca, popular hostility had been fanned by Pétain's propaganda machine, while the original idea of moving the administration to North Africa had been submerged by more dramatic events and would not be publicly revealed until after the war.

North Africa was historically a base for anti-Semitism, despite a nineteenth-century law making Algerian Jews full French citizens, a privilege that the Vichy Government would cancel before installing even stricter anti-Jewish measures than those imposed on the mainland. Crowds at the dockside wanted to lynch Jean Zay and he was slapped by a fellow officer.

To the anti-Jewish press, Zay was the man who had corrupted French youth as the Popular Front's Minister of Education, and his enemies stressed his Jewish background, although he was actually a Protestant. His father was Jewish, but his mother and his wife were Christians. This was enough Jewish blood to attract hatred even for his unborn child. His pregnant wife was refused medical treatment on the ship and could not find a midwife in Morocco because of anti-Jewish feeling and a fear of official reprisals. 'Not even unborn Jews have any rights,' the future Madame Mendès France noted.

When the passengers disembarked in Casablanca on 27 June 1940, they were threatened by Fascist supporters of the Parti Populaire Français, a movement founded by a renegade Communist, Jacques Doriot. A press campaign claimed that the ship was loaded with Jews and Freemasons fleeing to South America, rumours fed by the disproportionately high number of Jews aboard. Before Mandel could settle ashore, and after he had made several vain attempts to contact British envoys, he was arrested. His seizure effectively killed off the first credible resistance movement outside France.

Later, revenge would be taken against the four serving officers among the MPs, with more severe treatment being given to the two Jews among them. Pierre Mendès France had no reason to suspect reprisals, having taken the ship with a regular travel warrant to join his unit. Nearly two months later, he was arrested for desertion only a week after Jean Zay had been accused of the same offence. In the intervening two months, the *Massilia* Affair had been used to the full by Vichy in a search for scapegoats.

Mendès France was an excellent example. He was a Jewish MP and a Freemason. His subsequent imprisonment and trial can be compared with the Dreyfus Affair for its twisted justice.

While his family background in a clothing business in Le Sentier was familiar to so many contemporaries, Mendès France was a Sephardi who traced his origins back to Bordeaux in 1684. At the age of nineteen, he became the country's youngest lawyer and in 1938, when he was given a Treasury post at the age of thirty-one in Léon Blum's second Government, he became the youngest Minister.

By the time Mendès France was brought to court on 9 May 1941, at Clermont-Ferrand, there was no chance of a fair trial from a Government-controlled military tribunal headed by a colonel-judge who was an Action Française militant. The court was packed with 300 people invited by the prosecution, with only six invited by the defence, while the anti-Semitic press, such as *Gringoire* and *Au Pilori,* stirred up hostility by describing the MP as 'a carpet-dealer trembling with fear' or as 'a Jew, thief, traitor and deserter who has no right to add France to his name'.

Even though they were under threat of punishment themselves, Air Force commanders confirmed that he had been ordered to go to North Africa, and they praised his courage. Their defiance was useless. Only one of the seven judges disagreed with a verdict and sentence condemning Mendès France to be stripped of his rank and to endure six years in jail. In the previous October, another court had been even harder on Jean Zay, who was also strongly defended by his Air Force colleagues. He was sentenced to deportation.

In contrast, the two non-Jewish serving officer MPs on board the *Massilia* were treated leniently. Pierre Viénot thought he had no chance, having served in a Popular Front Ministry and organised anti-German propaganda during the first months of the war. He was given an eight-year suspended jail sentence and set free. Alex Wiltzer, the other non-Jewish MP, was acquitted without a trial.

On 21 June 1941, the first anniversary of the *Massilia* sailing, Mendès France, fearing execution, cut his way out of Clermont-Ferrand prison, near Vichy, and escaped to fight from London. He returned to join De Gaulle's Government as national economy minister after the Liberation of Paris. In 1954, Mendès France himself became Premier.[3]

There was to be no post-war revenge for Jean Zay. He refused to escape because he feared reprisals against his wife and two children. On 20 June 1944, the fourth anniversary of the day he boarded the *Massilia*, Zay was taken from Riom jail by Pétain's Milice and shot in the back. His body was not found until more than two years later.

CHAPTER FOUR

Work, Family, Fatherland

THE GOVERNMENT WHICH left Paris as an open city for the German Army finally settled in Vichy on 1 July 1940. For Pierre Laval, there was an inauspicious start when his official car broke down just before the town boundary and he had to walk the rest of the way.

An air of ridicule was to hang around the new French capital until the Vichy regime collapsed four years later. Even without the treachery of collaboration and repeated cowardice in the face of German pressure, it would be difficult to allot this period an honourable place in the nation's history. The comic-opera atmosphere of the little spa, noted for its liver cures, made it a subject of irony even for its leaders. Laval, twice Prime Minister, called it the Republic of Gérolstein, a Ruritania where tank commanders rode on bicycles, where ceremonial infantry paraded without weapons and where an eighty-four-year-old defeated military leader acted like a new King of France.

Many of the fateful choices made by the Vichy regime between 1940 and 1944 can be attributed to the isolation of the seat of government. The jaded Second Empire health resort owed its past prosperity to the patronage of Napoleon III's Empress Eugènie. The spa's only real attraction as a national administrative centre was its high number of hotels, now needed for offices and staff accommodation, but it was badly served by rail even for big southern cities like Lyons and Marseilles, both under Vichy control.

Operating from overcrowded hotel rooms, a casino or in the shadow of the fin-de-siècle pump room, the administration was out of touch with the realities of French life, particularly in German-occupied Paris, 220 miles to the north. Only a formidable propaganda machine, feeding on the semi-deified image of the Maréchal, kept up the illusion that France was being protected.

Writing of his conception of the French nation in his *Mémoires,* Charles de Gaulle, who was condemned to death in his absence by a Vichy court in August 1940, said he instinctively felt that Providence had created the country for complete greatness or exemplary misfortune. By choosing a capital in a faraway town of 30,000 people among the volcanic hills of the Auvergne, Pétain emphasised the fact that never in its history had France fallen so low as in the summer of 1940.

At the beginning of July, at about the same time that the Government caravan of dozens of vehicles reached Vichy, millions of Belgian and northern French refugees were making their slow return home. An estimated 50,000 Belgian Jews decided to stay in the unoccupied area of France, which now sheltered at least half the French and immigrant Jewish community.

Seen from Paris, where about 150,000 Jews still lived, the decision to establish a government at Vichy was just another mystery in a period of confusion. Pétain's administration had been forced to move out of Bordeaux when the Germans moved in, swapping the Atlantic port for Lyons, which had also been taken as an open city. The big south-eastern industrial and textile centre would have been an ideal temporary capital. Led by Charles Maurras, most of the anti-parliamentary movement and anti-Semitic press took refuge there. But Lyons was not considered suitable for the Government because the Mayor was Edouard Herriot, the National Assembly chairman who thought so much of Mandel and had little respect for the Maréchal's reformist and defeatist entourage.

Clermont-Ferrand, in the Auvergne, was politically much more suitable. The Michelin tyre family ruled the city with the sort of paternalistic authority that inspired the new Government. It was a centre for Pétainist supporters led by the local Senator, Jacques Bardoux, and his son-in-law, Edmond Giscard d'Estaing, father of a future President. But Clermont-Ferrand's industrial atmosphere was considered too depressing.

The caravan moved on thirty miles northwards to Vichy, generally considered as just another stopover before a return to Paris or Versailles. The inertia which kept the administration there for another four years had several origins. Alibert liked the spa because he was undergoing a slimming cure.

Meanwhile, Pierre Laval, drafted into the Cabinet as Minister of State with ominously undefined powers, was on familiar ground. His picturesque home town, Châteldon, where he had been brought up in his father's café and where he owned the baronial château, was only a few miles away. He was also in close touch with a variety of business interests ranging from his own mineral-water spring to the influential Auvergne newspaper, *Le Moniteur,* in Clermont-Ferrand.

Vichy's small-town atmosphere also suited Pétain, who was born in the north of France to a farming family. The almost empty rural Allier *département* (county) around Vichy was not unlike his birthplace. The spa's parks, concert halls, pump room and intimate restaurants provided a tranquil sanctuary where the true extent of the disaster could be forgotten. As armed resistance developed, the security factor provided by Vichy's isolation became increasingly important because it was difficult for opponents to get in and out of such a small area without being spotted.

The impossibility of protecting the rest of the country's 40 million citizens from such a remote place seems never to have been seriously considered. This was part of a series of tactical errors that made German domination easier. One of the most serious blunders had been made within hours of Pétain's appointment as Premier in Bordeaux, when French troops were still fighting a rearguard battle. In a hurry to stop the war, Pétain made a broadcast to the nation on 17 June saying that it was 'with a heavy heart that I tell you today to end the fighting'. Hundreds of thousands of soldiers in the field took the message literally, despite a correction of the broadcast recording and the published communiqué in which the key words became: 'We must try and end the fighting.' The mass surrenders of an Army that had lost 100,000 dead in six weeks proved over the next four years to be the biggest bargaining counter the Germans held. At the peak, 1.9 million men were in captivity, paralysing Vichy's room for negotiation and defiance, while Germany used this enormous reserve of potential hostages as political currency.

The Armistice was signed on 22 June in the same railway carriage at Compiègne, north of Paris, which had been used for the 1918 Armistice. While Hitler visited the conquered capital, the new French Government made the best of what were considered reasonable terms, even including Article 19, in which Germany reclaimed its political refugees, many of them Jewish.

Pétain's regime was left in full control of two-fifths of the national territory, an area which covered the second and third biggest cities, Marseilles and Lyons. The Germans took over the north and the Atlantic coastline. Meanwhile, Alsace and Lorraine, regained in 1918, were returned to Germany, which also forcibly attached the Nord and Pas-de-Calais *départements* to its Belgian administration and established a long strip of annexed territory along the Rhine frontier for German colonisation.

The Italians invaded France in the last days of the battle and occupied a strip of France east of the Rhône, mainly Alpine border territory. A benign Italian administration later provided a haven for Jews, saving thousands of lives despite threats from both the Germans and the French.

Technically, French or Vichy law was valid throughout the country, although the invading Army's decrees had priority in occupied areas. The French were solely responsible in the Zone

Non-Occupée, usually called the Nono. The choice of Vichy as a capital added another advantage for the Germans. The Demarcation Line between the two zones ran through Moulins, the Allier *département*'s chief administrative centre, only thirty miles to the north. Nazi stormtroopers were permanently posted there as a potential menace to the neutered French Government, which was left with nothing except a standing defence force of 100,000 lightly armed men.

The Armistice terms made one generous concession that turned out to be an accidental masterstroke for the victors, enabling them to destroy the chances of resurrecting France's alliance with Britain. The French were allowed to keep their Fleet, which was intact and barely less powerful than the Royal Navy. On 3 July 1940, Winston Churchill ordered the destruction of some of the most important vessels in their Algerian port of refuge, Mers-el-Kebir, because he feared that the French would eventually hand over the warships. More than 1290 French sailors were killed fighting from ships which were being disarmed. As Pétain's entourage was predominantly anglophobe, not least the Navy chief, Admiral François Darlan, France even contemplated declaring war on its old ally, frequently identified as a key partner in the international Jewish conspiracy to ruin Catholic France.

Vichy leaders were convinced that Britain would also have to sue for peace. The certainty that Germany would win the war, a belief that did not falter for at least three years, was at the basis of bad decisions from the moment that Vichy's hotel guests were evicted to make way for Government staff, while the casino and theatres were turned into offices by arranging hundreds of cardboard boxes of archives to give the impression that they were independent, partitioned-off departments. From this chaos, a comforting feeling grew that a complacent and co-operative France would soon be given a privileged place in a German-dominated Europe.

Outside the Auvergne hideout, there was a widespread belief

that the most adulated military leader of the century was planning a revolt, inspired by an area of the Auvergne where the Gauls had once resisted Caesar.

Inside Vichy, there was little except self-delusion, even over claims that Pétain's prestige had brought the German Army to a halt. In fact, the idea of a Free Zone was Hitler's own strategy. On 18 June 1940, the day de Gaulle made his first historic call from London in favour of a resistance movement, the German leader told Italy's Mussolini that it was indispensable that France continued to administer the country. 'This would be far preferable to a situation in which the French Government rejects German proposals and goes abroad to London to continue leading the war from over there without having to think about the disagreeable administrative responsibility which the occupying power would have to assume,' he said.

The urgent task for Pétain's Cabinet, which included two Socialists nominated by Léon Blum, was to create new institutions for what became the National Revolution with the motto 'Work, Family, Fatherland'. Despite the incredible disorder of the first few days, the reforms were ready within a week, put together with a resolution and speed totally absent during the crisis.

The force behind the new constitution that destroyed republicanism was Pierre Laval. He had been called into the Cabinet on 23 June 1940, just before his fifty-seventh birthday. Six years earlier, after the rioting outside the National Assembly, conservative newspapers held a nationwide opinion poll with the question: 'If France has need of a dictator, who would you choose?' Pétain was the most popular choice, with Laval just behind. The two men would now dispute the role in one of the strangest partnerships in history.

Laval was proud of the fact that he was born in 1883, the same year as Stalin and Mussolini. They were both 'men of the people and revolutionaries like me', he said. In 1935, after a legal, political and business career that had made him a huge fortune, he was appointed Prime Minister on a pacifist programme following an earlier term as Premier four years before and after holding office at the head of several ministries. A renegade Socialist, he had developed a special relationship with Mussolini and believed that this could be exploited to negotiate a lasting peace with Germany. His hopes were destroyed when he lost the premiership with the arrival of Léon Blum's Popular Front.

One of the more significant events of Laval's few months as Prime Minister had nothing to do with government. On 20 August 1935, his only daughter, Josée, married Comte René de Chambrun. The marriage brought Laval closer to Pétain. Although they had first met in 1931 on an official voyage to the United States, the two men had little contact when they were Ministers in the 1934 Doumergue Cabinet, but the Maréchal was a close friend of René de Chambrun's father, a military man. Using this family connection, one of Comte René's first acts was to persuade Pétain to become chairman of a French Information Centre he was setting up in the United States with Laval's blessing.

This minor political alliance was probably the only really amiable transaction between the two best-known figures of collaboration, even though Laval openly campaigned for a Pétain presidency from 1937 and the Maréchal reluctantly accepted Laval as a political partner on Alibert's repeated recommendation. Presumably, the Vichy leader saw Laval only as a hatchet man; indeed, he despised his future colleague, whom Pétain's wife, Eugènie, compared to a Moroccan carpet-dealer.

This allusion to Laval's possible mixed racial origins was one of many cheap insults from his enemies, who tried to fathom out why the future collaborator was ugly, dark and rapacious. The most common suggestion was that he was Jewish, a remark he dismissed with the words: 'I am neither *sidi* [Arab], Jew nor Freemason. If I was all that, or just part of it, I would say it was very honourable. But I must confess I have a fault. I am Auvergnat.' This remark was made in answer to hecklers at his Paris electoral base in the working-class suburb of Aubervilliers, where he was Mayor. He was remembered there for easy contact with local manual workers and for his deep, slow speech marked by the traditional Auvergne characteristic of rolled Rs.

While awaiting trial in 1945, Laval wrote his defence in a book published as *Laval Parle,* in which he said that it was an insult to accuse him of persecuting Jews. 'I was often characterised as a Jew myself. For many years, Maurras never wrote my name without preceding it with the word Jew, or without adding that my wife was a Portuguese Jew. It was during the repression against Jews that I fought most strongly against the Germans and their French accomplices.'

Racial exchanges were not limited to one side, for Madame Jeanne Laval used to refer to Madame Pétain's spurious Jewish origins. In the case of Pierre Laval, remarks about a dark family secret had been made since school, where he was called Jamaick, a nickname which led to frequent fights. This marginality was probably behind his passion for success, behind his need to break out of a small town where Laval was the most common name and where the first family photographs showed the little Pierre serving drinks at his father's café.

After studying law against the wishes of his parents, who needed him for the family business, he accumulated a financial empire partly based on media interests, including Radio Lyon. The radio station's advertising was handled by Marcel Bleustein-Blanchet, a young Parisian Jew whose agency, Publicis, became the most powerful company in France after the war, having recovered from seizure under Vichy legislation.

Laval's newspapers included *Le Moniteur,* whose printing presses in Clermont-Ferrand were to monopolise Vichy publications. His hobby was promoting his mineral water, La Sergentale, reputed to cure impotence and sold on French trains and Atlantic liners.

Laval's ugliness, his dark skin offset by a permanent white tie around his almost non-existent neck, predestined him to become the villain of the Vichy era. He was executed in 1945 by a firing squad as much for destroying the parliamentary system as for collaborating to the hilt during his second term in office from 1942 to 1944.

There has been more caution in recent judgements, particularly as Laval's dangerous compromises were inspired by a fanatical pacifism. After his first five months in office as Vichy's Prime Minister, he was sacked by Pétain against the wishes of the Germans, a true indication of the relative shares of real power held by the two French leaders. On Laval's second appointment in 1942 he was presented with a legal structure, including anti-Jewish laws, that had been put together by his predecessor as Premier, Admiral François Darlan, at a time when Pétain's faculties were considerably sharper than his supporters later claimed in his defence.

Pétain's greatest talent was to shift responsibility for the most distasteful decisions on to Laval, who seemed only too glad to assume them. Laval was also the pole of attraction for a previously unreconcilable group of political misfits. They included the fanatical anti-Semitic lawyer, Xavier Vallat, violent Socialist renegades such as Marcel Déat and Adrien Marquet, political enemies of Leon Blum like Charles Spinasse or Paul Faure, who were former members of the Popular Front, and the anti-Republican pacifist, Gaston Bergery.

In a series of brilliant manoeuvres in July 1940 during days of backroom lobbying, Laval persuaded the Senate and the National Assembly to scuttle the Third Republic and set up a state which wiped out the Revolutionary slogan, 'Liberty, Equality and Fraternity'. Meeting as a Parliament in Vichy's casino, MPs voted by 569 votes to 80 to 'crucify' the Republic, in Spinasse's description, so that the country would not sink into anarchy. Most Socialist MPs elected in the Popular Front triumph backed this execution, voting to hand over full powers to Pétain.

Léon Blum opposed the reforms and wrote in his *Mémoires:* 'In two days, I saw men change, become corrupt before my eyes as if they had been plunged into a toxic vat. What caused it was fear.' Laval had panicked Parliament into abandoning power, but his belief that the Maréchal would be content with a figurehead role was quickly dispelled.

CHAPTER FIVE

We, Philippe Pétain

THE THIRD REPUBLIC had set a tradition of weak, ceremonial Presidents who delegated government to their Prime Ministers. There was no reason to think that Pétain would want more than the prestige as the legitimate autocratic head of l'Etat Français. Laval assured himself the role of nominated Dauphin, a title which underlined the pseudo-monarchy of Vichy. It seemed only a matter of time before age or illness would get the better of the Maréchal, leaving his nominated successor in charge.

Laval quickly realised his mistake. After apparently engineering the type of technocratic government he wanted, as well as taking revenge on a Parliament that had 'vomited' him in 1936, Laval saw the immensity of his error as soon as the Head of State signed the constitutional act beginning: 'We, Philippe Pétain'.

The formula was a throwback to the style of kings and had been dictated to Alibert, the jurist, by Pétain without Laval's knowledge. There was no question of delegating power. The Maréchal was invested with more legal authority than any ruler since Bonaparte. He was in charge of the armed forces and responsible for all laws and for civil and military government appointments. He was also in charge of all negotiations and treaties.

It was not Pétain but his Ministers who had been reduced to participants in the National Revolution. As Alibert grew more and more influential with the Maréchal's authority behind him, Laval needed all his political cunning to survive. In the event, he lasted only until a palace coup in December 1940. It was enough time to create the animosity that guided much of his second term as Premier in 1942, when he sought his revenge.

Apart from their personalities, Pétain and Laval were divided by their concepts of government. The Premier was a professional politician whose ambition was to go down in history as a good manager by using a recognisable system to gain legitimacy. He was pragmatic, egocentric, paranoiac and often motivated by a desire to avenge slights, but he was not autocratic and he continually felt the need to justify his decisions and explain his errors. For his trial in 1945, he prepared a defence that became the basis of the posthumous book, *Laval Parle,* but in a mockery of a hearing that he called a 'judicial crime' he was given little or no chance to speak.

In contrast to Laval's repeated attempts to tell his story Pétain refused to give evidence at his own hearing, just as Louis XVI snubbed the Revolutionary Tribunal. The Maréchal was a monarch by instinct. He was accustomed to commanding and being obeyed without discussion as the holder of the highest military rank. He surrounded himself with followers and syco-phants, mostly military men used to accepting orders, while purging his Administration of anyone who could throw a shadow over his authority.

One of his speechwriters, Emmanuel Berl, the Jewish author, who supported the National Revolution in its opening weeks, recalled reports that Pétain secretly loved the Germans, but said that the old man 'didn't even like the French'.

'The Maréchal did not like anyone,' Berl added. 'He had a huge taste for power and great pleasure in taking it. When you're old, if there is no one coming to you for interviews, autographs and decorations, what have you got?'

After Philippe Pétain was sentenced to death for high treason in 1945 and before being reprieved by de Gaulle he was sent to Portalet, a fortress jail in the Pyrenees where he was given Cell 5, the same damp, dilapidated room where Georges Mandel had spent his first months in captivity. Mandel's murder in 1944 weighed more heavily in the final verdict than any other single factor and it was no coincidence that Pétain, then aged eighty-eight, was flown to the mountain prison. Soon after his arrival, a letter sent to his wife was intercepted by his jailer, Captain Joseph Simon. In it the Maréchal wrote: 'The place is deplorable. If I had known what I am living through now, I would not have sent my worst enemies here.'

Among others who were held there by Pétain were three former Premiers, Blum, Reynaud and Daladier, who were blamed for the 1940 defeat. Throughout his trial, and in many written and spoken statements up to his death in 1951 in another prison on the Atlantic Ile d'Yeu, Pétain would repeatedly claim that he had been ignorant of what had been done in his name. That is a view still widely held in preference to Berl's cruel judgement, which amounted to accusing Pétain of betraying France for personal vanity. Pétain's great age and past glory inhibited historians from judging him with the same severity as Laval, preferring de Gaulle's excuse that age was a shipwreck and that Pétain had 'delivered himself to people who were clever at covering themselves with his majestic lassitude'.

In his first months in office, Pétain had a different view of his own level of responsibility, notably when he told his friend Senator Lémery that the country had put its confidence in him by granting full powers. He alone was accountable to the nation and Ministers were accountable to him. Later, after meeting Hitler on 24 October 1940 at the small town of Montoire on the Loire, he recommended collaboration in a radio broadcast, and was even more explicit: 'It is me alone that history will judge.'

Although the chaos in Vichy and Pétain's lack of political experience encouraged ambitious Ministers to push through reforms with a minimum of consultation, there was little in the actions of the French state that contradicted Pétain's fundamental beliefs. On the Jewish question, in particular, he had been brought up in a period of anti-Semitism that, because of the Dreyfus Affair, had damaged the Army more than any other institution. His closest advisers were openly anti-Semitic and Pétain personally signed a formidable structure of racial laws built up under Admiral François Darlan in 1941 and 1942 to convince the Germans of France's good faith.

Putting aside the explanations of passivity or culpable ignorance over what was being done in his name to thousands of innocent people, it has always been difficult to pin down Pétain's attitude. He was extremely cautious about going on record and equally cunning in covering up his tracks. However, the nearest thing to an official history of the Vichy period made no concessions in its harsh judgement. In *L'Abime,* published by the Imprimerie Nationale in 1982, Jean-Baptiste Duroselle, Director of the Institut de l'Histoire des Rélations Internationales, swept aside all reticence on Pétain's attitude. 'The Maréchal was profoundly anti-Semitic in the same way as Charles Maurras,' Duroselle wrote.

No historian has shown that Pétain personally approved the Final Solution or was informed by the Germans that deported Jews were being summarily executed en masse, although this accusation was circulating in the Resistance press in France as early as July 1942, when La Grande Rafle took place. He was unquestionably cruel in his indifference, especially to the fate of immigrant Jews, reflecting a majority view among those who exploited his prestige in the little spa town.

While he made weak protests in certain cases such as those concerning war veterans or relatives of close friends, the rest were treated as if they had brought punishment on themselves by being born Jewish. Even the most pathetic appeals from children to save their parents from deportation or letters from war heroes were ignored, while French Jews in the Free Zone were left to fend for themselves after being ousted from the civil service and the professions.

If Pétain had an active grudge, it was centred on Freemasons. 'A Jew is never responsible for his origins, a Freemason is always accountable for his choice,' he said. Unfortunately, Jews were disproportionately numerous in Freemasonry. The esoteric movement was one of the strongest forces inside the pro-Dreyfus Radical Party, whose most prominent leaders included Jews like Mandel.

Pétain's family background, his career and his friends made him a model of French conservatism, a natural follower of the broad sentiments of Action Française, although he did not swallow all of Maurras' philosophies. For instance, Protestantism was acceptable in Vichy and among many influential Protestant advisers was the Maréchal's own speechwriter, René Gillouin, who eventually resigned in protest over the treatment of Jews.

Born into a big northern French Catholic family in 1856, Pétain was strongly influenced by his uncle, Father Jean-Baptiste Legrand, who had taken part in the Napoleonic wars. The Prussian victory of 1870 and the seizure of Alsace and Lorraine inflamed a natural patriotism in Pétain. He grew into a handsome but humourless artillery officer, and spent much of his career planning the defence of his home region around Béthune, one of the Great War battlegrounds.

His extraordinary national popularity after his victory at Verdun in 1916, where a million French and Germans died, was raised even further by his opposition to the useless sacrifice of the French Army in head-on offensives the following year. Even Socialists praised his handling of the 1917 mutinies and, more than twenty years later, Léon Blum described him as the most humane of French generals. However, Daniel Mayer, who led the Socialist Party while Blum was in prison, said there was nothing humane about Pétain's methods in stopping the revolt by French soldiers. 'He picked out every tenth man, whether he was a hero or a coward, and had him shot,' Mayer said.

The truth about the executions, during which, according to

official figures, only fifty-five soldiers were put before firing squads, has remained obscure. If Pétain's methods were more brutal than the public realised, his gift of turning failure to his advantage was shown at Vichy, where he even escaped blame for France's poor preparation for modern warfare.

Some of the heaviest responsibility for France's 1940 defeat was directly attributable to Pétain's lack of foresight. For at least ten years after the Great War, he was the dominant influence in defence planning and was War Minister in 1934. His prestige continued to influence the General Staff long after he retired, inspiring defensive policies that led to the construction of the Maginot Line, a chain of outdated underground fortresses crossing north-eastern France. Many of the mistakes he attributed to politicians were of his own making, not least because he refused to listen to de Gaulle's repeated warnings on the need for mobile defences to counter tank warfare.[4]

It was to cover up Pétain's bad military planning that Vichy was so assiduous in seeking scapegoats and it was in order to forget the humiliation of defeat that the nation all but deified Pétain in the first months of Vichy.

His striking military bearing, piercing blue eyes, white hair and obligatory officer's moustache were projected as outward signs of a benign great protector. The finest poets of the day, including Paul Claudel, sang his praises and his bust was reproduced hundreds of thousands of times, becoming an object of cult in both town halls and shop windows. A sycophantic song, 'Maréchal, nous voilà', virtually replaced the 'Marseillaise' and was sung every day by schoolchildren standing in front of the national flag or Pétain's portrait.

The Free Zone press devoted pages to his charismatic personality, and his saintlike appearance was even credited with working miracles. Behaving like an *ancien régime* monarch, the Maréchal held regular court for flocks of faithful who came to Vichy from all over the country and sent him 3000 letters a day.

Souvenirs, ranging from mugs to quasi-religious medals, were sold by the thousand while versions of the Lord's Prayer and the Credo were written with Pétain as the earthly god.

While war veterans led the cult, the most active supporters were the Catholic clergy, who distributed the Maréchal's speeches and used them as the basis for sermons inspired by the National Revolution's call for moral rectitude. Even the Archbishop of Toulouse, Monsignor Jules-Géraud Saliège, who later led opposition to anti-Jewish persecution, enthusiastically backed one of Pétain's themes, blaming the defeat on moral decline, traceable first of all to the Popular Front, which had reduced working hours and granted paid annual holidays.

As Saliège was one of the most courageous men of this dark period, it is worth recalling his comments, which reflected a national sentiment that France had been justly punished. 'For having chased God from the schools, for having accepted unhealthy literature and prostitution, for the degrading promiscuity of our workshops, offices and factories, Lord, we ask Your pardon. What use have we made of the victory of 1918? What use would we have made of an easy victory in 1940?'

Pétain won the support of a morally strict middle class, largely because he praised severe, repressive Catholicism with its accent on sexual purity. Although he was regularly seen beside cardinals and archbishops, who projected Pétain as an exemplary Christian, he did not feel bound by moral strictures himself. He never claimed to be a model of sexual abstinence nor a man who respected Christian marriage laws.

He was sixty-four before he married a friend's wife with whom he was having an affair at the time he was called on to deal with the 1917 mutinies. She was divorced and they were not married by the Church until 1943. After the war, Pétain told his jailer, Captain Joseph Simon, that he had caused his wife much pain by constant infidelity. His 'last night of love', he told the Captain, was in 1942 at the Hôtel du Parc, his official residence at Vichy.

It had been spent with a young woman who later sent him a long letter thanking him for a 'folle nuit d'amour'. Women had always been kind to him, he revealed, and there had been areas of the Hôtel du Parc where he could carry on illicit affairs.

Besides showing him to be still sexually active at the age of eighty-six, the liaison also gives an interesting insight into the Maréchal's state of health. His colleagues noted how the sudden elevation to supreme power of this taciturn, secretive man acted like a tonic, making him talkative and bursting with apparent good health. His main problem was a slight deafness that he probably exploited to his advantage, but there was no record of illness except occasional sore throats. Throughout the Vichy period and during his trial and imprisonment, there were indications that Pétain knew how to exploit old age to gain sympathy and it was probable that the impression he made on people during the first months depended on whether he wanted to be seen as a vigorous ruler or a manipulated old man.

If he was senile when the worst Vichy measures were taken against Jews and the Resistance movement, this could only be known for certain through the records of his personal doctor, Bernard Ménétrel. Nobody thought to ask the doctor for his opinion before he was killed in a car crash in 1947 while under investigation for his part in Vichy's treachery. No one blamed Ménétrel for looking after Pétain, nor for being his most trusted confidant. The doctor had a much more sinister role as his personal secretary and the most violent anti-Semitic in the head of state's entourage.

In a report by the Renseignments Généraux – the Special Branch – submitted for Pierre Laval's 1945 trial, the discredited Premier was quoted as saying to a senior police interrogator: 'Pétain never existed. It was me who created the political Pétain. I thought of everything except that France would be governed by a doctor, Ménétrel.'

In trying to deal with Pétain by classic political methods, Laval was attempting to break through an irrational screen in which the last and most effective barrier was Bernard Ménétrel. The doctor was one of the few people with whom Pétain had a genuine affectionate relationship, and the Maréchal was in no way perturbed by Ménétrel's virulent anti-Semitism. The doctor represented the visceral and illogical middle-class hatred of Jews, a hatred which he had inherited from his father, a Paris GP who refused Jews as patients. The father became Pétain's personal doctor before the Great War. His neighbours were old Army friends of Pétain, who was a lieutenant-colonel at the time.

There were rumours that Bernard was Pétain's natural child, a report contradicted by the Maréchal himself when speaking to his jailer, Joseph Simon. Referring to his many affairs, the old soldier said he had never left a 'modèle', a euphemism for a child. 'I always made sure women washed themselves,' he added.

As a baby, Bernard filled an emotional gap in the life of the austere bachelor Colonel, who often spent much of his leave in the Ménétrel house playing childish games with Bernard or his sister. When the father, Louis Ménétrel, died in 1936, Bernard became Pétain's personal physician at the age of thirty. The relationship was so close that, when Pétain hurried back from Madrid in May 1940 to join the Government, he stayed with Bernard Ménétrel and his young family. As a conscripted Captain, Ménétrel was leaving for the Front when Pétain ordered him to stay at his side. Ménétrel's two children would later be used in Vichy propaganda pictures playing with the grandfatherly soldier-protector.

There was nothing outwardly sinister or corrupt about the small and corpulent doctor, a family man pushed into the centre of immense power, capable of protecting the Head of State even from his cunning Prime Minister. Ménétrel lived on his Army doctor's modest pay, following Pétain to all the important rendezvous of the next four years until the Nazis separated the two men when they were forcibly transferred to Germany in September 1944.

His reward during the Vichy period was the power to favour his friends. Of the 2500 new French state medals, called the Francisque, Ménétrel personally awarded more than 270.

The doctor was never tried for helping the enemy because he was known to hate the Germans, nor was he ever seriously questioned about his influence on the Maréchal over the treatment of the Jews or any other issue. But there is little doubt that he made his anti-Semitic views heard. Serge Klarsfeld, the lawyer son of an immigrant Roumanian Jew, discovered a 1943 letter in the German archives in which Ménétrel wrote of his admiration for 'the resolution with which the Germans are putting to work the final annihilation of the Jews'.

By then rumours of massacres in concentration camps were circulating in Vichy and even Pétain must have been aware of the probable fate of deported Jews. There was no way of knowing whether Pétain shared his doctor's satisfaction at the Final Solution, although one might conclude that Ménétrel must have repeated his opinions openly while acting as the Maréchal's most trusted adviser.

Many of the letters sent by Jews to Pétain as a final resort are filed in the National Archives and some are annotated in Ménétrel's handwriting. His views can be summed up by a pencilled note on a request by a Frenchwoman asking that her war-veteran husband should be exempted from racial legislation. Ménétrel's comment reads: 'Typical Jew naturally demanding to escape the law.'

Even requests from Pétain's friends were sifted by Ménétrel, as was confirmed in a conversation between Eugènie Pétain and Xavier Vallat, the Commissioner for Jewish Affairs. René Gillouin, one of the official speechwriters, recalled that Madame Pétain had asked for dispensation for a Jewish friend and was told by Vallat that she was well placed to intervene personally. 'Of course, but I can't act without Bernard's knowledge, and when anyone speaks of Jews, he sees red,' Madame Pétain replied.

If Pétain had any doubts about anti-Jewish measures, Ménétrel was well placed to alleviate them, although he was not the only man Pétain consulted. The Vichy leader wrote to Charles Maurras and Pius XII asking for advice on the Jews. Maurras went to Vichy in 1940 to meet Pétain for the first time and provided no discouragement. The Pope, who was credited with the expression 'the Pétain miracle' in reference to the moral renaissance, appointed a nuncio to the Pétain court but ignored his own clergy's appeals to denounce deportations.

Alienated from the sufferings of the Jewish population both by the spa's geographical remoteness and by the natural sentiments of his Administration, there was never any likelihood that Pétain would play the role of protector in the Final Solution. One of the few excuses in his favour was that the process of persecution started before he came to power and that concentration camps were already full when his offices were installed on the third floor of the Hôtel du Parc, above those of his nominated Dauphin, Pierre Laval.

CHAPTER SIX

Le Statut des Juifs

LONG BEFORE THE Vichy regime was created and Pétain took the decision to intern foreign Jews, France already had what were officially called *camps de concentration*. These had caused international scandal. In 1939, barrack-style wooden huts surrounded by barbed wire were hurriedly constructed to house refugees from the Spanish Civil War. About 900,000 defeated Republicans, including members of the International Brigades representing more than fifty nationalities, poured across the border after Franco's victory. Nearly half were confined in primitive conditions.

Overcrowding, poor food, bad administration and callous treatment by warders from gendarmerie units showed how poorly prepared France was to look after refugees. Most camps were in or near the Pyrenees, far removed from official inspection. Nothing was done to improve accommodation when mass internment of potential enemy aliens began with the outbreak of war. Most internees were German or Austrian Jews who had fled Nazism. Leading anti-Hitler intellectuals were among at least 15,000 men arrested in the first weeks of the war, nearly half of whom would be released before winter. An even bigger operation took place during the chaos of May and June 1940, when women were also interned.

With the country mobilised against invasion, internment of enemy aliens was a precautionary measure that other nations at war, including Britain, put into operation. Nowhere was indifference to the fate of stateless foreigners more marked than in

France. British and United States newspapers protested against the conditions revealed in a description by Arthur Koestler, the Hungarian-born Jewish writer. He was a victim of administrative chaos, ordered to report for registration soon after war broke out even though Hungarians were not considered enemies. Koestler was sent to the small town of Le Vernet in the Pyrenees, which may have looked geographically well situated from Paris but was one of the coldest places in France during the winter. In his 1941 book, *Scum of the Earth,* Koestler recalled that among the 2000 occupants were several Germans who had spent the previous four years in Dachau, where they considered conditions to be better than at Le Vernet.

In the French camp, each hut housed 200 men in a space thirty yards long by five yards wide. Down each side, there were upper and lower platforms of planks only a yard across. These were 'beds', divided into compartments in which ten men slept in rows of five on thin layers of straw. Squeezed together on the yard-wide plank, everyone had to turn over if one changed position. There were no stoves nor blankets. Daily rations consisted of boiled beef at midday and a thin concoction of chick peas, lentils or vermicelli at night.

If that did not give the impression that refugees were enemies of the state, gendarmes forced home the message 'with fist and crop', according to Koestler, during the four daily roll calls or during road building. By December 1939, temperatures had fallen below zero and some internees died of poor treatment or committed suicide. When Koestler was released after it was admitted that he had been detained by error, dysentery was commonplace. Later, he went to England and was again interned as an alien, but this time in comparatively humane conditions.

While France's treatment of refugees during this period contained a measure of cynicism reflecting the denigration of foreigners over the previous decades, administrative failures were also an indication of the general breakdown in the national way of life which led to such a rapid defeat in 1940. Two years before, when laws were passed to control the entry of foreigners, there were an estimated 180,000 refugees in the country, which also served as a transit point for exiles from Fascist Italy, Spain or Central Europe. The experience of Lisa Fittko, a German-Jewish refugee who set up an escape route across the Pyrenees, added to the picture of incompetent civil servants and policemen over-whelmed by a bigger refugee influx when war broke out than that into any other Western country.

Lisa Fittko, born in Uzhorod in the Ukraine, was thirty in 1939 and had learned the art of survival in Germany, Austria and Czechoslovakia as an active anti-Nazi. She had been distributing anti-Fascist literature with her journalist husband when she was stopped from leaving France because war had broken out. Her husband was arrested immediately but she stayed in Paris until ordered to register in May 1940 at the Vélodrome d'Hiver, a stadium that would become an inhuman temporary detention centre during La Grande Rafle in 1942. With 10,000 other women, Mrs Fittko was sent to the most notorious of all concentration camps, Gurs, in the Pyrenees, near the beautiful medieval hill town of Oloron.

Conditions were chaotic and there was so little food that inmates counted the number of chick peas in the soup, con-sidering themselves spoilt if they received more than fourteen. As the Germans swept across France, French authorities admitted that they had no way of sorting genuine enemies from the mass of political refugees. The latter were predominantly Jews, but at Gurs the internees included a convent of nuns from Alsace. Because none of the French police spoke German, Lisa Fittko was asked to carry out interrogations, a situation she exploited to rid the camp of known Nazis and protect political refugees.

Camp administration at most centres broke down as France collapsed, allowing detainees to escape in their hundreds, most of them settling among the huge French and foreign population which took refuge along the Mediterranean. While living there, Lisa Fittko played a part in a tragedy that underlined the individual human element of a slaughter whose significance was often lost in repetition of meaningless casualty figures.

The German-Jewish philosopher Walter Benjamin asked her in September 1940 to guide him across the Pyrenees after he had been held in a detention centre in central France and then taken refuge in Marseilles. Benjamin, one of the Frankfurt school of philosophers, was forty-eight at the time and looked like an absent-minded professor. Mrs Fittko was struck by his gentle manner and exceptional courtesy when she guided him to the Spanish frontier at Port Bou, leaving him at a hotel. But a minor bureaucratic wrangle prevented him from staying in Spain, and Benjamin committed suicide in despair.

When he set out on the ten-hour walk to the frontier, an agonising journey because he was suffering from heart trouble, the philosopher had been carrying a leather briefcase containing a manuscript. During the walk he told his guide: 'You know, this briefcase contains my most precious possession. It must not be lost. This manuscript must be saved. It is more important than my own body.' The briefcase disappeared after being taken from his hotel by Spanish police. Its contents remain one of the great literary mysteries of the century.

Lisa Fittko escaped in 1943 after leading hundreds of Jewish refugees to safety on her Pyrenean route and later settled in Chicago. Recently she returned to France to thank the French people who had saved the life of her hunted parents in the South of France and to visit the detention blocks at Gurs. Like Benjamin's manuscript, the campsite had disappeared without trace or monument, except for the graves of 1167 Jews.

The inability of a nation at war to care for civilian internees did nothing to stop the Vichy regime from aggravating the problem from the first days in power by creating an ever growing pool of refugees, among them its own citizens. Responding to years of accusations that foreigners, particularly Jews, had sought French citizenship to undermine the national fabric, one of the first stones in the new edifice of racial legislation was laid on 22 July, only six days after Philippe Pétain had chosen his title, Head of State.

A decree setting up a Commission for Denaturalisation was promulgated and one of the first to volunteer for the three-man board was André Mornet, who was to become public prosecutor at Pétain's trial in 1945. Mornet asked to come out of retirement as a judge to serve on the Denaturalisation Commission, which was to be responsible for decisions stripping nationality from 15,154 foreigners, including 6307 Jews, most of whom would be deported as stateless persons. When he was questioned about this by Pétain's defence lawyers, Mornet made what was to become a classic Vichy excuse, saying that his actions had prevented the Germans from carrying out more stringent measures.

Even before the denaturalisation reform, other decrees were introduced which, if not explicitly anti-Semitic, enabled measures to be taken against Jews. On 6 July 1940, when the Republic technically still existed, all entry visas were cancelled and foreigners already in France were forbidden to travel freely. On 18 July, the *Journal Officiel* published a decree banning employment in the civil service to anyone whose father was not born French. Five weeks later, Vichy repealed a 1939 decree banning press articles on race or religion intended to arouse racial hatred.

This reactionary step, reinstating a double-edged free-speech law of 1881, was intended to prepare public opinion for the Statut des Juifs, which was being put together from the first days that Pétain came to power. On 3 October, though the Statut was far from complete, it was made public by the Government in a reaction to a move by the German Occupation authorities, who had released their own anti-Jewish controls six days before. On 4 October, a new Vichy decision was announced allowing local authorities in the Free Zone to intern foreign Jews. Three days later, Algerian Jews were deprived of French citizenship, a right that had been granted automatically since 1871.

As the Statut des Juifs and previous disguised measures against Jews contained no suggestion of annihilating the community, there was nothing in the laws that had not been openly discussed before the war by the men who became Pétain's closest advisers. Public opinion had been well prepared in the long run-up from the Dreyfus Affair, while public apathy about restrictions placed on French Jews could be explained by the abysmal lack of information in moderate pro-Vichy newspapers, which published only the bare bones of Government communiqués.

If the monthly reports to Vichy from provincial officials were correct, internment of foreign Jews passed unremarked, probably because it was seen as a follow-up to detention measures already taken at the outbreak of war and in the chaos of defeat. No one at the time could have seen the camps as reservoirs for the 1942 deportations, because a decision on the Final Solution had not yet been taken by the Nazis. Meanwhile, worsening problems in detention camps were known only to charitable organisations and local administrators.

Even with the difficult working conditions in the new French capital, Vichy was not short of men capable of rushing through its early priorities. The civil service was reorganised to bring forward young, competent officials. Pétain's reputation helped recruit advisers from private business sympathetic to Vichy's crusade of national recovery led by a new generation of technocrats desperate to wipe out the shame of defeat. Although many of them were inspired by the emotional force of Action Française, their real passion was for economic reform to rival the German model or for changes in the education system to reinforce moral and physical goals. For most of them, the Jewish problem was a nuisance issue.

Even at Vichy, discrimination in the early months was often only theoretical. The author Emmanuel Berl, who was a relative of Henri Bergson, wrote some of the most adulatory newspaper articles on Pétain as well as drafting some of his speeches. Although Berl was Jewish, he shared the general feeling that foreign Jews should be excluded from French society. Another prominent Jewish writer, Daniel Halévy, was also a strong supporter of Vichy in the opening months, praising the National Revolution in the influential daily newspaper, *Le Temps*.

Protestants, who had been seen as enemies since the Dreyfus Affair, also played an active part in bringing into effect priorities outlined before the war in clubs and newspapers sponsored by big business, which along with the defence forces and the Church was one of the most important influences in Vichy.

The responsibility of industrialists in encouraging Vichy's excesses, particularly collaboration, has often been under-estimated, because few big companies were punished after the war and many continued to play a central role in French politics and commerce. Among other factors, they helped to tranquillise public opinion through controlling interests in the pro-Pétain radio and press.

While it was often falsely claimed before the war that Jews had a near-monopoly of news outlets, big business had powerful propaganda machines of its own, including the two most respected newspapers, *Le Temps* and *Le Figaro*, plus access to sympathetic broadcasting stations like Laval's Radio Lyon. *Le Temps*, controlled by the big steel families, moved to the Free Zone with *Le Figaro*, providing two of the main information sources for the 18 million people living outside German-occupied areas. Faithfully following the Government line, they gave minimum coverage to controversial laws or explained them by official press releases full of distorted logic.

Le Temps' assets were seized at the Liberation and used to found *Le Monde*, but *Le Figaro* still publishes as the country's oldest newspaper. *Le Figaro* contained many of the ironies of this period, not least the fact that its owner, Yvonne Cotnareanu, had previously been married to the fanatically anti-Semitic cosmetics manufacturer, François Coty, who owned *L'Ami du Peuple*. On 6 December 1940, the Paris-based anti-Semitic weekly *Au Pilori* denounced her new husband, a Roumanian businessman, as a Jew.

Figaro's editor-in-chief, Pierre Brisson, had been a censor in the Phoney War and had escaped from German captivity by swimming the Allier river. He was hardly a rabid anti-Semite as he had a close business association with the millionaire Jewish publicist Marcel Bleustein-Blanchet, who also worked for Laval's Radio Lyon. Despite this friendship, Pierre Brisson made no exceptions when he wrote under his own initials in December 1940 that all Pétain's reforms 'were inspired by the realistic sentiment of necessity' and added: 'They show a determination for purification and moral revival . . . worthy of one of the most decisive tests in our history.'

The newspaper's credibility was reinforced by the quality of its wartime contributors like the poet Paul Valéry and the authors François Mauriac and Georges Duhamel. Readers were not aware that the newspaper was subsidised by Pétain's Government, receiving more than 2 million francs in aid in 1941. Like most Vichy supporters, despite collaboration, the newspaper was implicitly anti-German and scuttled itself in November 1942 when the Germans occupied the Free Zone, an act which justified resurrection in 1944 with the same editor-in-chief.

Le Temps was even more of a direct link with big business as it represented the 200 richest families, who were said to run France until the war. Some of the eminent industrialists sponsoring National Revolution policies were named in an article by the clandestine version of the Communist paper, *L'Humanité*, when, on 3 October, it approved Government confiscation of assets belonging to the exiled Maurice de Rothschild. 'Très bien, but to expropriate a capitalist because he is a Jew and leave the others solves nothing,' the paper said. 'The de Wendels, the Schneiders, the Renaults, the Lehideux, the Michelins, the Baudoins or others must be expropriated as well.'

All these families provided leading Vichyists, while big-industry protégés, like Alibert, became Government Ministers directly responsible for administering anti-Jewish laws. They worked against any return of a Popular Front-style administration which might reinforce Socialist and Communist power in a bid to break employer dictatorship. There was also the simple question of accumulating money, which was achieved through voluntary collaboration to provide Germany with war material from the Free Zone. As a bonus, some businesses also benefited from the destruction of Jewish competition when firms and property were confiscated and handed over to aryan trustees.

None of the many historians who have sifted French and German archives has come up with any proof that Vichy acted under Nazi pressure in passing racial laws in 1940. Instead, they have emphasised an atmosphere of competition between France and Germany to become the most anti-Semitic nation, not least because French legislation was more specifically racist than the occupying Army's. In the first few months, French policy lines often clashed with those of the Germans, who deported their own Jews to the Free Zone while France tried to expel them.

Apart from coping with the huge exodus from the North, local provincial communities that had rarely seen Jews were suddenly confronted by the enforced arrival, among others, of 3000 Alsatian Jews, thrown out by the Germans in July 1940, or of 6500 German Jews from Baden and Saarpfalz who were des-patched in October in sealed trains to Lyons, part of an unfulfilled plan to send 270,000 German Jews into Vichy territory. The French protested, while the Jews were shuttled backwards and forwards for three days until they were sent to Gurs, where many died. The survivors were returned to Germany for extermination in 1942 and 1943.

An estimated 22,000 eastern French Jews had been expelled into Vichy territory before the end of October, joining thousands of other non-Jewish deportees from Alsace and Lorraine and refugee foreigners, who contributed to a general wave of xenophobia.

Even though Pierre Laval told the Germans several times in the summer of 1940 of planned exclusion measures for Jews, the question does not seem to have been officially discussed by Cabinet before 10 September, nor did Pétain ever refer to forthcoming restrictions on Jews in his many speeches. There was even reluctance to admit official anti-Semitism as late as 12 September, when the Interior Minister, Marcel Peyrouton, referred to a 'certain category of people' in justifying measures that restricted access to medicine and the Bar to nationals with French fathers, a move aimed at cutting down the number of Jews in those professions. Peyrouton, whose police would soon be involved in mass arrests, produced another standard Vichy excuse when he was tried in 1945. He claimed that Ministers had been no more than agents carrying out Pétain's orders. 'I am not a Republican nor an anti-Republican,' he said. 'I am an official.'

Two weeks after Peyrouton's camouflaged attempt to squeeze Jews out of the professions, the Germans specifically identified the enemy within by introducing strict controls on Jews in the Occupied Zone. Perhaps relieved that the Nazis had brought the issue into the open, a Vichy Cabinet meeting on 1 October approved the Jewish statute presented by the Justice Minister, Raphaël Alibert. It was publicly revealed two days later. The six-day difference between publication of German and French anti-Jewish laws has been the basis of claims by Pétain's supporters that France only responded to Nazi threats.

While extreme caution has to be used in quoting any of the leading Vichy protagonists, who often lied blatantly at their trials to shift blame for the Jewish slaughter, the Foreign Minister in October 1940, Paul Baudoin, said that Pétain himself was the 'most severe' during the Cabinet meeting on 1 October and insisted that the 'judicial and educational systems should contain no Jew'.

Baudoin, who recalled his period at Vichy in a book, *Neuf Mois au Gouvernement,* was delegated to explain the measures to American newsmen accredited to the shrunken French Administration. He said his Government intended to 'limit the action of a spiritual community, which, regardless of its qualities, has always stayed outside the French intellectual community'. He promised that neither people nor property would be touched and there would be no humiliating discrimination. This would have sounded a strange reassurance to reporters if they had met Jean-Louis Tixier-Vignancour, responsible for radio at Vichy and well known as a Jew-baiter with a particular hatred for Léon Blum.

In discussing French willingness to provide victims for the Holocaust, much is made of the major difference between French and German legislations. Vichy defined a Jew by race while the Nazis spoke only of religion. For once, the French were less hypocritical while satisfying an obscure matter of conscience. *Le Figaro,* which reported the first Statut des Juifs without comment, explained the Government criteria when the statute was updated the following year. Publishing an official Vichy information-service text, the newspaper said that 'the Maréchal's Government never intended, in effect, to attack the freedom of this religion, because, contrary to what has been said on many occasions in newspaper articles, it was never intended to turn the Jewish problem into a religious problem.'

By then, Jews had already been rounded up, murdered, stripped of their property or hounded out of jobs by both Germans and French without being told whether it was because they went to a synagogue or because of their ancestry. The legal basis of French discrimination, applicable in both Occupied and Vichy France, was published in the *Journal Officiel* on 18 October 1940, where the seven articles of the decree were detailed under the opening words, 'Nous, Maréchal de France, chef de l'Etat français . . . décrétons', and was reported on *Le Figaro*'s front page the following day between items on Turkey's policies on Islam and a raid by 200 German bombers on London.

A Jew was defined as anyone with three Jewish grandparents or only two grandparents if the spouse was also Jewish. A list of excluded professions or official posts, ranging from Head of State to cinema manager, included the officer corps, all elected offices, teaching, most civil service appointments, the judiciary, press and entertainment. The clause on entertainment was particularly aimed at the cinema industry, which was blamed for undermining morale and censoring anti-Jewish material.

Among those excluded was the director Max Ophuls, a German-Jewish immigrant. He made a comeback after the war while his son, Marcel, took personal revenge on Vichy with a 1971 film called *Le Chagrin et la Pitié*, revealing the extent of collaboration and anti-Semitism in Vichy's chief satellite town, Clermont-Ferrand. In 1989, he won a Hollywood Oscar for his documentary on the Barbie trial, called *Hôtel Terminus*.

Over the next few months, the Statut des Juifs would be refined by decrees to make it even more difficult to escape being labelled Jewish and to restrict even more professions. In the meantime, a witchhunt had started that involved the best-educated and most qualified sections of the population in racial discrimination against their colleagues. Nowhere was this more intense than in education, where even future left-wing activists like Simone de Beauvoir signed papers denying Jewish blood. Whether the author of *The Second Sex* would have been able to keep her lycée post without this implicit rejection of her Jewish friends is doubtful.

Official instructions said that even if colleagues were only thought to be Jewish they should be denounced and that any name changes should be checked with earlier generations, if necessary by looking at family tombstones.

Exceptions were reserved for Jews with honourable war service, a rule that turned out to be a moral fraud. Hundreds of national heroes and their families would eventually be sent to gas chambers for the sole reason that they were part of a new, legally created sub-species. Among them would be many of the 30,000 foreign Jewish volunteers, representing most of the male population old enough for service, who joined special regiments or the Foreign Legion at the outbreak of war. They were given no protection after demobilisation and, under internment laws, were sent as slave labour to help build the Trans-Saharan railway. Most of them survived the war, unlike many of their friends interned in France.

CHAPTER SEVEN

Collaboration

PHILIPPE PÉTAIN'S UNINTERRUPTED presence as head of the French state from July 1940 until he was forcibly taken to Germany in 1944, gave a false image of continuity to Government policies in the spa town. Stability was no more impressive than that of a Third Republic administration. The Vice-Président du Conseil, the full title of Pétain's Prime Minister, was changed four times. There were three Cabinet reshuffles in the first five months alone while portfolios changed hands with bewildering speed as men and policies fell out of favour or as France accepted or rejected German pressure. In the first year there were four different Foreign Ministers, five Ministers for both the Interior and Education and six for Industrial Production.

There was constant rivalry over control of propaganda outlets. Eight different Information Ministers succeeded each other in the space of four years while there were fifteen junior Ministers responsible for radio. Pierre Laval, twice Premier, had different powers in his two terms in office.

Sometimes specialists would dominate policy; at other times the military gained the upper hand. Even major guidelines were contradictory. Pétain liked to be called the Maréchal-paysan, idealising a return to traditional rural-based values linked to the influence of the Catholic Church. However, his new wave of government specialists, many of them graduates from Grandes Ecoles which trained future civil servants and industrialists, usually worked to create the modern, materialistic society demanded by big industry.

Apart from the Maréchal's prestige, the most identifiable
thread during the Vichy period was the unshakeable belief that
Germany would win the war, thus making concessions to Berlin
an essential part of policy. Collaboration, though, was uneven and
was cut into two periods of about two years each. In the first,
Vichy tried to promote the National Revolution while making
only piecemeal compromises with Nazi priorities, despite a
meeting between Pétain and Hitler on French soil in October
1940.

From mid-1942, after Laval returned for a second term, little
separated the main lines of Vichy's programme from German
priorities. The closer Germany came to defeat, the more Vichy
was prepared to support the Nazi cause, claiming that France was
in the front line of the fight against Communism.

The tragic mould was set in the last six months of 1940 when
collaboration was officially sealed by a French government
anxious to offset crippling Armistice terms. These involved the
payment of 400 million francs a day for the Occupation Army, an
exorbitant sum which the French claimed could pay for 18
million men. Laval, whose pacifist record went back to the Great
War, tried to develop joint policies with Germany by using
traditional diplomatic channels. Like Pétain, he was sure that
Britain would soon be defeated and that Europe's political future
would be decided in Berlin. His own pre-war record of
conciliation with Fascist powers was considered a guarantee
of French co-operation. He offered an invaluable bargaining
counter, the wealth of France's Empire.

On the general idea of a working relationship with the Nazis,
Laval's thinking did not run contrary to Pétain's analysis. The
Maréchal, who was also concerned about keeping the Empire
intact and restoring normal peacetime conditions, sent out
parallel diplomatic feelers to the German Air Force chief,
Hermann Göring, through the Great War fighter ace, René
Fonck.

Because post-war knowledge of German atrocities has changed historical perception of French attitudes in the first period of the war, it should be remembered that these contacts took place when it was felt that a reasonable deal on a permanent peace could be arranged in a civilised way. Hitler's promised outrages in *Mein Kampf* and his well-known revengeful hatred for France were disguised by the superficially correct behaviour of German officials, some of whom shared the dream of a fair French–German peace agreement.

In essence, French approaches were made in the spirit of the Munich agreement, a naive belief that Hitler was a reasonable leader in need of friendly co-operation with France to defeat the common enemy, Marxism. In the first few deluded weeks, French leaders, among them Pétain himself, were inspired by the Prussian recovery after Napoleon's lightning victory in 1806, which was followed by a period of collaboration.

Pétain also drew on contemporary examples for encouragement, seeing himself as representing a European-wide movement towards autocratic government. His personal model was the Portuguese dictator, Antonio Salazar, and he kept the French edition of Salazar's book, *Estado Novo,* on his desk for visitors to see. The third French edition in 1942 carried a preface comparing all the main lines of Pétain's National Revolution with those of Salazar's regime.

The idea of an eventual meeting with Hitler went back to well before the war. During his first few weeks in power, Pétain talked to many people about projected top-level discussions in which his own prestige would be decisive. The first recorded mention of the project was during a conversation with the American Ambassador, William Bullitt, on 1 July 1940, even before Laval had convinced parliamentarians to scuttle the Republic.

After many approaches to the German authorities, particularly by Laval, the Nazi dictator agreed to talks when he saw the chance of testing French readiness to confront Britain. This followed a naval engagement at Dakar, Senegal, on 23 September 1940, in which French ships beat off a British-backed invasion attempt by Charles de Gaulle's Free French. When Germany's Battle of Britain air offensive faltered in the autumn, one of Hitler's main hopes of destroying British resistance was a plan to invade Gibraltar through Spain with Franco's help. In October 1940, his personal train, *Amerika*, took him to Hendaye on the Spanish frontier for a meeting with Franco, but the Spanish dictator refused to co-operate.

Just before that meeting, on 22 October, Hitler met Laval while the official train was parked in the small French town of Montoire on the Loire river. On his return from Hendaye, Hitler talked to Pétain in the same railway station. By then, the importance of an eventual military deal with the French had diminished because of Franco's rebuff. Discussions between the French and German leaders turned into little more than polite and evasive exchanges.

German accounts agree with French claims that Pétain offered no deal and that Hitler was just as non-committal in the two hours of talks, held through an interpreter. No document was signed, nor was there any definition attempted of the scope of collaboration. The Jewish question was not raised directly.

The meeting at Montoire was the first time that Pétain crossed into the Occupied Zone and was to prove the most tragic of all his mistakes. Pride and vanity pushed the Maréchal into assuming responsibility for a decision to collaborate, destroying his own claims to being 'a shield' for the French people and identifying him as an enemy for the nascent Resistance movement.

He even lied about the results of the talks rather than let it be thought that Hitler had humiliated him or that new concessions had been made. Six days after shaking the German leader's hand, Pétain gave the impression on radio that he had talked Hitler into offering a fairer deal than the Armistice. 'I did not give in to any diktat from him, nor any pressure,' Pétain said, insisting that he had gone to Montoire of his own free will, a fact confirmed by Hitler, who said he had responded to an invitation from the Maréchal.

Later in his radio speech, Pétain provided the basis for a charge of high treason by saying: 'It is with honour and to maintain French unity – a unity of ten centuries – in the framework of constructive activity in the new European order that, today, I enter into the way of collaboration.' To justify this, he added what amounted to a fantasy. 'Therefore, in the near future, the burden of sufferings of our country could be eased, the fate of our prisoners improved and the cost of occupation lightened. The Demarcation Line could be made more flexible and facilitate administration and food supplies for our territory.' In the past, he said, he had spoken as a father and now he spoke as a chief. 'This policy is mine. It is me alone that history will judge.'

Only three weeks later, the Germans showed their contempt for the idea that France might have a special place in Nazi-controlled Europe by expelling 70,000 people from Lorraine, despatching them to Lyons in sixty-one trains. On Friday, 13 December, Pétain dismissed Laval, blaming him for the Montoire fiasco, in what proved a dangerous act of defiance. Soon afterwards, a new Prime Minister, Admiral François Darlan, would be obliged to offer Germany military help.

Collaboration in its true sense of working together had proved another illusion. Instead, the word quickly became a synonym for a sinister and treasonable alliance in which the Germans took what they wanted from a supine, disorganised French administration sinking in the mire of its own contradictions.

Laval was dismissed for what amounted to *lèse-majesté* in a palace revolution which revealed the true centre of power. After the expulsions from Lorraine, Pétain saw that he had been duped and his anger concentrated on his Dauphin. Among many comments recorded by one of Pétain's advisers, Henri du Moulin de

Labarthète, Pétain described Hitler as 'a little nothing, an inflated parvenu and a mediocrity'. He even claimed to have warned Hitler during his talks that his attitude was impolite.

Pétain's pride had been stung and, by 9 December, he decided to get rid of Laval, who irritated him in many other ways, not least by chain-smoking in his presence. 'Who does he take himself for, enfin?', Pétain was quoted as saying. 'Is it him or me whom France has called on?'

One of the key plotters in Laval's fall was Raphaél Alibert. He pushed Pétain into believing that a German invitation to Paris, arranged by Laval, was a conspiracy to kidnap the Maréchal, leaving his Dauphin as the real ruler. Hitler had offered to send back the ashes from Vienna of Napoleon's heir, the Aiglon, and a ceremony was planned for Les Invalides. Pétain gave the impression that he was ready to attend rather than insult the Führer and then held a Cabinet meeting in which all Ministers were asked to resign in preparation for a reshuffle. Only Laval's resignation was accepted. 'I no longer have confidence in you,' Pétain said. 'You are dragging France much too far. You made me go to Montoire by surprise. You accept nearly everything the Germans ask you and you keep me informed of nothing.'

On the evening of 13 December, Laval was arrested at the Hôtel du Parc by members of the Groupe de Protection, an ultra-right-wing parallel police force which guarded Pétain. The group had developed out of the pre-war terrorist movement, Les Cagoulards, the hooded ones, who were involved in plotting during the riots of February 1934.

There was pressure to assassinate Laval, notably from Dr Ménétrel, but he was put under guard at his home in Châteldon and later rescued by German troops, led by the Ambassador, Otto Abetz.

Several lessons could be drawn from Laval's dismissal. It proved that during the opening months of Vichy, when the Statut des Juifs was drawn up, Pétain's authority dominated. Secondly, despite Hitler's anger at a personal insult over Pétain's refusal to attend the ceremony and at Vichy's ousting of the Minister most favourable to collaboration, there was no move to occupy the Free Zone nor to take revenge on French prisoners of war. Pétain had called Hitler's bluff and got away with it. The Germans could not afford to waste men administering all of France at a time when the air offensive against Britain continued and plans to invade Russia were advancing.

Laval had the last word in the row. Before he set off for Paris, now under German protection, there was an angry scene in the Maréchal's office where Laval made a prophetic judgement: 'You couldn't care less about honour or dignity. You are a puppet, a windbag and a weathercock which turns with the wind.'[5]

It was no less than the truth. Getting rid of Laval had been an act of personal vengeance that had nothing to do with pressure for collaboration, which developed more rapidly without Laval. Within weeks, French and Germans were voluntarily working side by side in a number of areas, notably harmonising treatment of Jews.

One of the reasons for the Vichy Government's mistakes during Laval's first period in office was an inability to identify the real influences in the Nazi Administration. This was partly due to disarray in the French bureaucracy following internal purges of reluctant Pétainists, but German forces were just as prone to policy contradictions and personal rivalry over military, diplomatic or security priorities. Unfortunately, the French never tried to exploit this early confusion to put off fateful choices. Instead, in the immediate aftermath of Montoire, there was a flurry of activity, notably by Laval, to try and turn the spirit of contact into concrete advantage.

The Premier continued his policy of concentrating on traditional channels through the German Embassy in Paris, a misinterpretation of the Nazi power structure caused by a refusal to see that war was destroying normal diplomatic influence. The German administrative system in Paris was spread into different channels that often worked against each other, with bilateral disputes supposedly handled by an Armistice Commission in Wiesbaden, Germany. The Occupation Army itself was at the mercy of Hitler's whims while regular officers resented pressure from Nazi policymakers like Heinrich Himmler and his SS. Over and over again, promises were made to Vichy by Berlin that were never kept while the French all too often anticipated Nazi demands in the vain hope of gaining favours.

This was the case with the Jewish issue. Coherent German demands for repression did not emerge until the SS gained the upper hand in 1942, taking over complete control of law-and-order administration in France from the military command. The initial urgency, as far as Hitler was concerned, was to drain France economically while avoiding controversies that might force Germany to assume administration in the south. Discussion on the Jewish question did, however, preoccupy the invaders from the first days, because every command sector had its rival Jewish section.

At the beginning, overall administration policy was in the hands of the German Army's French Military Command, Militarbefehlshaber in Frankreich or MBF, working from the Hôtel Majestic near the Arc de Triomphe in a building that has become a government international conference centre. The MBF had both military and civilian chiefs. The uniformed men were predominantly professional Wehrmacht or Luftwaffe officers. The civilians included fanatical Nazis, like their chief, Dr Werner Best, a leading supporter of ridding Europe of its Jews. His economic staff was led by Dr Elmar Michel, who was later implicated in the aryanisation of Jewish businesses. Despite its anti-Jewish officials, the regular defence forces would never be more than marginally involved with deportations, believing that fighting soldiers would object to being mobilised for police work.

The German Embassy, situated in the rue de Lille near the National Assembly, had its own Semitic theorists, including the Ambassador, Otto Abetz, the strongest influence on Pierre Laval. His main role would be as a political go-between and he convinced the Premier that Hitler would grant favours if France stepped up anti-Jewish measures.

The Ambassador had a clear advantage over most of the occupying forces as he could speak French. He was a francophile with a French wife, although this did not prevent him from fleeing France with a mistress in 1944, taking a hoard of looted treasure. A man of considerable charm, Abetz had studied art in Paris and led Franco-German conciliation moves in the thirties, when he was also Ambassador, before being expelled as an *agent provocateur.*

Abetz continually overestimated his own influence on Hitler but, for a time, he persuaded Laval that he was the Führer's privileged spokesman, charged with organising a special Franco-German relationship. He was also a favourite of Parisian right-wing intellectuals, many of whom opposed the Vichy of generals and churchmen. They were more attracted by Abetz's programme for a popular anti-clerical European mass movement with anti-Semitism as a rallying cry.

The Embassy had its own Jewish Affairs section which, from 1941, took part in regular Tuesday meetings with other Jewish branches in the Army and the German police. The Embassy department was headed by a fanatical Nazi, Karl-Theo Zeitschel, a former Navy doctor who claimed to be the bastard son of the Kaiser. He often based his analysis on interpretations sent to him by the German Consul in Vichy, Roland Krug von Nidda.

There was regular contact between the Army, the Embassy and Vichy from the start because Pétain had his own delegate in Paris, Fernand de Brinon, a pro-German who would be executed after the war. De Brinon's main concern was to establish a relatively friendly working relationship with the occupiers, while the German

Army tried not to complicate its task by appearing repressive. There were only a million troops occupying the biggest area of national territory conquered by the Germans and the political priority was to persuade Vichy to stand firm in its opposition to Britain. It was only when Communist armed resistance developed in August 1941 that the occupying forces were directly drawn into action against Jews, who were blamed for sabotage attacks.

The Germans were concerned that repressive action against Jews would cause a similar situation to that existing in Holland, where arrests had caused popular reaction from the first weeks. Dutch Communists supported a series of protests by organising a national strike in February 1941, in solidarity with persecuted Jews. Agitation on the same scale in France, where the Communist Party tolerated collaboration until the invasion of the Soviet Union in June 1941, would have been a serious blow to the Nazi conception of France as its most important economic partner.

As a result, Pétain's authority and the role of an independent French government were scrupulously respected as far as the Free Zone was concerned, while Nazi pressure over discrimination against the Jews was at first purely theoretical. For some time, the French did not even know of the existence in Paris of what would become the real motor of extermination, a special department hidden inside Heinrich Himmler's SS and its Security Division, the Reichssicherheitshauptamt or RSHA.

The RSHA covered the Sipo-SD, the SS Security Police and the Secret Police, the Gestapo. Because the Gestapo was technically an internal German political police force its presence in the capital contravened the Armistice and it had to be installed secretly. But there was no complaint from France when the Gestapo came into the open, setting up sections in other big occupied cities where most of the plainclothes staff was French.

Vichy had some excuse for failing to see the eventual power contained in the complicated structure of the SS Sipo-SD Security and Secret Police with its deliberately enigmatic sub-sections and conflicting levels of command. Confusion continued even after the Liberation, complicating attempts to prosecute war criminals. Three of the most active SS members in Paris were not tried until 1979. Nor was rank any clear guide to ultimate responsibility in the persecution of Jews, as was shown by the 1987 trial of Klaus Barbie, who was only an SS-Lieutenant during his reign of terror in Lyons.

In Paris, long-term planning was in the hands of another lieutenant, SS-Obersturmführer Theodor Dannecker. He was twenty-eight when he came to Paris in summer 1940 to head the RSHA Bureau IVB4–J or the Judenreferat, the Jewish Affairs section. Dannecker was desperate to make a success of his task and often overreached himself, but he forced the pace of deportation despite the reluctance of senior SS officers more concerned with smooth economic collaboration. He must have been continually aware of the example in Holland, where many Nazi-imposed restrictions on Jews were introduced well before those in France. Among his rivals in Holland was Klaus Barbie, who was involved in physical attacks on Jews and arrests while Dannecker was still struggling with paperwork or theories on establishing a Jewish homeland.

Dannecker was chosen for the Paris post as the SS expert on what was known as the Madagascar Plan, a proposal to send European Jews to the French Indian Ocean colony. He was also the Gestapo expert on Assimilated Jews, which had led to a special study of the established French community whose leaders he would identify when arrests started.

The decision to slaughter the European Jewish population was not taken until 1942, but Dannecker had been well prepared for extreme action. He was a pure Nazi product, a member of the SS since 1932 when only nineteen. This rescued him from an unpromising career after only average secondary school studies in his home town of Tübingen and an early commercial job with a textile merchant. Within two years he was a permanent member of the SD, and before long he was working in Berlin with Reinhard Heydrich, Himmler's SS deputy and head of all Nazi police forces, including the Gestapo.

Dannecker's determination to succeed was intensified by competition with better-educated colleagues who were trained with him at the Gestapo's Ideological Enemy section under the control of a university professor, Dr Franz-Alfred Six, head of Berlin's Foreign Political Science Institute. Among Six's small group of students was Adolf Eichmann, logistical mastermind of the Final Solution, and Dannecker's future SS colonel in Paris, Helmut Knochen, the son of a university professor and an expert in English literature.

One of Six's most brilliant students was Herbert Hagen, who would also be sent to Paris as an SS-Major in 1942. With Six, Hagen wrote a popular pre-war anti-Semitic brochure on world Jewry, *Das Weldjudentem.* Six went on to lead an extermination commando unit in the Soviet Union.

As a Nazi theorist, Dannecker was put in charge of a number of conferences on anti-Jewish propaganda and later was an active man in the field, operating with Gestapo squads in Eastern Europe before Eichmann sent him to Paris. His modest rank of lieutenant did not prevent him from dealing on equal terms with superior officers both in the MBF military command and the Embassy during the opening months of Occupation, when he co-ordinated regular weekly meetings with other Jewish affairs experts.

His main difficulties were with SS colleagues, particularly the English literature expert, Colonel Knochen, a tall, good-looking Prussian. The Colonel had been a Nazi since the age of twenty-two in 1932, although he was never considered a fanatic. His pre-war work was mainly undercover intelligence, a role he played at the 1936 Berlin Olympics where he posed as a sports writer. When war was declared, Knochen engineered the capture of two

British agents in neutral Holland in a case which caused an international sensation. The Colonel's natural flair for diplomacy and innate political caution would make him a key figure in dealings with Vichy over both economic collaboration and the Jewish issue. He was a pragmatic rather than a visceral anti-Semite, which meant that Dannecker's often frenetic anti-Jewish demands met with opposition when they cut across the more important priorities of exploiting French industrial resources and flattering Pétain.

But Knochen's resistance to Dannecker was also inspired by contempt. A personality clash ended in autumn 1942 with Dannecker being forced to leave France on the strength of reports made by his colonel. Dannecker was equally misunderstood and disliked by the SS-General, Karl Oberg, a conscientious, lacklustre man of forty-five, whose shaved head and thin-rimmed glasses contrasted with the deliberately stylish look adopted by most of his subordinate officers.

Like many leading SS men, Oberg had more or less drifted into pre-war National Socialism to avoid unemployment after an unsuccessful venture as a banana importer. He was not sent to Paris until May 1942 when it was decided that the SS would take overall responsibility for security work. His authority rested on a close relationship with Himmler's deputy, Reinhard Heydrich, who came to Paris two months before La Grande Rafle as head of the whole Nazi RSHA security administration to negotiate with the French and reorganise German security. Oberg could not speak French and depended heavily on Colonel Knochen to develop a comparatively easy relationship with Vichy leaders, a relationship that softened many of Dannecker's extremist demands.

It needed the stubbornness and ambition of the fanatically anti-Semitic Dannecker to mount the first large-scale deportations. He even lied to Eichmann in order to be allotted more trains than he could hope to fill at a time when Oberg and

Knochen were set on putting him in his place. Serge Klarsfeld, the lawyer who has led an international hunt for war criminals involved in the Final Solution, said that no other member of Eichmann's team could have been so successful as Dannecker, whom photographs show to have been a stocky, broad-faced man, obviously proud of his black Gestapo uniform. 'He was the real architect of the anti-Jewish structure in France,' Klarsfeld said. 'Without him it would have been impossible to have obtained co-operation from the French authorities in the mass deportations of July 1942.'

If he was still alive, Dannecker would undoubtedly take that as a compliment, but he hanged himself in an American prison in 1945 before he could be tried.

CHAPTER EIGHT

The Arrests

IN THE SUMMER and autumn of 1940, none of the Nazi organisations had a definite programme for Jews except to get rid of as many as possible by sending them to the Free Zone while Dannecker got on with the practical details of the Madagascar Plan and accumulating intelligence material on the Jewish community.

An indication of Nazi reluctance to press for deportations was shown after the Armistice agreement which forced France to send back German political refugees. An invited Gestapo-led commission openly toured Vichy concentration camps, examining 32,000 detainees during the late summer of 1940. Of the 7500 Germans in more than thirty camps or detention centres, about 5000 were Jews; yet only 800 refugees were reclaimed, almost all of them aryan. Most of the important political Jewish suspects had escaped in the chaos of defeat and, despite French insistence, the Germans said they were not interested in repatriating ordinary Jewish citizens. Among those who were taken away was Herschel Grynszpan, whose murder of a German diplomat had sparked off Kristallnacht.

Forced repatriation of German political refugees did not signal the beginning of the deportation policy. Another eighteen months were to pass before the first trainload of Jews was sent to Germany. That departure would almost certainly have been delayed if Dannecker had not found an invaluable ally on the French side, the Vichy Commissioner-General for Jewish Affairs, Xavier

Vallat, a war hero and former MP. Although they often worked in opposition, the two men overcame the hesitations of their superiors and a lethargic bureaucracy to ensure that France was well represented when the Final Solution was decided in January 1942.

German authorities were initially cautious about any large-scale police action against Jews because they feared that popular condemnation would rebound on the Occupation forces. On 30 January 1941, three months after the Vichy Government had legalised a witchhunt against foreign and French Jews with the Statut des Juifs, the Sipo-SD second-in-command, SS-Captain Kurt Lischka, who was answerable to Colonel Knochen, drew up a report of a meeting between the military command, the MBF, and the Nazi Security Police. These talks agreed to leave future methods of settling the Jewish question to Vichy. 'As a result, German services will restrict themselves to making suggestions,' the report added. Even at the end of February the following year, an Embassy estimate by the Jewish Affairs councillor, Karl-Theo Zeitschel, warned that public opinion lagged behind the intentions of the French Government, who 'would be happy to be rid of the Jews in any way whatsoever without making too much fuss'.

In a Note to the Foreign Ministry in Berlin, on 28 February 1942, Zeitschel repeated the substance of information gathered at Vichy by the German Consul-General, Roland Krug von Nidda, who said that Pétain's Administration was ready to make the 'largest concessions on the Jewish question if we make complete and clear proposals'. On the other hand, Zeitschel said that a new propaganda campaign was needed in which every crime and minor offence committed by Jews was fed to the press in order to overcome the 'marked sense of justice among French people'.

If the French were not ready for repressive anti-Semitism, this was no fault of Xavier Vallat, the MP who had contemptuously greeted Léon Blum in the National Assembly in 1936. Although

Vallat detested the Germans, he and Dannecker made a perfect Inquisition team, the Frenchman providing pedantically legitimate texts to justify Nazi ideological torture.

Dannecker, whose determination to gather as much credit for himself as possible irritated his SS colleagues, claimed to have put up the 'suggestion' that led to the formation of Vichy's Commissariat-Général aux Questions Juives, of which Vallat became the first Commissioner in March 1941, setting up offices in Vichy's Hôtel d'Alger.

The imperative as far as the French were concerned was to establish Vichy control over Nazi spoliation of industry. German aryanisation of Jewish businesses in the Occupied Zone threatened the supposed authority of Vichy because it was believed that the Nazis were seizing French firms. Vichy was already worried by the pillaging of Jewish assets by the Einsatzab Rosenberg, a group that worked outside the control of both the Embassy and the Army.

Named after a leading Nazi theorist, Alfred Rosenberg, and working directly for Hitler and other chiefs like Hermann Göring, teams of robbers broke into museums and private houses, stealing collections of artworks, among them those belonging to the de Rothschilds, David-Weills and Wildensteins, who had all left France. The haul eventually covered nearly 11,000 paintings and as many other art objects.

However, as far as the official aryanisation of Jewish business was concerned, the Germans were much less greedy. Apart from industries involved in the German economy, the Nazis were glad to hand over the complicated management of all small companies and Jewish properties to Vichy-appointed trustees.

Xavier Vallat's qualifications for his job in administering the Statut des Juifs were inseparable from Vichy's fundamental identity and he naturally inherited Raphaël Alibert's central anti-Semitic role when the Justice Minister was dropped by the Maréchal in the spring of 1941. Vallat was a Vichy caricature, a southern provincial, born into a rural, Catholic family in 1891. He rightly told Dannecker that he had been anti-Semitic long before the Nazi was born, as his family were regular subscribers to the Catholic magazine, *Le Pèlerin*, which took up the anti-Jewish crusade started by *La Croix*.

His father, who had ten children, was a schoolteacher devoted to the ideas of Action Française, while Vallat himself taught French literature before being elected a conservative Deputy for the rural southern *département* of the Ardèche. He had an exemplary Great War record, having lost an eye and a leg in battle, and was associated at one time or another with most Fascist or right-wing movements between the wars. His first role at Vichy was Minister for Anciens Combattants and, under his guidance, old soldiers' movements were merged into the Légion Française des Combattants, a patriotic body owing allegiance to Pétain. The Legion was originally intended as the basis of a single national political movement.

The new Jewish Affairs Commissioner's attitude provided a clear guide to the mainstream of anti-Jewish thought at Vichy. He supported Maurras' idea of state anti-Semitism, to distinguish it from pure racism, in which the national interest demanded that Jews were excluded because they were incapable of being assimilated. Vallat explained the guidelines many times during the war and made no attempt to disguise his views when he was tried in 1945. Apart from the classic Catholic belief that Jews had committed deicide, he feared that they meant to form a state within a state with the aim of dominating, an opinion that even André Gide had subscribed to in his references to Léon Blum. According to Vallat, Jews were also 'foreign in thought and language' and were a parasitical element, draining host nations.

In April 1941, he told a press conference that his policies would be carried out 'without hatred or reprisals' and rejected the idea that any foreign nation could dictate methods of dealing with Jews, one of the reasons why he was replaced after Nazi pressure just before deportations began.

In the extreme terms of the Final Solution, Vallat could be considered a moderate anti-Semite, but he never reflected on the danger of isolating a minority which Hitler wanted to destroy, nor did he feel any concern for foreign Jews suffering and dying in Vichy concentration camps. Although he continually refined the Statut des Juifs, he did not outlaw intermarriage and he accepted the idea that a few Jews would be acceptable in French society in 'homeopathic doses'. These included about 25,000 established families, if they were kept out of influential jobs, while he was also ready to accept exemptions for war veterans with heroic service. He went even further and warned that over-radical measures would look like 'unjust and needless persecution' and create sympathy. On the other hand, in a roundabout reference to foreign Jews, he told students in the spring of 1942 that it was the victors' business to 'find means to settle the wandering Jew'.

Vallat's crusade led him into weird contortions as he set about defining the exact nature of a Jew, including a decision that a baptised person or the child of a baptised person was Jewish if three grandparents were Jewish. Even in cases where two grandparents were Christian, it was necessary to have been baptised before 25 June 1940 to claim Christianity, an arbitrary cut-off point determined by the day the Armistice was ratified.

By July 1941, when the Germans were demanding pure aryan certificates before letting French into the Occupied Zone, the rules were so complicated that there was a spontaneous demand for proof of being non-Jewish. The French issued Certificats de non-Appartenance à la Religion Juive, with doubtful cases being decided on guidelines from an ethnologist attached to the Commission staff. By the time Vallat was ousted in March 1942, when Darlan appointed a pro-Nazi Commissioner for Jewish Affairs, he was preparing a third Statut des Juifs which was never published. Neither religion nor race were to be decisive factors, just 'the beginnings of proof' that Jewish traditions were being upheld in a family.

Sometimes, Vallat's mission appeared to verge on insanity as he scrupulously pursued civil servants to ensure that even the most minor details of his laws, decrees and official guidelines were respected to the letter. As a result, the workings of the Jewish Affairs Commission have left millions of documents covering an entire floor of archive space. Attempts to sift out the most important findings include a three-volume résumé by a German historian, Doctor Joseph Billig, who gave evidence at some of the biggest war-crimes trials, among them Klaus Barbie's.

With this incredible ever-growing bureaucracy, Vallat was only blindly pursuing what he considered a patriotic duty and had neither the intelligence nor the compassion to see that his priorities paved the way to Nazi extermination. The most contemptuous judgement during the war period came from a leading Jewish paediatrician, Robert Debré, whose son Michel Debré joined the Free French and became de Gaulle's first Prime Minister when the Fifth Republic was founded in 1958. Robert Debré was such a highly considered specialist that he was one of the few Jews to be exempted from Vichy legislation. He believed he could persuade Vallat to tone down discrimination and he visited Vichy with another Jewish doctor, Gaston Nora, who had saved Vallat's life on the operating table in the Great War.

The appeals were a waste of time. In his memoirs, *L'Honneur de vivre,* Debré wrote off Vallat as having 'neither heart nor brain'.

At the Sipo-SD Jewish section's office at 31-bis avenue Foch, a road of elegant flats and mansions leading to the Bois de Boulogne from the Arc de Triomphe, Theodor Dannecker had every reason to believe that Vichy was dedicated to an ideological anti-Semitic policy that coincided with Nazi ambitions. Since Admiral Darlan had been appointed Prime Minister in February 1941, Vichy had steadily accepted all German suggestions, while adding refinements of its own.

From 5 April 1941, Xavier Vallat held regular meetings with

German officials and there was no sign of any French resistance either to the arrests of Jews in the Occupied Zone, with French police help, or to reinforcing controls in the Free Zone. After the first contacts when Vallat met the military commander, General Otto von Stülpnagel, in Paris's Hôtel Majestic, the General's civilian aide, Werner Best, drew up a report saying that the French were reluctant to accede to a German demand to intern Jews in the Occupied Zone. His doubts on Vichy's readiness to co-operate were quickly proved wrong.

Hardly a month later, French police, using a filing system set up by a special French squad trained by Dannecker, arrested 3747 Polish, Czech and Austrian Jews by the simple method of sending out summonses to renew their residence permits at police stations. The men were interned in French-run camps in the Occupied Zone at Pithiviers and Beaune-la-Rolande, two small towns near Orleans. That was the first of three police sweeps in the Paris region during 1941 which concluded with the mass arrest of prominent French Jews.

If there were problems and misunderstandings, most of them could be put down to the disorganised management of Vallat's Commissariat, which was attached first to Darlan's office and then to the Ministry of the Interior run by Pierre Pucheu, a businessman who represented the steel industry's Cartel d'Acier.

Jewish Affairs Commission employees were only temporary civil servants and there was a high turnover in the original staff of 400. The numbers and workload steadily grew as Vichy instituted its own aryanisation policy to compete with a similar move by the Germans, and about two-thirds of Vallat's staff were involved in keeping a check on provisional administrators or trustees put in charge of sequestered Jewish businesses and property.

Vallat's zeal never wavered despite an often inept and corrupt bureaucracy. A second Statut des Juifs was promulgated on 2 June 1941, completing the purge of Jews from worthwhile jobs. In the next six months, decrees would be issued which all but eliminated

Jews from the professions and crafts by means of a quota system, reducing the number of Jewish doctors, lawyers, architects and actors, among others, to only 2 per cent of the whole. Thousands of names were added to the list of internal refugees struggling to survive in Paris or the provinces by taking up menial jobs or giving private lessons.

A more sinister move was a census in the Free Zone in which all Jews, French and foreign, were obliged to fill in forms that included details of their family, property and income. This completed the census ordered by the Germans in the Occupied Zone a year before and undertaken by a French anti-Jewish police squad in charge of an elaborate cardfile system. The two census registers would be crucial to the success of the deportation programme.

The only issue which caused much controversy inside Vichy was the seizure of Jewish business interests, a move that inevitably touched on the sensitive question of the sacredness of property while spilling over into management areas of the Ministries managing the economy. Vallat overcame objections to a decree on 22 July 1941 empowering him to appoint trustees to take over Jewish firms by claiming that similar Nazi ordinances were disguised German nationalisation of French industry.

The French law, whose terms were negotiated with the Germans, inevitably led to wholesale corruption, attracting criminals who abused their trustees' mandates, which allowed them to manage or dispose of Jewish property as they wished. Technically, profits went into a Government fund but the opportunities for abuse were unlimited and encouraged the denunciation of Jewish-owned businesses by rivals. In his attempts to control the legalised theft, Vallat produced nearly seventy laws and decrees in a few months.

Werner Best's fear that the French were reluctant to become involved in arrests was based on Vallat's own wariness at being responsible for police action. After several weeks of discussion at Vichy, the Interior Minister, Pierre Pucheu, took on the responsibility himself and created a Police aux Questions Juives in the autumn of 1941 which was answerable to him. This followed an initiative by Dannecker, who had detached police inspectors from the Paris police headquarters. They were accommodated in premises off the boulevard Haussmann near the Galeries Lafayette department store, one of the first Jewish businesses to be seized by the Germans. This section later became part of the Vichy police force.

Dannecker's most important initiative of 1941 was to involve the Jews in their own extermination by forcing Vallat to set up the Union Générale des Israélites de France, UGIF, inspired by the Jewish Councils or Judenrate in Eastern Europe. The Nazi officer was under constant pressure from Eichmann to explain why Jewish interests were still only loosely controlled by both the occupying power and Vichy as late as autumn 1941. The simple answer was the lack of a common ghetto, like Warsaw, while Jewish associations worked independently through dozens of French and immigrant bodies, including religious and welfare groups. The need to co-ordinate these into a single unit was important for both the eventual Final Solution and to enable the Nazis to seize the Jewish community's assets.

Impatient at delays from Vichy, which were at least partly due to disorganisation in Vallat's office, Dannecker started working with some Consistory officials in Paris in the summer of 1941 and brought in two Jews from Vienna to work in his office on a draft programme for a French Judenrat. Vallat was forced into action, fearing that France would lose control of Jewish funds.

By 29 November 1941, Vichy had gone further than Dannecker expected by setting up UGIF, under the control of the Vichy Jewish Affairs Commission, with responsibility for both zones. All Jewish philanthropic organisations were forcibly absorbed into UGIF, while separate councils headed by French Jews were set up for each zone, moves that later led to controversial claims that community leaders collaborated in deportation.

Less than three weeks after UGIF came into being, the Germans fined the whole Jewish community 1 billion francs as a reprisal for the murder of German soldiers, although there was no proof of Jewish involvement. Raising the money, which was nothing less than a ransom, was left to leaders of the Jewish community, who became enmeshed in their own destruction.

Only a week before the fine was imposed, the Germans had struck at the heart of the secure, middle-class Jewish community that had been so sure of assimilation before the war. The previous two police sweeps in 1941 had been predominantly French affairs. Following the May operation, in which 3700 men had been arrested after being summoned to police stations, a more classic *rafle* was carried out between 20 and 23 August as a reaction to Communist agitation in the wake of Hitler's invasion of Russia. About 2400 Paris policemen, under the command of German officers, seized 4230 Jews before taking them to Drancy in city buses. They were the first Jewish detainees in the newly opened suburban concentration camp. Among them were 200 prominent French Jews, mostly lawyers accused of masterminding sabotage campaigns.

The attack on the established French community on 12 December 1941 was purely a German affair. Two hundred Gestapo and 360 Wehrmacht police, operating under Dannecker's command, arrested 743 men and seized another 300 in Drancy. They included company directors, lawyers, doctors, teachers, engineers, scientists and students, who were transferred as hostages to the German-controlled concentration camp at Compiègne, north of Paris, where the Armistice had been signed. Among them was René Blum, Léon Blum's youngest brother, who had been a close friend of the Jewish writer Marcel Proust. René Blum was the pre-war Director of the Monte Carlo Ballet and had returned from safety in the United States as an act of solidarity with the Jewish community. He was murdered in Germany in 1943.

In a German Note of 7 December 1941, the Ambassador, Otto Abetz, had advised that responsibility for killing Germans should be attributed to 'Jews and their agents in the pay of Anglo-Saxon and Soviet secret services'. On 14 December, German posters were put up in Paris announcing that 'a large number of Judéo-Bolsheviks, Communists and anarchists connected with the murders will be shot.' The following day, 100 men, including 53 Jews, were executed at the Mont Valérien fort in the Paris suburbs. Fifty had been selected in Drancy that morning by Dannecker.

The billion-franc fine was hurriedly put together by UGIF with Vichy help. Banks were forced to make short-term loans to the new Jewish organisation, which paid the money back from seized Jewish accounts held by a Government fund. While the transaction might have given the impression that the Germans had been bought off, it probably did not save a single life.

By then, a meeting had been arranged in a Berlin police building in a street called Grossen Wannsee, where senior SS officers assembled on 20 January 1942 to organise the Final Solution. The Madagascar Plan had been replaced by death camps.

CHAPTER NINE

The Ill Wind

B Y THE TIME the secret decision had been taken on the Final Solution, a peak had been reached in what one of the leading figures at Vichy called the 'rose et idyllique' period of collaboration.

The expression comes from the privately published memoirs of Alibert's successor as Justice Minister, Joseph Barthélemy, a Catholic jurist and a law professor at the Sorbonne whose father had been a left-wing mayor of Toulouse. In contrast to Alibert, Barthélemy was a brilliant academic and had been covered with honours between the wars when he was an MP. He joined the Cabinet in February 1941 at the age of sixty as its third most important member on the personal invitation of Pétain, a man Barthélemy admired as a 'conciliator'. There was nothing in the new Minister's record to show any attraction to Fascism or anti-Semitism, but he was drawn into helping construct oppressive measures against Jews, including a second Jewish Statute, that were overseen by the new Prime Minister, Admiral François Darlan.

The fourteen months of Darlan's leadership form the most revealing period for making a judgement on Vichy's voluntary identification with Nazi policies. The time of hasty decisions following the panic of defeat had passed. France was technically at peace and the Germans had not yet occupied all of France. These were the months most marked by Pétain's own choices over ministerial appointments, when he worked in harmony with a premier who had his total confidence.

François Darlan, a man who boasted of his lack of academic diplomas and who had an exaggerated taste for luxury, was sixty years old when he was chosen as Premier three months after Laval's dismissal. The Germans had rejected Laval's first successor, Pierre-Etienne Flandin, a Third Republic politician, and the boycott was so effective that Flandin escaped charges of treason after the war.

Darlan was a more sensible choice both for Pétain and for the Nazis. The Maréchal had suggested even before the Armistice that Darlan should become his deputy. There was no personality clash, while age and rank gave Pétain automatic authority. No Vichy politician was given so much scope as Darlan. At one time he was also Minister of Foreign Affairs, Information, Interior and Defence, holding more offices at any one time than any personality in the four years of Vichy, with the exception of the Head of State.

As Pétain's nominated Dauphin, Darlan quickly reassured Berlin that a more active form of collaboration was a priority. Just after Laval was dismissed, he went to see Hitler and had a second meeting in April 1941 at Berchetesgaden, the Führer's mountain bunker. He believed that he would one day be appointed the Grand Admiral of a united European fleet, an idea which strengthened his determination to ensure a German victory.

Darlan incarnated a traditional French Navy hatred of Britain and a desire for revenge for defeats long before Trafalgar. He brought France close to declaring war on its old ally and tried to contribute to a British collapse by ordering French troops to oppose a joint British–Free French invasion of Vichy-controlled Syria. If the Admiral never carried his hatred for Britain to a logical conclusion this was because he was not a fighting sailor, nor was there any Navy background in his family. Most French sailors were Bretons with a strong attachment to the monarchy. Darlan came from a small town in south-west France and his father was Justice Minister at the height of the Dreyfus Affair.

François Darlan's career was spent mostly in ministerial offices, notably as Permanent Secretary to a Navy Minister, Georges Leygues, a close friend of his father's. Nearly all of France's naval policies up to the war were personally overseen by Darlan, who was then given credit for saving the Fleet by not committing his ships to any important battle. His attitude during collaboration often seemed inspired by vanity. A small, pink-faced man, he tried to compensate for his size by living in a style that shocked colleagues like Barthelémy. The Justice Minister recalled that on official visits Darlan travelled by car followed by a special train to carry his own chef and a band of forty musicians.

The Admiral was another leader to escape judgement for his wartime role. He was assassinated in Algeria in December 1942 after rallying to the Allies following the invasion of North Africa. The background to the shooting has remained obscure. The Admiral's murderer, a young royalist, was executed almost immediately. Darlan's honour remained safe, even though a large bust of Pétain was put at the head of his coffin during the lying-in-state. In 1945, his body was transferred to the naval cemetery at Mers-el-Kebir and buried alongside sailors who had died fighting the British in 1940. His tomb was inscribed with the epitaph: '*Mort pour la France*'.

The legacy he built up as Premier until April 1942 was as treacherous as that of any Vichy politician and he made no effort to dismantle the trap closing on the Jewish community which tightened with the introduction of the second Statut des Juifs in June 1941. His Education Minister, Jerôme Carcopino, wrote after the war in a book called *Souvenirs de sept ans* that Darlan told him that stateless Jews did not interest him at all and that protection should be reserved for established families.

Vichy's increasing efforts to please Hitler during this period owed much to the fact that Berlin had not indicated any special role for France in a new Europe, as if it were waiting for some special commitment. As a result, Pétain was continually harassed into stepping up repression by a lobby of ultra-collaborationist politicians that had gathered in Paris around Pierre Laval. Nothing that Vichy did was good enough as far as the Paris lobby was concerned, as it plotted in favour of a recognisable Fascist administration. The pro-Nazi press in Paris accused Pétain of playing a double game and of failing to take vigorous measures against the enemies of Germany, identified as Communists and Jews. One of Laval's closest associates, Marcel Déat, described Vichy as 'an abortion clinic' which had botched National Revolution reforms.

It was to answer these critics that Pétain took the fateful decision to introduce legal machinery which destroyed any Vichy claims to being a benign, protective government. On 12 August 1941, he interrupted a performance of *Boris Godounov* at the Vichy Casino to announce a campaign to combat what he called 'an ill wind'. Before detailing twelve urgent reforms, he made a statement that again showed that he was personally responsible. 'Authority no longer comes from below,' he said. 'It is only what I propose or delegate.' Once again, the Maréchal had insisted that he had arrogated all powers to himself and was still prepared to let history judge him alone. In future, all executives such as police chiefs, senior civil servants, judges and soldiers had to swear oaths of allegiance to Pétain himself.

Among the twelve emergency measures was the creation of special tribunals, called Sections Spéciales, with powers to judge alleged terrorists even for offences committed before the system was introduced. The first victim of the courts was an immigrant Jew, who was guillotined. It was the start of a campaign in which both Vichy and the Nazis deliberately linked the Jewish community as a whole to Communist resistance, preparing public opinion for the round-ups to come.

The excuse for Pétain's increased support for the Nazis was linked to the German invasion of the Soviet Union in June 1941. The crusade against Communism gave Vichy a logical reason for justifying collaboration. It was a message easily understood by a population prepared by years of propaganda to believe that outside forces, notably Marxism and Judaism, had undermined France's national will.

Just before his 'ill wind' reforms, Pétain had given an indication of the severity to come by appointing Pierre Pucheu as Interior Minister, responsible for the police. The promotion was unexpected, but it can be explained by a remark recorded by Barthelémy: Pucheu said he was ready to execute 20,000 Communists. His hatreds also included Jews and he had campaigned before the war for France to be purged of 'foreign scum and the Jewish leprosy'. According to Barthelémy, Pucheu had a taste for intrigue, conspiracy, obscure transactions and the cult of violence. 'Without saying it, he was completely penetrated by Nazi doctrines,' Barthelémy wrote.

Pucheu proved to be one of the most efficient of all Pétain's Ministers, but his allegiances were far more complicated than Barthelémy made out. He belonged to what was called the synarchy, a group of young technocratic Ministers and civil servants whose main ambition was to remodel French industry to compete with Germany's. While Pucheu's ideas may have been Fascist in inspiration, he was distrusted by the Germans, who demanded his replacement in April 1942.

Pucheu's passion for a muscular capitalist system had arisen from a sudden conversion while studying at the Ecole Normale Supérieure in Paris when he was a near contemporary of figures as diverse as Robert Brasillach and Jean-Paul Sartre. Unlike these two middle-class writers, Pucheu had come from a poor background in south-west France. His father, a jobbing tailor, had been killed in the Great War. Pucheu won a scholarship to one of France's most famous Grandes Ecoles in the hope of filling an ambition to become a writer. But on reaching Paris he quickly decided on a business career, expressing a fascination for the 200 capitalist families that ran France's industry. Their dominance was especially marked in the steel industry's Comité des Forges, where Pucheu later headed a number of monopoly interests including the Cartel d'Acier.

The events of 6 February 1934 pushed him into politics, first as a member of the nationalist Croix de Feu and then as an ally of a Fascist, Jacques Doriot, the renegade Communist head of the Parti Populaire Français whom he abandoned in 1938 because of financial links with Germany. In February 1941, sponsored by his big-business friends in the steel industry who financed *Le Temps*, Pucheu was made Minister of Industrial Production at the age of forty-two.

His image of a soberly dressed, bespectacled businessman with a strong attachment to family life belied his callous attempts to impress the Germans when he became Interior Minister in July. Pucheu himself was directly involved in a series of summary executions of hostages by the Germans. He personally chose the ninety-eight hostages who were executed on 22 and 23 October 1941 in reprisal for the murder of German officers. More than half were Jews picked from the French-run camp at Drancy.

Pucheu's intervention defused a crisis between Berlin and Vichy. This had arisen because Pétain opposed the original German plan, which would have meant shooting non-Jewish war veterans. Pucheu's hostages included Jewish war heroes but the solution appeared to satisfy the Maréchal. Pétain made no mention of the incident on 24 October 1941 in an exchange of messages with Hitler on the anniversary of the meeting at Montoire that launched collaboration. Instead he congratulated the Führer on German victories over Bolshevism in the Soviet Union and promised more co-operation from France after a Nazi victory. 'Along these roads of high civilisation, the German people and the French people are certain of meeting and uniting their efforts,' he added.

Hitler remained unconvinced. In his reply on 10 November, he complained that collaboration was not working. He compared alleged atrocities by the French Occupation Army in 1918 with the supposedly model behaviour of the Wehrmacht in France. The Führer's message to Pétain concluded: 'Only the German Army is capable of overcoming the terrifying force which has been assembled against Europe: the Bolshevik danger.' If it were to win, French Jews would have triumphed.

Over the next few months, although France gave more proof of its willingness for further co-operation, Hitler remained sceptical about dealing with Vichy. On 13 May 1942, while the first wave of deportations was in progress, he expressed his feelings to his deputy, Martin Bormann, who recorded the conversation on a disc. 'What strikes me above everything about present French politics is that in wanting to sit on every seat they sit on none,' Hitler said. 'That's why the country's soul is torn apart. In the same Vichy Government, numerous tendencies are represented: national anti-Semitism, clerical philo-Semitism, royalism, revolutionary spirit, etcetera. In addition it lacks a man of energy.' Of Pétain, he added: 'I would say it would be just as well to give a grand role to an old singer covered in glory and, in the presence of a lamentable result, to be consoled with the thought that thirty or forty years before he had gold at the bottom of his throat.'

Although Hitler's views on Vichy's contradictions and Pétain's authority contained a large measure of truth, he had no reason to believe that France might change its mind about an eventual German victory, despite signs that the world political scene was swinging in favour of Berlin's opponents. The United States had entered the war in December 1941. Chances of a Nazi victory over Britain were waning. Fascist Spain had not wavered in its neutrality while Germany's Axis with Italy was already under pressure. De Gaulle's London-based resistance movement was gradually becoming a credible factor at a time when ordinary French people felt increasing resentment for the rigours of occupation.

In these circumstances, Vichy could have tried to gain more

time, particularly as the American Embassy in the spa town had stepped up negotiations for a secret alliance. Instead, complicity in the deportation of Jews marked the point of no return in collaboration.

During his last weeks in office, Darlan was tempted by a military agreement with Hitler and placed his hopes in approaches made to Berlin by the German Ambassador, Otto Abetz. On 5 January 1942, Abetz went to see Hitler and returned to Paris with the news that Germany was ready to sign a peace pact 'which would stupefy the French people', if they were ready to march alongside the Nazis until the end of the war. The offer was recorded by Darlan's delegate, Jacques Benoist-Méchin, an arch-collaborator and junior Minister. In 1984, Benoist-Méchin wrote his own memoirs of the period in a book called *De la Défaite au désastre,* in which he said he was convinced that a new era had opened up with Abetz's offer.

On 11 January, Bénoist-Méchin informed Pétain of the supposed deal at a Cabinet meeting. Darlan allegedly said: 'It is peace with the Reich and war with the others.' According to Bénoist-Méchin, even Pétain was ready to accept a plan in which France's alliance with the Nazis would be built up gradually as its military potential developed.

Abetz, unwilling to accept that his own influence had long been overtaken by the SS, took the French answer to Hitler only to find that the Führer had lost interest. On 24 February 1942, with Abetz already in partial disgrace, one of the Embassy's senior counsellors, Ernst Achenbach, was sent to Vichy with a different message from that conveyed only the month before. Darlan was no longer trusted and Germany demanded the return of Laval, who had recovered from an assassination attempt in August. The implied alternative to a refusal to accept Laval was the appoint-ment of the SS deputy leader, General Reinhard Heydrich, as Gauleiter.

On 18 April, after a secret meeting with Pétain, Laval was

reappointed Prime Minister. He inherited a situation in which treatment of Jews had worsened dramatically. Three weeks earlier, on 27 March 1942, the first deportation train had left for Germany. A breach had been opened which would ensure that French deportees would be among the first to be killed when gas chambers started operating at Auschwitz in mid-July.

CHAPTER TEN

No Hiding Place

ALTHOUGH MORE THAN two months had passed since the go-ahead had been given to the Final Solution in Berlin, the decision to transfer French nationals and stateless Jews to German concentration camps was carried out in an atmosphere of deception. The Nazi leadership hid its extermination programme both from the French Government and from its own military command in Paris, the MBF. After the war, leading SS men in Paris, like Colonel Knochen, claimed that they had been unaware that the ultimate destination was the gas chambers.

An international argument over the execution of hostages provided the excuse for the first deportation trains. Vichy's anxiety at losing control over police operations in the North was coupled with the concern of the MBF commander, Luftwaffe General Otto von Stülpnagel, that mass shootings would increase popular resentment of the German Army. He believed that deportation of Jews and Communists would be a more effective intimidatory measure. Von Stülpnagel resigned over the issue in February 1942 and was replaced by his cousin, General Karl Heinrich von Stülpnagel, in April. The new General supported a vigorous deportation programme, but by the time he had arrived in Paris the matter was out of his hands. Hitler had issued an order which approved both the murder of hostages in case of terrorist action and the imprisonment in Germany of 500 Jews and Communists for each attack.

The first trainload of Jews to leave France was justified as a reprisal measure and not racial persecution as such. Most of the hostages were taken from the German-run concentration camp at Compiègne. The train that left for Auschwitz on 27 March contained 1112 men aged between twenty and forty-eight. There were some unusual factors about this first departure when compared to later trains. The men were loaded into third-class carriages supplied by the SNCF state railways, rather than the cattle wagons used afterwards. Half the men were French Jews, an unusually high proportion, especially as most of them were leading members of the Paris community.

Throughout the war, established Jewish families, recently naturalised citizens and first-generation French represented less than a third of all Jews sent to Germany from France and most were seized after 1942 when the Nazis occupied the whole of France. Those assigned to the first train had been held in the German-run concentration camp since the round-up of 743 prominent Jews on 12 December. They were due to have been deported immediately but there were no trains to spare. In the meantime, more than 100 detainees had been released for health reasons.

To fill empty space on the first train, other carriages were occupied by foreign Jews, mostly Poles, who had been held in the council-flats camp at Drancy following the other two round-ups in 1941. The Drancy contingent had been picked up earlier in the day from Le Bourget station, which was to become the main point of departure after La Grande Rafle in July 1942.

The German High Command did not want to supply troops for the escort. It was decided that French gendarmes would travel as guards to the German frontier, but at the last minute sixty German military police were ordered to join the train from Paris. Theodor Dannecker, whose energy and Nazi convictions had ensured French complicity in the Final Solution, rode triumphantly on the train all the way on its three-day journey to Auschwitz, where most deportees later perished. Out of 1112, only 22 survived the war.

The despatch of the train was an important test of Vichy's sincerity over the protection of its Jewish citizens. A strong protest would not have been out of line as many of the deportees were not only well-known Parisians whose names were revealed in *Paris-Soir* but also decorated war veterans whose families had appealed directly to Pétain. Instead, Vichy accepted the German version that the men were being 'despatched for forced labour' and made no serious attempt to discover what happened even to French citizens. It was too late for Vichy to protest that the men were innocent victims. French police provided the names of the arrested men on the basis of political information contained in detailed census files.

Pétain's silence encouraged the Germans to plan more departures in northern France in order to make space in camps for other Parisian Jews considered to be a high security risk. On 5 June, a second train left Compiègne, this time with freight wagons instead of carriages. Three more were to follow from Occupied Zone concentration camps before July, by which time 5000 Jews had been taken to Germany. Most died less than three months after reaching Auschwitz, many of them not even living long enough to be sent to the gas chambers, where the first French victims were murdered on 19 July.

All the first deportees were from the German zone, where treatment of Jews had always been more severe than in the Vichy-controlled area. There were 150,000 French and foreign Jews registered as living in the Paris area and they had to suffer the double burden of German and Vichy laws. The original Vichy definition of a Jew on racial rather than religious grounds added to the scope for persecution applied under Nazi ordinances, as there was no escape for converts to Christianity. Nearly all police action was carried out by the French, often acting on Nazi information.

The Germans were always in advance of the French in

physically identifying Jews, even before the yellow star was enforced in the Occupied Zone in June 1942. From the beginning, businesses had to put up signs declaring Jewish ownership, facilitating the planned confiscation of 38,000 firms or blocks of flats that were to be handed over to French trustees.

A northern-zone census in 1940 had made it easier to accelerate the eviction of Jews from the professions and civil service under the Vichy Statut des Juifs. As the months passed, additional personal rights were removed one by one under German decrees. Jews were ordered to surrender their wireless sets at French police stations. Later their bicycles were confiscated, while segregation was tightened so that Jews mixed as little as possible with other Parisians. They were forced to travel in the last carriage of the Métro trains. Cafés, cinemas, theatres, museums, lifts and telephone boxes were put out of bounds, while children's parks were eventually closed to Jewish children. Defiance of these restrictions entailed heavy fines or detention, the latter meaning inevitable deportation.

Because hotels were closed to Jews, on visits to Paris they were often forced to sleep in the open like vagabonds, making them a target for French anti-Jewish police squads. Shopping was restricted to an hour in the afternoon when most rationed supplies had run out. It was impossible to join relatives in the Free Zone except by paying *passeurs* to lead escapers past German posts on the Demarcation Line, while no Jew could cross back into the Occupied Zone. Jews caught travelling illegally risked being interned or even executed. Many French Jews were deported as 'criminals' because they were caught near the Demarcation Line.

From the first days of the Occupation, the Germans found no shortage of anti-Semitic allies to support Nazi measures, which started with the drawing up of a list of proscribed books and authors by the Ambassador, Otto Abetz. French journalists and printers continued to publish the *Paris-Soir,* the capital's biggest newspaper, which the Germans had seized along with Radio Paris, whose contributors included well-known writers.

The radio was perhaps the most effective anti-Semitic medium, because it broadcast daily programmes to encourage listeners to denounce Jews, emphasising the alleged links between leading Jews and Communist or Gaullist resistance to Pétain. Denunciations poured into the French police and Gestapo, particularly from shopkeepers and other traders keen to remove competition. An estimated 3 million letters were sent to the German authorities during the war containing betrayals of Jews or resistance workers or throwing suspicion on business rivals.[6]

The most anti-Semitic of Parisian newspapers was the weekly *Au Pilori,* which held a competition in December 1940 offering a prize of silk stockings for the best suggestions on how to eliminate Jews. Ideas from the paper's 60,000 readers included dumping them in the jungle among wild animals or lepers or burning them in crematoria. Another newspaper, *La France au Travail,* began its campaign on 18 July 1940 with a long and detailed description of the genetic make-up of Jews, a theme taken up by a major French publisher, Robert Denoël, who issued a book called *Comment réconnaître un Juif.* Robert Brasillach's *Je Suis Partout* employed writers of an exceptional intellectual standard but they too stooped to gutter language in their demands to exterminate Jews. His friend Lucien Rabatet, a man of considerable culture, also wrote in another paper, *Le Cri du Peuple.* On 8 November 1940, Rebatet described Jews as being as odious as rats or plague carriers.

Among hundreds of anti-Semitic articles published at the time, insults were accompanied by practical information revealing the names of Jews in hiding or identifying businesses that had not yet been seized. Jews were also continually blamed for organising the black market, while petty criminal cases involving Jews were given prominence by the press and radio.

This daily assault was backed up by conferences and exhibitions. The most notorious public show was called 'Le Juif et la

France'. It opened in September 1941, in a building on the boulevard des Italiens occupied by the Berlitz language school. The Nazi-sponsored exhibition attracted thousands of people, who were lectured on ways to recognise Jews. The huge poster outside was taken up by a portrait of a caricatural Shylock, but attempts to show Jews as grotesque, greedy figures in astrakhan coats were probably counter-productive. Wartime photographs of poor Eastern European Jews showed that most of them looked no different from the average small, dark-haired Frenchman.

Despite the intensity of anti-Jewish propaganda in Paris there was no popular action against Jews except for isolated attacks on synagogues by French Fascists financed by the Germans. Propaganda was probably perceived by most people as a residue of discredited pre-war hysteria and was usually met with indifference. The average Parisian, hit by successive severe winters and strict rationing, was too preoccupied with a constant search for food, fuel and work to have time to turn on the inhabitants of the Pletzl or Belleville, where living standards were often considerably worse.

As the Vichy press did not circulate in the North, Parisians were cut off from the reality of conditions in the Free Zone. The constant criticism of Pétain in the Nazi-controlled press added to the illusion that safety and protection lay across the Demarcation Line. Jewish organisations did all in their power to help Jews cross into the French zone, in the belief that it was governed by a benign regime as well as providing access to escape routes into Switzerland and Spain or to the Italian Zone. The presence of foreign embassies in Vichy, notably the United States and the Vatican, gave hope of finding a land of refuge outside France, despite an obvious reluctance among non-European countries to accept new intakes of Jews. By early 1942, Vallat informed Darlan that there were about 150,000 Jews in the Free Zone compared to his estimate of 5000 before the war.

The influx was on a bigger scale than anything Paris had

experienced in the thirties. Local resentment grew steadily throughout 1941, if reports by provincial administrators can be trusted. The impact was increased by the enforced grouping of refugee Jews, who were disliked either because they were poor and needed help or because they were rich and lived better than the local people.

In some cases, complaints were partly justified. Among thousands of letters sent to Pétain, there was a long protest from the village of Tournon d'Agenais in the rural south-western *département* of Lot and Garonne. The population of 275 people had been told that their commune was a designated detention area for 175 'undesirable' stateless Jews. The letter recalled that the village had welcomed successive waves of refugees and now had to put up with the 'unjustified occupation of our buildings by a load of individuals which other towns and villages have rejected without pity'. Even so, the population said it was prepared to accept the sacrifice if Pétain ordered it because they were aware 'that Jews are human beings who are obliged to find their resting place somewhere'.

Most resentment was kept for rich Jews, particularly Parisians who settled on the Côte d'Azur. In the Alpes-Maritime, a 1942 census showed that 12,217 Jews had declared their presence, including 7554 foreigners. They were most noticeable in Cannes, which the anti-Semitic press said should be renamed Kahn. At one time, the Mayor tried to introduce restrictions but gave up in the face of protests by hoteliers and shopkeepers who had never done such good business.

The Jewish exiles recreated in Cannes the social life of pre-war Paris, since the town was also a refuge for much of French show business and the fashion world, notably Maurice Chevalier and Christian Dior. The actor Jean-Pierre Aumont, whose real name was Salomon, used Cannes as his base until he escaped to join the Free French and later developed a career in Hollywood.

The safest refuge for Jews was in Nice and the border area with

Italy. This had been occupied by the Italians, who resisted both German and Vichy attempts to arrest Jews. But like everywhere else, the Jewish population had been deprived of nearly all means of finding worthwhile jobs and had to live on savings or find manual work.

Although official restrictions under Vichy covered posts as different as midwives and estate agents, some minor civil service jobs were still open. Jews were recruited as warders in psychiatric hospitals, where conditions for patients were at least as bad as they were for Jews detained in concentration camps. According to a recent study, 40,000 mental patients in the Free Zone died of malnutrition or exposure because of Vichy's neglect of mental outcasts.

Until 1942, living under the Vichy administration, either as a foreign Jew in a camp or as a French Jew surviving by his wits, obviously provided a more hopeful prospect than life in the Occupied Zone. There was, however, no let-up in Vichy's anti-Jewish propaganda. Anti-Semitics like Charles Maurras continued their virulent attacks from Lyons, where *Le Figaro* became more explicit on the issue in December 1941 by publishing a long article justifying further updating of the Statut des Juifs. It had been issued by the official Havas News Agency, which had German interests, and argued that the Statut had been introduced to force Jews to work in the open rather than anonymously. The article summed up, in relatively rational terms, some of the main arguments that had been refined well before the war.

Jews were said to have held a mortgage on French institutions and to have ensured the triumph of policies in which the French nation had been sacrificed in a desperate defence of Jewish interests. Opponents had shouted warnings but Jews controlled the entire media, leaving no way for an anti-Semite to warn public opinion. The slightest allusion to the Jewish question in a film script ruled out an eventual commission. Jews were also accused of refusing manual labour, such as farming, and of living from speculation.

'Trade is not for him a useful way of sharing out produce but an art: to sell as much as possible at the highest price,' the paper said. 'Success in selling you what you do not need is a point of honour and his masterstroke is to sell you what you own already.' The accusations continued for a full column in a message with obvious undertones during a time of increasing dependence on the black market. Throughout 1941, police action against black marketeers concentrated on Jews, particularly in Marseilles and the Riviera, resulting in hundreds being sent to concentration camps or restricted residence centres.

In this atmosphere of vindictiveness, Vichy took revenge on Léon Blum and other political leaders considered responsible for the 1940 disaster. They were put on trial in February 1942, just before the first deportation train was despatched. Blum appeared in the courtroom at Riom, south of Vichy, with Edouard Daladier and General Maurice Gamelin, who was accused of bungling military action. Pétain insisted on staging the trial against the advice of some of his aides, personally appointing the judges and overseeing the procedure.

Although this new attempt to blame the Popular Front for all France's ills ended in ridicule without a sentence being passed, this did not stop Vichy from deporting Blum and the other accused to Germany at the end of 1942. The trial was an act of spite that turned to Pétain's disadvantage. Blum's defence and accusations against the Head of State were circulated in Resistance underground tracts and widely reported abroad. Hitler was furious at Blum's criticism of collaboration in the court and, after publicly condemning the whole procedure in a speech in Berlin on 15 March, he told the Ambassador in Paris to order Pétain to call off the prosecution. The Führer's anger was partly directed against Darlan and hastened the Admiral's departure as Prime Minister on 10 April 1942.

Four days later, Pétain suspended the Riom hearing, and the

world's press hailed this as a victory for Blum. The *New York Times* said the former Socialist Premier had shown the 'intelligent and heroic face of France which every human being loved and respected'. In the *New Yorker*, a commentary declared that, thanks to Blum, imprisoned France had again become the guardian of European values. This reaction increased Blum's value as a hostage but, before he was sent to Germany, his only son Robert was taken from a prisoner-of-war camp where he had been held since 1940 and jailed as a political detainee by the Nazis.

Blum expected no sympathy from an implacable enemy like Pétain, but hundreds of other Jews believed that they only had to write to the Maréchal and the persecutions would stop. The National Archives were soon filled with letters from Jewish leaders or ordinary families appealing for his intervention, especially on behalf of war veterans supposedly exempt from the worst aspects of anti-Semitic law. The most distinguished of the letters, probably sent in March 1941, was signed by a paediatrician, Professor Robert Debré, a judge, Léon Lyon-Caen, and the Secretary-General of the Association for Injured Veterans, Edmond Bloch. Protesting against the worst aspects of both German and Vichy laws, the letter said: 'It is not possible that this wounded country, wholly united behind its chief, could abandon thousands of its children without a word.'

As many less distinguished correspondents discovered, Pétain could and did abandon even the old soldiers who worshipped him. On 11 August 1941, eighteen veterans, with seventy medals between them, made a vain trip to Vichy to ask for anti-Semitic propaganda to be dropped from official Army publications. Not even when military citations had been signed personally by the Maréchal was there much hope of justice, as André Gerschel found out when he was dismissed as Mayor of Calais and forced to live in poverty.

The flow of letters increased after arrests began. Among those involved in the protest in December 1941 was Jacques Helbronner, head of the Jewish Consistory. He had been a close friend of Pétain since the Great War. As an officer on the General Staff, Helbronner was partly instrumental in ensuring Pétain's promotion to lead the French Army. In appealing for intervention, the Jewish leader described the Head of State as a man who had 'always shown me so much kindness and confident affection' and asked him to end the anti-Jewish campaign. The Maréchal, he said, was his sole comfort and support, a factor which did not prevent Helbronner and his family being sent to Auschwitz to be gassed in 1943.

One of the angriest letters was written by the head of the Paris Bar and former Senator, Pierre Masse, after the first Statut des Juifs stopped Jews from becoming Army officers. 'I would be obliged if you would tell me what I have to do to withdraw rank from: my brother, a second-lieutenant in the 36th Infantry Regiment, killed at Douaumont in April 1916; from my son-in-law, second-lieutenant in the Dragoons, killed in Belgium in May 1940; from my nephew, J.-F. Masse, lieutenant in the 23rd Colonial Regiment, killed at Rethel in May 1940,' he wrote. 'Can I leave my brother his Médaille Militaire won at Neuville-Saint-Vaast, with which he has been buried? Can my son Jacques, second-lieutenant in the Chasseurs Alpins, wounded at Soupir, in June 1940, keep his rank? Can I also be assured that no one will retrospectively take back the Sainte-Hélène medal from my great-grandfather?' Masse was arrested in Paris in 1941 and later sent to die in Germany.

An aunt wrote to Pétain to report that her nephew, Jacques Cohen, had been informed that he must quit his senior civil service post. He had been killed in action more than a year before, she said. Another case referred to a Jewish soldier, wounded in action, who was decorated with the Croix de Guerre and the Médaille Militaire after being repatriated by the Germans in February 1941. Eight months later, his father, awarded the

Médaille Militaire in the Great War, committed suicide when his wife was taken to Drancy and then deported, despite repeated appeals by her invalid son.

Pétain's failure to intervene on behalf of war veterans has resulted in long-lasting resentment even in the association that remembers his Great War victory at Verdun. The chairman of the survivors' organisation Ceux de Verdun, Jean Créange, interviewed returning deportees at the end of the war as an intelligence service colonel. Among those he hoped to meet was his brother Pierre, a poet. In July 1942, the brother had been betrayed by his *passeur* when crossing the Demarcation Line and taken to Drancy.

Jean Créange went to Vichy to ask Pétain for his help, confident that their joint experience at Verdun would oblige the Maréchal to act. He was interviewed by the Education Minister, Jerôme Carcopino, who had taught the two brothers. It turned out to be a wasted visit; Créange learned later that his brother had died in Auschwitz in 1943. 'All that was needed to save him was a single gesture from Pétain,' Créange said, acknowledging lasting bitterness against a man who had been his personal hero.

Many of the letters sent to Vichy were forwarded to the official Government delegate in Paris, Fernand de Brinon, a pro-German whose Jewish wife was forced to wear the yellow star except when visiting her home in the provinces. Some of the letters were annotated by the Maréchal himself and later the Germans officially informed him that there was no point in sending any more. Pétain probably did not see all the protests mailed to him, because Bernard Ménétrel sorted his post, but the many individual and moving cases definitely brought to his attention did not make him react publicly to ameliorate the increasingly suffocating effect of anti-Jewish policies that bore his signature.

Among the many approaches which proved that Pétain was not prepared to honour promises to Jewish soldiers whom Vallat had said would be protected was a letter containing a photograph of Victor Faynzylber. His left leg had been amputated during the

1940 disaster and in a picture he sent to Pétain he stands on crutches and wears his two decorations, a Croix de Guerre and a Médaille Militaire. His two children, a girl of about seven and a boy of about five, stand beside him. The girl wears a yellow star because she is more than six years old. The boy is too young, and the father is also exempted as a decorated war hero. Faynzylber appealed to Pétain to seek the release of his wife, who was being held in a concentration camp. Although Pétain acknowledged the letter, Madame Faynzylber was never set free. Her husband was arrested soon afterwards and both were murdered in Germany.

CHAPTER ELEVEN

Preparing La Grande Rafle

THE POLITICAL UPHEAVAL that followed the return of Pierre Laval also saw the departure of most of Darlan's closest associates. Some resigned because they objected to Laval's close links with the pro-German lobby in Paris. Others, like Pierre Pucheu, were sacked because they were considered unreliable by the Germans. One of the most important changes as far as Jews were concerned was the nomination of a new Commissioner for Jewish Affairs to replace Xavier Vallat.

A decision on a successor had been taken a month before Laval assumed his new official title of Chef du Gouvernement, taking control of the most important Ministries such as Foreign Affairs and the Interior. Berlin had been worried about Vallat's hostility to Germany, which dated back to the Great War, and he could not be depended on to co-operate with future deportations. His successor at the Commissariat-Général aux Questions Juives was a pro-Nazi Jew-hater, Darquier de Pellepoix.

The Germans had pressed for a year to get rid of Vallat and had put forward a list of seven candidates, among them the author Louis-Ferdinand Céline, all of whom had a record of extreme anti-Semitism. But the chosen man, Darquier, whose wife was British, was also corrupt and he eventually discredited himself with a swindle that led to his dismissal in 1944. His aristocratic claims were a fraud, for his real name was Louis Darquier. He was forty-five when he took up the post and had served heroically in both wars, reaching the rank of second-lieutenant. An undistinguished, stocky man, he had been at the forefront of violent anti-Semitism for many years.

In 1934, during the Stavisky affair, he was injured in the rioting and set himself up as chairman of an association for protesters injured in the clashes. The following year, while working as a journalist, he was elected to the Paris City Council on a national anti-Jewish platform. Council debates were regularly interrupted by slanging matches with Jewish councillors and, in 1937, he joined with other agitators to set up the French anti-Jewish Committee. In May the same year, he made his programme clear by telling a public meeting: 'The Jewish problem must be resolved urgently either by expelling Jews or by massacring them.'

Writing in the first publication of his own newspaper, *L'Antijuif,* on 3 June 1937, he set out a Statut des Juifs which broadly predicted Vallat's proposals in 1940. The following year, the newspaper became *La France Enchaînée,* devoted entirely to revealing Jewish 'plots', ranging from Jean Zay's supposed plans to corrupt French children as Minister of Education to a conspiracy to take over the Presidential Palace. Darquier was repeatedly involved in violent actions against Jews and in 1939 was jailed for three months for inciting racial hatred.

As the new Commissioner, he was given nominal charge of the arrangements for La Grande Rafle while his private secretary, Joseph Galien, a German agent, had the responsibility for arranging a transit camp at the Vélodrome d'Hiver. In fact, Darquier was present at only two preparatory conferences, and Galien made a scandalous mess of his task, a reflection of the incompetence of Darquier's administration. If Darquier had been left the entire responsibility for the fate of Jews, his natural inefficiency and laziness might have worked in their favour. In addition, he was despised by the Premier, who later publicly regretted not having got rid of him immediately. Laval's contempt for Darquier was shared by Pétain, who called the Commissioner a 'torturer', yet took no moves to dismiss him.

However, the greatest danger to the Jewish population came from Laval's appointment of a brilliant professional, René Bousquet, as national police chief. Bousquet's priority was to prove that the French could be more efficient than the Germans, and by the end of the year a Nazi report gave him credit for the success of mass arrests of Jews and praised his sense of 'camaraderie'.

René Bousquet was a key figure in Vichy and perhaps the man who best represented the image that the French state was trying to show to the world. Unlike the many revengeful politicians, opportunist leaders, unreliable anti-Semitics or well-intentioned dupes who formed the various administrations over the four years, Bousquet was a much-praised civil servant untainted by the scandals of pre-war years. He was a young, resolute nationalist and a cultured family man with a self-confidence in facing up to the Germans which won admiration even from the Nazis. Wartime photographs show a tallish, impeccably dressed man either shaking hands with Reinhard Heydrich or smiling among uniformed SS officers during a visit to Marseilles. The Nazis seemed to think he was destined for even higher office, possibly as a replacement Premier for Laval.

Among those who were 'strongly impressed' by Bousquet was Heinrich Himmler, the SS chief. They met in Paris on 3 August 1943 and talked for five hours. The German Consul-General in Paris, Rudolf Schleier, noted that Himmler said afterwards that Bousquet was a 'precious collaborator', forecasting that he would play a leading role in French policy but would become a 'dangerous enemy' if he was pushed into the other camp. In fact, the Germans later became worried by Bousquet's influence and brought him forcibly to Germany at the end of 1943. According to SS-Major Herbert Hagen, the decision was taken because Bousquet 'had decided not to give in to us on anything that cut across French interests'.

At his trial after the war, Bousquet was given only a nominal

sentence of five years' national disgrace, a penalty lifted immediately because of unspecified 'acts of resistance'. The British were
said to have intervened, behind the scenes, stating that Bousquet
had been working for their intelligence service. Cleared of
ignominy, Bousquet went on to head some of France's biggest
colonial companies in a brilliant business career.

Recent research, however, has shown that Bousquet was the
man who freely proposed the transfer of foreign Jews from the
comparative safety of the Free Zone and persuaded a hesitant
Laval to offer complete French police co-operation in La Grande
Rafle. His motive was to rehabilitate his police force, particularly
in the Occupied Zone, in order to reinforce the campaign against
Communism and other elements undermining Vichy. There was
no evidence that he acted out of blind anti-Semitism. Prag-
matically anti-Jewish in much the same way as Laval, his first
priority was the fight against Marxism. Laval's and Bousquet's
ideas on the issue were more in tune than those of any other
Interior Minister–police chief partnership in Vichy.

The Premier obviously admired the young official. The future
police chief had been something of a civil service phenomenon
since coming to Paris to study law from Montauban in the south-
west, where his father was a barrister. At the age of only twenty-
one, René Bousquet had been decorated with the Legion
d'Honneur for courage in saving dozens of people from drowning
during floods, and during the Battle of France he won a Croix de
Guerre. As the regional Prefect in the Champagne, he was in the
front line negotiating working agreements with the Germans and
had shown none of the sycophantic attitude of many local
administrators. His nearest equivalent on the Nazi side was the
elegant Colonel Helmut Knochen, the expert on English
literature in charge of the SS police sections. They were the same
age, had much the same background, except for Knochen's Nazi
indoctrination, and they got on well. In another era, they would
probably have been senior European Community officials.

Between them, Bousquet and Knochen removed the Jewish issue from its emotional and political context and treated it as if it were a commercial transaction over waste disposal. Their contempt for the fanatical, less intelligent ideologists, Darquier and Dannecker, was evident throughout well-documented discussions that led up to La Grande Rafle.

Most of the documents which revealed the build-up to La Grande Rafle came from Gestapo files abandoned by SS officers at the Liberation of Paris. Additional material has come from brief notes of Vichy Cabinet meetings. Recent research has destroyed the image of a defiant Bousquet, which he projected during his trial. He often lied over his responsibility in planning the round-up, even covering up a crucial meeting with SS chiefs.[7]

The files also reveal several dramatic swings in French policy, ranging from over-eager collaboration to a sudden change of mind only a fortnight before the operation was due to take place. Unfortunately, the documents do not show clearly why French policy changed so brusquely before agreement was given to use French police in such numbers. Often, there seemed to be an element of bluff in the French attitude during talks conducted in a remarkably civilised way, especially after Darquier and Dannecker had been put on the sidelines.

In the end, whether Vichy's attitude was based on ruse or cowardly acceptance of Nazi demands, two advantages were gained from Laval's point of view. Thousands of stateless German and Austrian refugees in the South, whom Vichy had been trying to get rid of for two years, were sent back to Germany, while thousands of French Jews threatened with deportation were given a reprieve. Bousquet, meanwhile, saved the French police from being relegated in the general fight against Communism and Gaullism. La Grande Rafle, followed by police action in the South, was accepted as proof by the Germans that Vichy was willing to handle law-and-order operations in a way that would please Berlin.

Any doubt should have been dispelled long before Bousquet took up his post in 1942. French police co-operation with the Gestapo began in January 1941 when Dannecker placed an SS officer in the Paris Prefecture de Police. In August, an independent anti-Jewish squad of eleven French inspectors advised by a Gestapo officer was set up and in December this was officially incorporated in the national police force. In a memorandum dated February 1942, Dannecker described the squad as 'an elite troop' and acknowledged the value of the French-run Jewish records service which had developed an elaborate filing system. The records, in which details of French and foreign Jews were filed under different colours, had 'considerably eased' the Gestapo task during the three round-ups in 1941, he said.

There was no lack of French police ready to work directly for the Gestapo. By the end of the war, it was estimated that about 30,000 French were working with Nazi services. In Marseilles there were 1000 French for only 50 German staff, while in Saint-Etienne, near Vichy, there were only 10 Germans for 344 French. In Paris, the Germans advertised for 2000 French recruits and received 6000 applications. These volunteers were not included in the official French police force of about 100,000 men, among them 30,000 in Paris, who made up a unit as big as the Armistice Army.[8]

Bousquet would have been unaware on his appointment that the Nazis had already started the process that led up to La Grand Rafle. In March 1942, after Dannecker had been promoted to captain, he said in another internal document that it was time to propose 'something really positive to the French'. His superior in Berlin, Adolf Eichmann, planned to ship 5000 Jews from France to German concentration camps during 1942. Within a fortnight of this note, Dannecker escorted the first deportation train on its three-day journey to Auschwitz where gas equipment for the Final Solution was being installed.

By June, the numbers of Jews to be shipped out had risen

sharply. Dannecker reported that because transportation of German Jews to the East would have to be suspended during summer, Eichmann had decided to make up the numbers with 15,000 Dutch Jews, 10,000 Belgian Jews and 100,000 French Jews between the ages of sixteen and forty. The decision was taken at a meeting of Gestapo Jewish affairs experts, including Dannecker, in Berlin. The figure of 100,000 for France had been suggested by Dannecker but he quickly saw that he had exaggerated the possibilities and scaled down his quota to 40,000, while the Dutch programme was increased to 40,000.

In the meantime, Dannecker had circulated a note on a conversation with Darquier de Pellepoix, in which he declared: 'As shown during an interview on 15 June 1942 with the French Commissioner for Jewish Affairs, we can count on several thousand Jews from the Non-Occupied Zone being put at our disposal for evacuation.' This was the first written evidence that discussions had started on proposals to deliver Jews outside German-held territory, but it appears to be a follow-up to earlier contacts at a much higher level. Another German report, written after the round-ups started, specifically named Bousquet as the first French official to ask for Jews in the Free Zone to be sent to Germany. The original offer was made during a meeting with Heydrich in Paris on 6 May 1942. Details of the talks, also attended by the SS chief for France, General Karl Oberg, were given in a consular note by Rudolf Schleier on 11 September 1942, soon after the transfer of Jews from the Free Zone had begun.

Heydrich headed the entire SS police and had come to France during visits to several capitals to outline arrangements for the Final Solution and for reorganisation of Nazi police units. During his week-long stay in France, he told Bousquet that trains were being prepared to take Jews in Drancy 'to a destination in the East with a view to employing them for work'. According to Schleier's report, Bousquet 'then asked Heydrich if Jews interned for more than a year and a half in the Non-Occupied Zone could also be evacuated with the first departures'. The SS General was clearly surprised at the offer as, according to Schleier, the 'question was left open at the time because of transport difficulties'. It was the last occasion that Heydrich took a direct interest in the French question; he was fatally wounded by Czech assassins in Prague on 27 May 1942, two days before Jews of more than six years old in the Occupied Zone were ordered to wear a yellow cloth star on their clothes.

Detailed preparations for French deportations were held up for a few days because the Gestapo's Jewish office in Paris was being reorganised with the arrival of SS-Lieutenant Heinz Röthke, a former theological student, who would soon take over from Dannecker. Co-ordination among Nazi Jewish services in Paris remained Dannecker's responsibility for some weeks and on 26 June he reported a meeting with Jean Leguay, Bousquet's delegate, when a proposition to arrest 22,000 Jews in the Paris region was discussed. Leguay again raised the question of Jews in the Free Zone, according to a report by Dannecker which made it clear that Vichy was more anxious than the Germans to get rid of Jews in the South.

The principle of transferring 10,000 Jews into German-controlled France had been agreed by officials on both sides without a clear commitment from the Vichy Government on the final number. Dannecker's internal report added:

> As Leguay claimed that it would be preferable to take more Jews from the Non-Occupied Zone, I said that I well understood the French interest but the occupation force on the other side had stated their demands for arrests in the Occupied Zone. I nevertheless left complete latitude for an increase in the figure of 10,000 as far as Jews in the Non-Occupied Zone were concerned.

By then, 83,000 Jews in the North had been issued with yellow stars, which they had to buy with their own clothing-ration coupons. The task of identifying future deportees had been made much easier.

On 28 June 1942, the last of the initial five trains had left the camp of Beaune-la-Rolande among the wheatfields of the Beauce near Orleans with 1004 men and 34 women, many of them imprisoned for trying to cross into the Free Zone. Most were Polish immigrants but twenty-three of the women were French, among them the youngest deportee, a fifteen-year-old girl, the first child to be sent to a death camp from France.

The meeting between Dannecker and Leguay on 25 June 1942 was important for another reason – the Nazi officer demanded that arrests in Paris should include 40 per cent naturalised French. It was a provocative request because it infringed Vichy authority over the fate of French citizens. But it probably reflected Dannecker's belief that Vichy was in favour of the total elimination of Jews from France, following its offer to transfer foreign Jews under its protection.

Dannecker's over-confidence was quickly deflated. On the following day, Leguay went to see him to say that the demand to arrest naturalised Jews was being discussed by the Government but that Bousquet denied ever having offered 10,000 Jews from the Free Zone. On the same day, the Vichy Cabinet met and, according to a brief résumé, Laval said that French opinion would never accept a German solution to the Jewish issue and that he had never given any approval for action against Jews by French police, either in the Free Zone or in Paris.

This disavowal of all that went before has led to speculation that Bousquet, Darquier and Leguay discussed La Grande Rafle with the Germans without consulting the Prime Minister. Considering the close relationship between Bousquet and Laval this seems an unlikely interpretation. Bousquet must have been well aware of Laval's priorities. When giving evidence at Pétain's trial, Laval made a point of praising Bousquet as a 'fonctionnaire remarquable' and insisted that the police chief had his 'entire confidence'.

The Vichy Government's sudden hesitation was more likely to have been due to a misinterpretation of Nazi policy than to a lack of communication between the Premier and his police. Like all Vichy leaders, the Prime Minister was eager to get rid of foreign Jews, who were both a welfare and a security problem in the two zones. Until Leguay handed on Dannecker's demands for the deportation of French Jews, it was probable that Government Ministers and officials thought they were dealing only with the eventual expulsion of unwanted immigrants. The use of French police acting under Nazi orders to arrest French Jews was not only an indirect attack on Vichy's sovereignty, but could also have stirred up popular reaction.

After the war, Knochen revealed that the Germans had no choice except to comply with French conditions if the plan to send 40,000 Jews to Germany was to be fulfilled. The entire German police force in France, including drivers and telephonists, amounted to only 2400 men and women, most of them involved in protecting the German Army from terrorist attacks. From the beginning of the occupation, the regular Army had refused to take part in arresting Jews, which was considered police work. 'If the French police had not helped us, we couldn't have done anything at all,' Knochen said.[9]

Dannecker must have been in near panic at Leguay's sudden announcement that Vichy co-operation was no longer sure. There were only a few hundred Jews left in northern-zone concentration camps at a time when dozens of trains were being scheduled. A new agreement had to be arranged or La Grande Rafle would have to be abandoned. In desperation, Dannecker asked Eichmann to come to Paris. The logistical mastermind of the Final Solution arrived on 29 June and was probably as worried as Dannecker that he was about to suffer a humiliating setback just as the mass-murder programme got under way.

Among the documents Eichmann studied was a report from a German agent at Vichy which stated that Pétain's Government could not ask French police to intervene because of a fear of 'attracting extremely difficult reaction'. Presumably, there were many background discussions which went unrecorded during Eichmann's forty-eight-hour stay, because the day after he left the French position swung dramatically again.

On 2 July 1942, René Bousquet went to meet General Oberg and senior SS officers. Both sides resented Eichmann's intervention, which was seen as a threat to the authority of both Nazi and Vichy police chiefs. Dannecker was excluded from the talks by Oberg and Knochen. The 2 July meeting was crucial, because it resulted in what was called the first Oberg–Bousquet agreement, which reinforced the French law-and-order role in exchange for Vichy's co-operation over deportations. The French also won their point over exemptions for recently naturalised citizens.

A report of the 2 July discussions was made by SS-Major Herbert Hagen, a man with a perfect knowledge of French and Oberg's most trusted aide. The tone of the meeting seemed polite and began with Bousquet regretfully announcing that Laval had been told by Pétain that French police could no longer carry out arrests in the Occupied Zone. On the other hand, Pétain and Laval proposed to 'arrest and transfer only Jews with foreign nationality from non-occupied territory'. The French, he was reported as saying, had no objection to arrests in themselves, it was the use of French police that was 'génant'. The French word for 'bothersome' or 'embarrassing' was noted in its original form in the text.

Colonel Knochen led the discussions on the German side. He told Bousquet that Hitler had insisted on no other matter as much as 'the absolute necessity for the definitive solution to the Jewish question'. 'If the French Government puts obstacles in the way of arrests, the Führer would certainly not understand,' Knochen was quoted as saying. Without giving details of what was probably a long bargaining session, Hagen's report of the meeting added:

> That is why we agreed on the following arrangement: because it is not possible for the moment to arrest Jews of French nationality, following the Maréchal's intervention, Bousquet said he was ready to make arrests of the number of foreign Jews we wanted throughout French territory during the course of unified action. Bousquet insisted on the fact that, as far as the French Government was concerned, it was an entirely unprecedented way of acting and that one had to be aware of the difficulties that will result.

Later, the report stated, Bousquet said the real reason for Pétain's refusal was the problem of Jews from Alsace, as he had a number of connections with the province.

When he was questioned in prison after the war before his token trial, Bousquet did not mention the 2 July meeting. There was no official French version available as it was locked in the police archives. As a result, the reasons for Bousquet's sudden turnaround have to be guessed at. It was unlikely that he offered co-operation without being sure that he would be endorsed by Laval, just as it seemed unlikely that he would have agreed to round up Jews in the Free Zone if he had not been covered by his Premier, who, as Interior Minister, had the deciding word on police action.

The French priorities were simple. They wanted to get rid of foreign Jews and did not want to create an unpredictable problem by rounding up French Jews. They also wanted to be reassured that the visits of Heydrich and Eichmann did not presage an increase in German authority over Vichy security forces. Knochen, with his political flair, would have understood the issue without a long explanation. Both he and Oberg knew that any action which threatened economic collaboration or increased armed resistance would be regarded unfavourably in Berlin, whatever the Führer's supposed priorities were. The net result of the discussion nonetheless gave the Germans what they wanted – the delivery of 40,000 Jews by the French police, without compromising the occupation army.

An indication of Bousquet's certainty in making this unprecedented deal was reflected in the speed with which Laval gave the go-ahead. The Vichy Cabinet was convened on 3 July 1942, when the Prime Minister apparently gave as little detail as possible except to promise a new census in the Free Zone to distinguish immigrant Jews from the French. Pétain was quoted as telling his Ministers that 'this distinction is fair and understood by public opinion'. Laval was cruder, suggesting that a fundamental difference had been established between 'Juifs français et les déchets expediés par les Allemands eux-mêmes' – French Jews and waste matter sent by the Germans themselves.

Whether Laval would have sacrificed collaboration to save the French Jews, many of whom would be arrested anyway, was by no means certain. A fortnight earlier, on 22 June, the Premier had tied his destiny inextricably to Germany's with a speech in which he uttered the words: 'I desire a German victory because without it Bolshevism will be installed everywhere.' The speech, full of praise for German sacrifices, was approved by Pétain, who asked Laval to change only one word. Originally, the Prime Minister wanted to say that he 'believed' in a German victory but the Head of State told him that he was not a military man and was not capable of predicting the outcome of the war. Laval, though, had derived his opinion from solid signs, including German victories in Russia and British defeats in Libya, with the fall of Tobruk opening Rommel's way into Egypt. It was not the moment to revise Vichy's fundamental belief that France was dealing with a victorious Germany. Jews were fair downpayment for a worthwhile place in Hitler's empire.

On 4 July, Laval gave spectacular proof that much of his earlier supposed reluctance was hypocrisy and that Bousquet had probably been given clear instructions for the crucial 2 July meeting with Oberg and Knochen. The Premier went to Paris on 4 July and met Nazi officials. Two days later, Dannecker sent an urgent telegram to his superiors in Berlin. 'Laval has proposed that during the evacuation from the Non-Occupied Zone, children of less than sixteen years old should be taken as well. As far as the children who stayed in the Occupied Zone were concerned, the question did not interest him.' Up till then, to support the fiction that the Jews were being sent to labour camps, it had been planned to deport only those foreign Jews aged between sixteen and forty-eight. Dannecker had overreacted several times before in his eagerness to impress Eichmann. This time there was no mistake.

On 10 July, at a Vichy Cabinet meeting with Pétain present, Laval confirmed that 'contrary to the first German proposals' children from the Free Zone would be authorised to accompany their parents, a decision approved by the Cabinet for 'humanitarian reasons'. It was obvious that most of the children would have been born in France, but Vichy had no wish to look after abandoned boys and girls.

By 6 July 1942, Bousquet, Darquier, Dannecker and Knochen had got down to planning details of La Grande Rafle. Whether or not Bousquet's brief lack of co-operation was a bluff, he seemed to have got what he wanted: total control of police operations including those against Jews. In mid-June, he had written a letter to the SS chief, Karl Oberg, saying that the reinforcement of Vichy authority in law-and-order issues was crucial for morale. Given that the major point of discussion at the time was the Jewish issue, the letter had a special significance, particularly the following paragraph:

> You know the French police. It undoubtedly has its faults but it also has its qualities. I believe that if it was reorganised on a

new basis and energetically led, it would be capable of rendering the greatest services. Already, on numerous occasions you have been able to remark on its activity and the efficiency of its action. I am certain that it can do even better.

The proof was La Grande Rafle and the Free Zone sweeps that followed. There was no operation during the war when the Paris municipal police were mobilised on the same scale, although most of the policemen who arrested Jews in 1942 took a leading part in the Liberation of the capital in 1944, when the whole force was decorated for bravery.

CHAPTER TWELVE

La Grande Rafle

THERE IS NO authentic photographic record of La Grande Rafle of 16 July and 17 July 1942, two dates obscured by myth and misunderstanding. Nor is there definite proof that the Germans codenamed the operation Springtime Wind, as is often said, while the number of policemen who took part is disputed. Most accounts speak of 9000 but official documents suggest that it could have been half that number, although every Paris police official must have been involved at least indirectly because no Germans took part.

There is also no way of checking claims that police alerted thousands of Jews, except to point out that more than 25,000 file cards were issued to arresting teams and only half that number of Jews was caught. Rumours of a police sweep had been circulating for days. UGIF officials, representing the only approved Jewish welfare body, had been told to collect blankets and provisions, while civilian bus and rail representatives had been involved in preparations. Yiddish and French tracts were circulated to give warnings at least twenty-four hours before. Most of those who escaped were men who went into hiding. The 1941 round-ups had not affected women and children and no one suspected that entire families would be seized. The absence of many husbands may have increased the anxiety of wives and children but reduced the number of those who suffered at the Vélodrome d'Hiver indoor bicycle stadium, where more than 8000 people, including 4115 children, were interned in vile conditions for five days.

The operation began on time at four o'clock in the morning with fifty Paris city buses and their drivers requisitioned to drive Jews either to the stadium or to the flats at Drancy. About 100 suicides were reported as police commandos, sometimes helped by 400 thugs from Jacques Doriot's Fascist Parti Populaire Français, concentrated mainly on poor immigrant quarters. Roadblocks were set up to catch anyone who tried to flee but there was little resistance, partly because the police usually acted without brutality.

The real violence was inflicted in the giant covered stadium in the 15th *arrondissement,* which was a venue for both six-day cycle races and political meetings before the war. The best-remembered political rally was held in 1937 to greet Charles Maurras when he was released from jail after the attack on Léon Blum. Joseph Galien, Darquier's deputy, the official responsible for accommodation, had been told that as many as 20,000 arrested Jews would be held in the Vélodrome, where there were benches for only 15,000 people. Because so many escaped arrest, there was only half that number. Even so, sanitary conditions were hopelessly inadequate with only six lavatories, and they soon became blocked. The summer heat worsened the effect of scarce food and water supplies while only two doctors were allowed to treat the sick and dying, many of them suffering from dysentery. At night, it was very cold and there was insufficient space for everyone to lie down.

Georges Wellers, a Paris lawyer and one of the most active Jewish resistance workers who helped found the Jewish Contemporary Documentation Centre in Paris, described the horror of the Vélodrome d'Hiver. 'All these wretched people lived five horrifying days in the enormous interior filled with deafening noise, among the shouting and weeping of children, and of adults at their nerves' ends, among the screams and cries of people who had gone mad or the injured who had tried to kill themselves,' he recalled.

Those who were taken later to the camps at Beaune-la-Rolande and Pithiviers in police trucks had a few hours of mistaken liberty before being plunged into another form of chaos and neglect. Families driven directly in city buses to Drancy were already suffering from equally appalling conditions while deportation trains were arriving from the South, bringing victims of round-ups in other towns. Among them were hundreds of supposedly exempt French Jews.

Throughout La Grande Rafle, Laval was in Paris, but there was no record of his taking any interest in the outcome. Dannecker was absent on a week-long tour of the Free Zone on a Vichy invitation to advise on the handing over of Jews in French concentration camps. It was his last big assignment before being sent back to Berlin by Knochen and Oberg.

The greatest single atrocity arising from the nationwide arrests that coincided or followed La Grande Rafle was the murder of about 6000 children deported in 1942. Nearly all were gassed immediately on arrival in Germany. Deportation of children began on 20 July in a train despatched from Angers in the Occupied Zone. Half the trainload of 824 Jews were women and there were 200 people of French nationality, among them a thirteen-year-old girl and four children aged fourteen.

Cruelty and neglect began long before the trains reached the border and even children who were not sent to Auschwitz under-went appalling suffering. After the horrors of the Vélodrome d'Hiver, conditions were equally miserable at Drancy where 4000 children between the ages of two and twelve were temporarily interned following their stay in the cycle stadium. Among dozens of eyewitness reports of the suburban camp run entirely by the French police, Georges Wellers recalled the brutality inflicted on children barely able to walk.

The flats at Drancy were unfinished and there were few separating walls. The internees had to sleep on cement floors. The children were put in dormitories, each containing about 100 with a few adults to look after them. 'Buckets were placed on the landing because many children were unfit to walk down the long, difficult staircases to the lavatories,' Wellers said.

> Little ones incapable of looking after themselves had to wait desperately for the help of welfare workers or another child. This was the time of cabbage soup at Drancy. It wasn't bad but it was not suitable for children's stomachs.
>
> All very quickly suffered from terrible diarrhoea. They fouled their clothes and they dirtied the mattresses where they spent all their time, day and night. Because there was no soap, their clothes were rinsed in cold water and the children had to wait almost naked until they dried.

According to Wellers, one of the French intellectuals who had been interned in December 1941, the smallest children did not even know their names and could only be identified after their friends had been questioned. Each one was tagged with a small piece of wood hung around the neck. 'Every night, from the other side of the camp, we heard the uninterrupted weeping of desperate children and, from time to time, the appeals and piercing screams of children who could no longer hold themselves back.'

From 21 July to 9 September, about 5500 children passed through Drancy. About a fifth had to receive hospital treatment for serious diseases or malnutrition. The majority had been shuttled between camps in the North while others were brought from the Free Zone. When they arrived in sealed cattle wagons their physical condition shocked welfare workers, who found themselves having to deal with weeks of neglect. Long before the end of the year, nearly all the children were sent to Germany in groups of forty or sixty, packed into railtrucks assembled at the Quai aux Moutons. Deportees were selected by the French police under the command of Jean Leguay. Later, he was to deny that the

French police even took part in La Grande Rafle and was officially reinstated in the Prefects' Corps in the civil service while working for the scent firm, Nina Ricci, in the United States. He returned to an executive business career in France, retiring in 1975, four years before he was charged with Crimes against Humanity in a private prosecution. He died without having been tried in 1989.

The Germans, who had originally set the lower age limit for arrests at sixteen, did not want the responsibility of deporting children and at least 1500 others were forcibly returned to the Free Zone. It was several weeks before Berlin, which had made no preparations for gassing children, eventually gave permission for those still in French detention centres to be deported.

Some of the most moving accounts of what happened after La Grande Rafle were written by those who escaped being sent to Auschwitz. Annette Muller was nine when the rumour grew that the Paris round-up was about to take place. Annette's father went into hiding, like many of his friends who remembered previous police action in which only men had been seized. No one was aware of orders to arrest entire families.

With her mother and small brother, Annette Muller was first taken to the Vélodrome d'Hiver and then sent on a five-hour lorry drive on a beautiful summer day to Beaune-la-Rolande, a camp run by the French in the middle of wheatfields in the Occupied Zone. In August, it was decided to separate children under the age of twelve from their mothers, who had been told they were being sent to labour camps in the East.

'Everybody was assembled in the middle of the camp,' Annette Muller remembered forty years later.

> The gendarmes hit out with the butts of their rifles and their truncheons or sprayed us with firehoses full of ice-cold water to force the children to leave their mothers, who wouldn't let them go.
>
> There was wild scuffling, shouts, weeping and screams of

pain. The gendarmes tore off the women's clothing looking for
jewels or money. Then there was a great silence. On one side,
hundreds of children and on the other side, the mothers and
some older boys and girls. In the middle were the gendarmes
giving brief orders.

Left alone except for a few voluntary workers, the children were
later forced to sew yellow stars on their clothes, and their heads
were partially shaved. For several weeks they were kept on starvation rations and given poor medical care; as a result, some of
them died before the rest were marched through the village to an
austere railway station set in a huge empty square.

Cattle trucks took them to Drancy where a selection process
was carried out under the supervision of Jewish officials from
UGIF, who seized on every opportunity to claim exemption. The
Muller children were reprieved because they were born in France.
They were transferred to a huge refuge in Paris run by voluntary
workers of the Oeuvre de Secours aux Enfants, OSE, a child-care
association started in the Soviet Union, which had been incorporated into the UGIF. As they sat in the police van which took
them to the refuge, the children – believing despite the presence
of four gendarmes that they were going home – started singing
and shouting. 'At a certain moment, I turned towards the policemen sitting behind us,' she said. 'They were listening to us in
silence, crying. I realised we weren't going home, so I cried too.'

Eventually, her father found his two children and took them to
safety. 'Sadly, for my mother it was too late,' Annette Muller said.
It was also too late for most of the 41,951 Jews sent to Germany
between 27 March and 11 November in forty-five trains provided
by the French state railways. Most of the 6000 children who died
were deported during the eleven weeks between 17 July and 30
September, when an average of about 3000 Jews were put into
death trains every seven days.

CHAPTER THIRTEEN

The Church Protests

More than forty years after the event, following a long campaign by Resistance and Jewish groups, accurate descriptions of La Grande Rafle and its consequences were included in school textbooks for the first time. Feature films, documentaries and articles inspired by events like the trial of Klaus Barbie or attempts to incriminate collaborators have made the scenes of violence and degradation familiar images. Personal recollections have also made up for the absence of any newspaper reports at the time or of a photographic record – with the possible exception of pictures kept in the closed Paris police archives.

In contrast, the round-up of Jews in the Free Zone, an entirely French responsibility, has remained obscure even though it involved at least 10,000 police. From the beginning, it was a Vichy decision and was discussed by the Cabinet with Pétain present. The victims were families who had taken refuge in the Free Zone, believing they were protected by the French.

The most intensive sweep took place between 26 and 28 August with a manhunt spread throughout Vichy-controlled territory in which military-style opérations were mounted to run down Jews hiding in forests or in the mountains. Some of the atmosphere of the Free Zone police round-ups was captured by an undated Communist tract:

> Executing Hitler's orders, Laval and Pétain have unleashed a
> wave of terror in the Non-Occupied Zone with bestial

repression against Jewish families. At Marseilles, Lyons, Narbonne, Sête, Toulouse, Agen, Cahors, Montauban and in other towns, monstrous round-ups have taken place which makes it shameful to be French. Swarms of police have attacked sleeping Jewish households, tearing them from their beds and herding them like cattle into police vans. Children have been torn from their parents and their papers ripped in front of their mothers and fathers so that the little ones cannot be identified.

Once again, the role and the true face of Pétain have appeared in their hideous nudity. It is Pétain, with Laval, who has ordered this horrible manhunt.

The tract finished with an appeal: 'Français. Françaises. Jews are our brothers, Jews are our sisters. They are human beings like us. It is our most elementary duty to save them.'

Vichy newspapers and radio stations remained silent on police operations, a pointless censorship because Swiss newspapers circulated widely in the Free Zone and gave accounts later broadcast to France by the BBC.

The *rafle* might have had less impact if sufficient stateless Jews had been held in Free Zone concentration camps, but Dannecker's week-long tour, accompanied by the head of the French Police for Jewish Affairs, Jacques Schweblin, proved a disappointment. He expected to find 40,000 interned Jews but detentions had dwindled sharply since 1940. At Gurs, where Dannecker counted on 20,000, only 2599 people could be legally deported. Prefects, the local governors who had been given the right to intern foreign Jews in October 1940, interpreted the rulings more loosely after supply and welfare problems followed indiscriminate arrests.

Difficulties in running camps, where at least 3000 Jews had died of culpable neglect, were partly solved by seizing on every excuse to disperse internees to labour camps or by settling them on reluctant villagers under a form of house arrest. Hundreds of

Pétain and Laval, his Prime Minister, in 1940.

A propaganda poster compares pre-Vichy and Vichy France as two houses built on different foundations. Among the factors undermining the house on the left is 'Juiverie'. The six stars in the sky of the right-hand house are Pétain's Maréchal insignia.

Xavier Vallat, first Commissioner-General for Jewish Affairs.

Darquier de Pellepoix, second Commissioner-General for Jewish Affairs.

Inside the main courtyard at the Drancy concentration camp near Paris.

Drancy flats in 1989, soon after the memorial wagon was installed in the former camp's courtyard.

Pétain takes his daily walk with his doctor, the fanatically anti-Semitic Ménétrel.

René Bousquet, head of Vichy Police (smiling, with cigarette and fur collar), with SS chiefs during a round-up.

A plainclothed French policeman helps SS men carry out an identity check at Paris's Gare de L'Est. The uniformed police are French gendarmes.

Pétain with Hermann Göring, Head of the Luftwaffe, at a meeting in France.

A Jewish man wearing the yellow star in Paris, 1942.

Monsignor Jules-Géraud Saliège, Archbishop of Toulouse, who led attacks on Vichy over the deportation of the Jews.

French concentration camp at Beaune-la-Rolande, near Orléans.

Léon Blum gives evidence at Pétain's trial in 1945.

Memorial to Jews interned at Drancy.

Jewish detainees were technically protected, either through supposed age limits or because they had been issued exit visas by a protecting power or came from a country allied to Germany. Many others were recently naturalised French who could claim exemption. A special camp had been set up for British and American Jewish detainees among hotels in the Vosges spa town of Vittel, eastern France.

It was obvious that thousands of arrests would have to be made outside the camps to fulfil German demands, but Laval still promised to deliver 14,500 stateless Jews, saying that he would not be 'dishonoured' by the decision. Secret instructions were issued by Bousquet's deputy at Vichy, Henri Cado, ordering local administrators to be prepared to hand over all foreign Jews who had entered France since the beginning of 1936, the first sign that France intended to bend nationality rules to ensure that quotas would be fulfilled. Bousquet sent an even stronger Note on 22 August ordering Prefects to rid their areas of all foreign Jews and to 'crush all resistance'. Questions of principle had been pushed aside and the only priority was to meet Nazi demands.

Because of the disappointing results of La Grande Rafle, on 11 August Vichy began transferring stateless Jews from the camps at Noé and Récébédou, south of Toulouse, to ensure that scheduled trains to Auschwitz would be full. One of the witnesses of these departures was the Noé camp chaplain, Rabbi René Kapel, who had previously served in the Fifth Army Corps, also as chaplain. He was responsible for other camps in the South, including Gurs, but was at Noé when the first deportation train left. Kapel, previously a rabbi at Mulhouse on the Swiss frontier, said that while he had been intensely moved at seeing the old and sick inmates of Noé being herded into cattle wagons, he had not been aware that they were being sent to their deaths.

Four trains left Noé in August and September and their passengers included a rabbi's wife, Ruth Altmann, and her six children, one of many big families to be deported together. Her husband, Jacob, a German refugee, had installed a synagogue in one of the huts and organised social work among the 800 Jewish internees. He died soon after his family was taken away and was buried in the camp cemetery.

The camp at Récébédou was situated in the suburbs of Toulouse in an area now covered by housing estates and a new shopping mall. Rabbi Kapel, who later became chaplain to a Zionist Resistance movement called L'Armée Juive, watched the departure of the third train from Récébédou, which, like Noé, was reserved for the sick and old:

> The deportees were obliged to walk more than a mile under freezing rain to the station at Portet-Saint-Simon. They had to climb into cattle wagons while invalids were put into third-class carriages. The local population was shocked by these scenes, which was why the Vichy authorities then took the precaution to organise departures only at night, so there would be no witnesses.

Another description of conditions at Récébédou at last stirred the conscience of the Catholic clergy. Monsignor Louis de Courrèges d'Ustou, auxiliary Bishop of Toulouse, was at Archbishop's House in the south-western city when a woman Catholic social worker came to see the Archbishop, Monsignor Jules-Géraud Saliège. She asked for Church intervention over the treatment of Jews. The Bishop recalled:

> The Archbishop was given a description of a pitiful spectacle – a procession of the old, sick and crippled, stumbling across fields for more than a mile while old ladies had to stop every few steps with tears in their eyes.
>
> Monsignor Saliège was told of awful scenes, attempts at suicide, collapses and crises of madness caused by the violent separation of families. He was deeply moved and scribbled a

letter that was to have an echo far and wide and which was like
a resurrection of the human conscience.

Archbishop Saliège, himself a sick and crippled man of seventy-two who could move only in a wheelchair, defied orders from the Vichy Government and issued what became the most famous of all protests against Vichy's persecution. A Pastoral Letter read in most parishes of the Haute Garonne *département* on 23 August declared that Jews were being treated like a 'foul herd' and were being separated from their families to be sent to an unknown destination. 'In our diocese there have been horrifying scenes in the camps at Noé and Récébédou,' Saliège added. 'Jews are men, Jews are women. They are part of humankind. They are our brothers like anyone else. A Christian cannot forget that.'

Saliège became a hero for the Jewish community and in 1951, to commemorate his sixty years as a priest, the Grand Rabbi, Isaïe Schwartz, presented him with a 400-year-old Bible and a gold plate inscribed with the opening words of his 1942 Pastoral Letter. The Archbishop's courageous act, however, was not a sudden conversion. Before the war he had led criticism of racism and was one of the few Christian Democrat prelates in a conservative hierarchy.

When Vichy was set up, he sent a priest to the spa town who returned with the advice that he should keep his distance from a government dominated by supporters of Action Française. Even so, the Archbishop welcomed the moral renewal of the National Revolution and was irritated when his Pastoral Letter was interpreted as a personal attack on Pétain. He issued a statement affirming his complete loyalty to the Head of State. This took nothing away from the Pastoral Letter's impact and it was published by underground newspapers, broadcast by the BBC and reproduced by journals in Britain and the United States.

Saliège's act of defiance was reinforced by Monsignor Pierre-Marie Théas, Archbishop of Montauban, the city where Bousquet was born. He issued a Pastoral Letter on 30 August giving 'voice to the outraged protest of Christian conscience' and proclaiming that all men were brothers because they were created by the same God. Anti-Semitic measures showed contempt for human dignity and were a violation of the most sacred rights of people and families, he said.

Other Church leaders made explicit or implicit attacks on anti-Jewish policy, splitting one of the most reliable areas of Pétain's support. The Maréchal had returned to regular Mass-going as part of an opportunist relationship with the Church which led to his being married in a religious ceremony in January 1943 – a proxy wedding carried out by the Cardinal Archbishop of Paris, Emmanuel Suhard.

No other institution was so closely identified with the National Revolution as the Catholic Church. Even the defence forces were split between Vichy and de Gaulle. In the first weeks of the new French state, Pétain had received a rapturous reception in Lyons where the Cardinal Archbishop, Pierre-Marie Gerlier, said ecstatically, 'Pétain, c'est la France et la France c'est Pétain.'

Gerlier was the most senior churchman to be seen regularly at Vichy. The round-up in the South would turn him into the regime's most dangerous critic.

Archbishop Théas's Pastoral Letter was read from pulpits only hours after what became known as La Nuit de Vénissieux, the climax of three days of frantic attempts to save children and adults destined to be deported to the German zone from the Lyons region. The night of Saturday, 29 August 1942, was to mark a turning point in the attitude towards Vichy inside the Church and official charitable bodies, including Jewish organisations, who had tried to work within the law.

Overnight, the first clandestine operations to save Jewish children from the Nazis came into effect, creating a pool of popular resistance to Pétain that eventually involved thousands of people. Except for the armed movement to rally to de Gaulle in London or Africa, no event before the end of 1942 mobilised more people in a concerted initiative to undermine Vichy and German policies. In many cases, courageous pacific opposition to deporting Jews led to the establishment of armed groups. The fact that about 250,000 Jews survived the war can be largely traced to a growing awareness of Vichy's treachery exposed in events before and after La Nuit de Vénissieux which at last made Archbishop Gerlier aware of the inevitable impact of anti-Jewish legislation.

Countless former Vichy supporters became accomplices in dangerous undercover rescue work either as volunteers or as paid assistants. It would have been difficult to find any Jew still alive in 1944 who could have survived without the vast network of organised or spontaneous illegal support provided by an anonymous mass of ordinary French people who, until the summer of 1942, had put their entire faith in Pétain's priorities.

Vénissieux, an industrial suburb of Lyons, was one of the key staging posts for Jews arrested in the South. A former temporary barracks set in an old factory with fifteen-foot-high brick walls, the concentration camp was placed under the guard of colonial troops from Indo-China, commanded by a Frenchman. An estimated 4000 Jews passed through the camp, at least 1300 during the last week of August. The conditions were among the worst experienced by deportees. Suicide attempts were common, with twenty-six reported on one night alone.

Between 26 and 29 August, an ecumenical welfare group, Amitié Chrétienne, was given the responsibility of sorting potential deportees from those who could claim exemption. Representatives from other organisations including the Jewish OSE were secretly attached to Amitié Chrétienne in a race against time. The Christian friendship movement was jointly sponsored by Cardinal Gerlier and Pastor Marc Boegner, chairman of the Protestant Federation. It had been given the responsibility for finding homes for refugee Jewish children following a meeting of Christian and

Jewish charities, which set up a joint organisation in 1941 known as the Committee of Nîmes.

The suggestion came from a Catholic priest, Abbé Alexandre Glasberg, a converted Ukrainian Jew, who became a well-known figure in the concentration camps, not least because of his thread-bare soutane covered in patches. After helping many Jews to leave the camps, he was at the centre of the Vénissieux affair, when he smuggled out children in his black Citroën car, which the guards mistook for the Prefect's official vehicle. A squat, broad man with pebble glasses, Glasberg worked alongside a Jesuit priest, Father Pierre Chaillet, a close confidant of Cardinal Gerlier.

The chaos and suffering at Vénissieux was so unbearable that the French police officer overseeing the sorting process left on the first night, giving the welfare team the chance to intercept official orders from Bousquet which overrode all age and nationality exemptions. The orders were kept hidden and the team saved about 500 adults and 108 children who would otherwise have been sent to Drancy.

Often it was necessary to forge identities or help people to escape, but one of the easiest methods was to authorise hospital treatment. The camp doctor signed about 140 false medical certificates. By the time the deportation list was drawn up, welfare workers had spared all but 545 potential deportees, who were later transferred to Drancy.

Saving children presented numerous problems. Arrested Jews were under the impression that deportation trains were destined for labour camps or even a Jewish homeland. They had to be persuaded that their sons and daughters were in danger and that the Christian movement would not forcibly baptise them. The ages of stateless children over sixteen had to be altered to satisfy French officials unaware that the exemption for younger people had been summarily dropped.

Finally, it was decided to remove children from Vénissieux in the camp bus. On 29 August, 108 were taken to the headquarters of the Jewish Scout movement, Les Eclaireurs Israélites de France, in the Croix Rousse quarter of Lyons. About twenty of the older children were given Scout and Guide uniforms and sent on a camping trip in a rural retreat in the Haute Loire.

The frantic few hours that followed were to have far-reaching consequences. Angry at being tricked, the Lyons Regional Prefect, Alexandre Angeli, told Father Chaillet that he had to hand over the eighty-four children who had been hidden by Lyons families. The priest refused to disclose addresses, saying that the children's parents were 'bound for exile and, without doubt, death'. Cardinal Gerlier, in his role as honorary leader of Amitié Chrétienne, told Angeli that the organisation's gesture should be considered 'a protest by the Church against the handing over of Israélites to the occupying authority'. This was accompanied by a statement of loyalty to the Vichy Government which did not save Father Chaillet from being put under house arrest in a psychiatric hospital for three months.

On 2 September, the Cardinal's anger had increased and he issued a message to be read in all churches proclaiming that it was his urgent and painful duty to protest against an affront to his conscience and that his heart ached at 'the thought of the treatment undergone by thousands of human beings while believing that it could have been prevented'.

Almost without being aware of it, Gerlier had become the key figure in an opposition movement that made some amends for the long silence on anti-Jewish legislation. The specific question of discrimination had left the Catholic hierarchy more or less indifferent until La Grande Rafle, which took place just before a Church leaders' assembly in Paris. A weak private joint protest was made to Pétain, but on 17 August Grand Rabbi Jacob Kaplan and Pastor Boegner, a member of the Vichy constitutional advisory body, the National Council, persuaded Cardinal Gerlier to approach Pétain personally as part of an ecumenical initiative.

Later, the Pastor put his own fears in a letter to the Head of

State in which he referred to the terrible fate of deportees, adding: 'As you have said yourself, no defeat can force France to permit an attack on its honour.' This was followed by a prophetic remark on future judgement of Vichy's role: the Protestant leader pleaded with Pétain not to let France 'inflict a moral defeat on itself in which the burden will be incalculable'.

Among other Christian leaders to approach Pétain personally was the American YMCA delegate, Tracy Strong, who went to Vichy on 4 August. Two days later, the Head of State received Donald Lowrie, who led all charitable organisations as chairman of the Comité de Coordination des Oeuvres. Later, the Quakers also went to see the Maréchal.

Jewish leaders made a number of dignified protests which were based on detailed eyewitness reports. In late July, rumours of imminent action in the Free Zone were already circulating after reports in the foreign press and on the BBC. The Chaplain-General, Rabbi René Hirschler, who operated from Marseilles, made inquiries in Vichy before deciding to send twenty-four rabbis as observers in the main Free Zone camps and detention centres. Their presence, particularly in the Toulouse region, was crucial in alerting other religious leaders, notably Monsignor Saliège, who made the only public protest before the Vichy manhunt began.

Catholic leaders also kept the Papal Nuncio, Valerio Valeri, informed of precise details, which he relayed directly to Pétain on a number of occasions. Like the American delegates, Valeri insisted that the deportees were being sent to certain death. The Papal Ambassador, however, had to defend the Pope against allegations from Latin American envoys who accused the Holy See of 'hiding behind silence in the face of such inhuman persecution'. They detected no direct pressure on Vichy from the Pope, a fact which Valeri explained as 'a cautious period of waiting and wise reserve'.

Pétain may well have been inspired by the Pope's prudent example, for he did not intervene in the controversy except to approve the dismissal of General Robert de Saint-Vincent, who commanded part of the Lyons district. When it was clear that events at Vénissieux were out of hand, the General was asked by the local police chief to order his soldiers to help with the transfer of Jews to the deportation train. He replied: 'Never in my life will I lend my troops for an operation like that.' Within forty-eight hours he had been forcibly retired.

Cardinal Gerlier wrote his protest on 30 August 1942, and published it on 2 September, ordering it to be read from all pulpits on 6 September. He was aware of Vichy attempts to stifle the Pastoral Letters of Saliège and Théas and no doubt personally told Pétain of his initiative before his message was released.

By then, there had been time for Government officials to read reports from Prefects in the Free Zone detailing various degrees of popular condemnation. Most accounts referred to limited or non-existent popular sympathy, with Prefects claiming that Jews had made themselves disliked because of links with the black market. Other reports contained implicit warnings of hostile reaction which were probably spelled out more specifically in telephone conversations.

One of the shortest official notes, written on 1 September 1942 by the Prefect of Montpellier, was also one of the most dramatic. In the Mediterranean city, what the Prefect called the Jewish question had caused 'a crisis of panic and anxiety among Israelite elements'; he added: 'Part of public opinion has been moved by repression that it considers pitiless.'

Alexandre Angeli, the Lyons region Prefect, said that although only 545 'individuals' had been deported from Vénissieux, reaction could not have been greater if 100,000 had been despatched. He named both Gerlier and Father Chaillet, who ran the Lyons Catholic Institute, for refusing to divulge the address of the hidden children and said the two priests had blocked a Government plan on the pretext of moral obligation.

Pétain's Government had feared that Lyons would be a centre of opposition as early as July 1940. It was suspicious of the Mayor, Edouard Herriot, the National Assembly and Radical Party chairman, who had proved the ill-will he felt towards Pétain by refusing an official order to identify Jewish Members of Parliament when the Statut des Juifs was published. He was supported by the Senate chairman, Jules Jeanneney.

From Vichy, 100 miles from Lyons by road, the south-eastern capital was correctly seen as a potential centre of resistance, not least because it sheltered 35,000 Jews, most of them refugees from the North or Alsace. Newly founded Resistance movements operated almost openly in the city, from which the Germans were excluded. Losing the confidence of the Lyons Cardinal Archbishop would have had disastrous effects on Vichy's authority. Laval could see no way out except a hasty retreat, and he called off the police action.

On 2 September, the day Gerlier's Pastoral Letter was being delivered to churches around Lyons, Laval had lunch in Paris with the SS chief, General Oberg, the German Ambassador, Otto Abetz, and the Vichy delegate in the capital, Fernand de Brinon. Laval's position on the use of French police in the round-ups had swung from opposition to support in July, and then to excessive and unexpected collaboration in August when he offered to hand over children.

The SS report of the lunch, drawn up by Major Hagen, made it sound as if Laval was glad to have been proved wrong by the Church's reaction. Despite the dramatic events, the meal was a relaxed affair with repeated references to Laval's irony, particularly towards Darquier de Pellepoix, 'un bon garçon' who was incapable of doing his job properly. This was interpreted as pressure to sack the Jewish Affairs Commissioner and followed a request by the Vichy Premier for the Germans not to make any new demands over the delivery of Jews and to avoid setting a target figure.

'. . . Laval explained that the demands we have formulated

concerning the Jewish question have recently encountered unparalleled resistance on the part of the Church,' Hagen wrote. 'The head of this anti-governmental opposition happens to be Cardinal Gerlier.' Hagen also accurately caught Laval's colourful tone of speech: 'He asked us to believe in his complete honesty when he promised to settle the Jewish question but, he said, the deliveries of Jews were not like goods in a single price department store where one could take as many products as one wanted always at the same price.'

Laval's attitude was taken in good part by General Oberg, who assured the French leader that the SS would not be making any new demands. The Nazi General was probably in no more hurry over the Jewish question than Laval and may also have regretted giving in to the joint pressure of Dannecker and Eichmann. The Occupation authorities did not want to disturb the extremely satisfactory state of collaboration, which was soon to enter a new phase with the mass deportation of Frenchmen for compulsory war work in German factories.

Neither Oberg nor Colonel Knochen had been in favour of new demands from Eichmann's office which were based on a thousand deportations a day, a target that could only have been reached with more arrivals from the Free Zone. New round-ups in the South could only intensify Church protests and undermine both Pétain and Laval, destroying a key portion of Hitler's strategy for governing France without having to draw on more troops.

The Germans must have been taken by surprise by the strength of Church protest, because the Occupation authorities had reasonably good relations with the Archbishop of Paris, a factor which led to de Gaulle's shunning of Cardinal Suhard at the Liberation of Paris. Oberg may also have been less confident than Bousquet about police co-operation, especially in the Gendarmerie, which operated in the rural districts and provided guards for the trains and camps. Nazi agents reported cases of exhaustion after pursuing Jews who had gone into hiding in the Pyrenees, and there was probably resentment that general law-and-order operations were affected by Nazi priorities.

There was written evidence that the Gendarmerie, made up of professional soldiers, objected to escorting trains from Vichy concentration camps to Drancy. A detailed account of the journey of a train from Gurs on 1 September 1942 was drawn up by a Gendarmerie captain whose men were shocked at the squalid conditions in the cattle trucks. His escort was eventually involved in a humanitarian operation for which they received thanks from the deportees. He pointed out that the official treatment of Jews 'strongly and unfavourably impressed' French people, especially when his train was halted at stations. 'Professional soldiers looked after, fed, went to fetch water in the stations [for the deportees] and lived without sleep for twenty-four hours in an unbreathable atmosphere, standing beside the wagon doors or on filthy straw,' the Captain added. 'They comforted the depressed, gave hope to those who had become discouraged and morally disarmed those who wanted to escape.' In a laconic final comment, the Captain said: 'A better arrangement for these trains is profoundly desirable.'

A terse report by the Renseignements Généraux, the French Special Branch, also reported popular 'astonishment that the French Government should hand over people arrested for contravening laws in the Non-Occupied Zone'.

There was enough cause for concern for both Vichy and the SS to reconsider tactics. As a result, only half of Laval's promised 14,500 deportees from the Free Zone were rounded up in August, along with 3000 others taken from inside camps. But Laval maintained his promise to transfer stateless Germans and Austrians already in French hands to the Occupied Zone. Trains continued to cross the Demarcation Line until 15 September, by which time 10,522 people had been despatched by thirteen trains.

Desperate efforts were made to avoid the shortfall by

organising new police swoops in Paris and by continually changing rules to allow French police to arrest previously exempt national categories, including a thousand Greek Jews. Greeks made up three-quarters of the second-last contingent to be sent out in 1942 in a train on 9 November 1942.

A forty-third train was scheduled to leave Drancy on 11 November with another 1000 people, but only 700 were left in the block of flats. This was despite the arrest of nearly a thousand Roumanian Jews in Paris and another French police operation in provincial areas of the Occupied Zone on 9 and 10 October when 1742 Jews were arrested in nearly twenty towns. More than 600 were seized in the Poitiers region.

In an attempt to fill the last freight trucks, the SS officer responsible for organising departure schedules from Drancy, Second-Lieutenant Ernst Heinrichsohn, went to the Rothschild Hospice in Paris and seized thirty-five patients aged between seventy and ninety. Even so the train left partly empty. The old people were among 599 deportees, including 63 children less than twelve years old, gassed on arrival at Auschwitz. The others were selected for forced labour and died soon afterwards, except for two men who survived the war.

Earlier, Colonel Knochen, drawing directly on warnings from Laval of increasing Church protests, had vetoed the most controversial plan, the arrest of more than 5000 leading 'rich and influential' French Jews in Paris which was to have involved 3000 police. The raid was scheduled for 21 September, the same day that the Wehrmacht executed 116 hostages as reprisals for terrorist attacks.

Despite Knochen's concern that action against French Jews would arouse unfavourable reaction in Vichy and among the public in the Occupied Zone, this did not prevent about 3000 French Jews being included in the deportation trains in 1942. Vichy made no protest when it was claimed by the Germans that they were petty criminals. In fact they were mostly poor people, some of them arrested because they had no resources or because they had attempted to cross the Demarcation Line.

If the full extent of Eichmann's original plans had been carried out in 1942, at least another 45,000 Jews would have been shipped out. Their reprieve can be directly attributed to the pressure put on Pétain by churchmen. It would have needed a man of Dannecker's fanatical energy to have revived the programme quickly, but the SS-Lieutenant had already left Paris.

The cause of his departure was the final act in a long personality duel with Knochen, who believed that the Gestapo officer's arrogance and recklessness would destroy a carefully balanced programme to draw Vichy into deeper collaboration. Knochen's official excuse for replacing Dannecker was a complaint that he spent too much time in nightclubs in Pigalle. Bousquet said after the war that Knochen had also received strong support from Vichy, where Dannecker was considered 'a madman and a sadist'. After a short period overseeing deportation procedures on the Demarcation Line, the officer who had prepared the way for La Grande Rafle was recalled to Berlin and sent to Sofia to organise the murder of Bulgarian Jews.

CHAPTER FOURTEEN

Saving the Children

THE CHURCH PROTEST gained a four-month reprieve before deportations restarted, allowing time for underground operations which saved thousands of lives. Reaction to La Grande Rafle and the Free Zone round-ups made the Jewish community aware of the hypocrisy of Vichy promises of protection. It became easier to persuade families to go into hiding in the countryside, escape across the Swiss or Spanish frontiers or to send children to secret refuges.

Some historians, notably Serge Klarsfeld, believe that the Catholic Church's intervention was the decisive factor in frustrating plans to exterminate all French Jews. However, there are other historians, even inside the Catholic Church, who object to claims that the Church stood up to Vichy and Pétain. They point out that both Cardinal Gerlier and Cardinal Suhard went to see the Head of State on 29 October 1942 to pledge their loyalty at a time when deportation trains were still leaving for Germany. During this meeting, the question of Vichy subsidies for religious education in schools was raised. Two months before, René Bousquet had suggested that the offer of help for religious teaching could be used to buy the Church's continued support for Vichy.[10]

After the Cardinals' meeting with Pétain, no Catholic bishop publicly criticised Vichy's complicity over deportation of Jews. Renée Bederrida, a Catholic historian who was part of the anti-Vichy Témoignage Chrétien movement, said the opposition to

Vichy's policy on Jews should be seen as an individual response by Christians, not as an operation by the hierarchy. 'There were about eighty bishops and archbishops of whom only five or six went on record during the August protest,' she said. 'The real attitude of the Church as a religious organisation is still open to question.'

Silence did not mean that other bishops refused to help Jews, either through personal intervention or by turning a blind eye to Resistance activities by clergy and parishioners. Priests were a key link in escape routes and the main source of forged baptismal certificates. Senior clergymen refrained from criticising Vichy or Nazi policies in order to avoid attracting attention to underground networks depending on churches and monasteries.

Both Saliège and Théas, the two most courageous bishops, refrained from protesting when deportations began again in 1943 but provided cover for operations that saved hundreds of hunted people. In June 1944, Théas was arrested by the Germans for Resistance activities and taken to the Compiégne concentration camp. He was due to be deported to Germany when the camp was liberated. Other Church leaders maintained an ambiguous attitude until the fall of Vichy and some openly collaborated. Eight bishops were forced to resign at the Liberation for pro-German activities.

In the same month that Théas was arrested, several bishops, including Gerlier and Suhard, attended Requiem Masses for the Vichy Information Minister, Philippe Henriot, who had been murdered by the Resistance. He was responsible for the most violent anti-Semitic broadcasts on Vichy Radio, which continued after reports that deported Jews were facing certain death. The Archbishops of Marseilles and Bordeaux both read funeral eulogies for Henriot.

Distribution of blame or credit for the Catholic Church's official attitude over Jews will be impossible until the hierarchy opens war-time archives, which include a day-to-day diary by

Cardinal Suhard on contacts between the Church and the Nazis. Even direct appeals to Cardinal Lustiger by Jewish and Christian historians have failed, increasing the impression that the Church is embarrassed by what records would reveal. However, Lustiger's own wartime experience provides a favourable insight into Church involvement in rescue work, as well as throwing light on a spiritual journey that led to his becoming head of the French Catholic Church forty years later.

Joint Jewish and Christian welfare networks were in place well before the war. They took on a new significance in 1939 with the evacuee problem caused by families fleeing the big cities. When war broke out, the Lustiger family left their hosiery shop in Montmartre and took refuge in Orleans, a city chosen by chance. During the Phoney War, the family split up. Aron Lustiger, as he was then, stayed in the city dedicated to Joan of Arc while his mother returned to Montmartre. A year after demobilisation, his father went into hiding in the Free Zone.

On Maundy Thursday 1940, Aron, aged fourteen, entered Orleans Cathedral for the first time and was so deeply impressed by the atmosphere that he returned on Good Friday and decided to be baptised. Like many young Jewish refugees, he had come under the influence of a Catholic family which lodged him, but it was a genuine conversion, unlike some forced baptisms by religious zealots or the thousands of circumstantial changes of religion to obtain baptismal certificates. On 25 August 1940, Lustiger was received into the Church by the Bishop of Orleans. The baptism did not change his official status as a Jew, nor did his Christian name, Jean-Marie. He had to be declared to the Nazis because Orleans was in the Occupied Zone, and he was hidden by priests at the lycée where he studied.

In defiance of aryanisation laws, his mother continued to run the shop in Paris under the protection of a complacent Christian trustee. On 10 September 1942, she was denounced by a neighbour at a time when the Germans offered as little as 100 francs, the price of two black-market packets of cigarettes, for the names of Jews in hiding.

Later, the future Archbishop secretly crossed the Demarcation Line using a false identity card and joined his father working in a bitumen factory in Decazeville, a small industrial town in southern France. Within a few weeks, he was summoned to the police station where he was told, 'We know perfectly well what you are,' before his identity card was seized and stamped with the word 'Juif' in inch-high red letters.

In the spring of 1944, Lustiger took his father to a Jesuit agricultural college near Toulouse which was part of Saliège's network of refuges for Jews. While his father was issued with false papers enabling him to work as a farm labourer, Lustiger went into hiding, keeping in touch with Resistance workers from Témoignage Chrétien. The movement had opposed Vichy since the defeat and had issued its first pamphlets criticising anti-Semitic policies in 1941.

Seven years after the war, Lustiger was issued with a Government certificate confirming that his mother had 'disappeared', but it was not until 1985, when laws on the presumption of death in the case of deported Jews were eased, that a death certificate was issued. By then, researchers led by Beate and Serge Klarsfeld, had traced the destination and fate of every Jew caught by the French or Germans during the war, fulfilling a task which successive governments had ignored. The Cardinal at last knew that his mother had been sent to Auschwitz in deportation train No. 48 which left on 13 February 1943.

Lustiger's own life on the run during Vichy's four years was a commonly repeated story. Most of the time, Jews had to live on their wits, unable to distinguish friend from enemy. Their greatest fear was any contact with officialdom, whose identification with Vichy had been reinforced by a personal oath to Philippe Pétain.

Lustiger's experience in the South, when he was forced to carry the word 'Juif' on his identity card, was probably the result of a denunciation, but the civil servant who confronted him could have had him arrested for breaking anti-Semitic laws. By letting Lustiger go, the official was deliberately or accidentally part of a civil service passive resistance movement whose size or responsibility can never be estimated. As the likelihood of Allied invasion grew, many bureaucrats became active underground workers, warning guerrilla units of military operations or supplying information to Allied spy networks. As a result, judging individual civil servants' responsibility in the persecution of Jews is no easier than judging that of priests. Most provincial officials involved in action against Jews were transferred without blame to the Gaullist Provisional Government when Vichy fell. Only a few were punished for helping the Germans, while others were decorated for aiding the Allies and the Resistance.

In the first two years of the Vichy regime, there was no question where the civil service's political allegiance lay. Potentially anti-Vichy officials in the capital or the provinces were sacked and replaced by men prepared to swear personal allegiance to Pétain. Nearly 200 Prefects and other senior officials were dismissed or prematurely retired. Local mayors and councils were also purged to ensure that Vichy laws would be obeyed. To ensure promotion, civil servants had to show impeccable devotion to Pétain's ideals, including the Statut des Juifs. For at least one senior official, this blind devotion to Vichy on the Jewish issue would lead to a time of reckoning nearly half a century later.

On 5 June 1942, a promising young civil servant, Maurice Papon was appointed Secretary-General of the Bordeaux region, and took part in a ceremony in which senior administrators renewed their oath to Pétain. In 1989, he was formally charged with Crimes against Humanity in connection with the deportation of Jews.

There was little to distinguish Papon from most of his fellow bureaucrats when he arrived in Bordeaux at the age of thirty-one. He had been educated in Paris at the Political Science Institute where his political sympathies were considered to be moderately left-wing, an attitude he maintained until de Gaulle seized power in 1958.

Whatever his political convictions, Papon was a model bureaucrat who had to deal with an exceptional situation at Bordeaux, the second-biggest city in the Occupied Zone. His role involved administering a region under the control of a Prefect answerable directly to Vichy. Among Papon's special duties was responsibility for Jewish affairs.

He coped with the day-to-day problems of negotiating with the occupying power so well that the Germans wrote an appreciation on 5 April 1943 which read: 'As a result of his declarations and after private and public conversations with him, he turns out to be collaborationist. He is pleasant to work with.' Three months later, on 21 July, another report said: 'He co-operates without any problem with the Feldkommandantur. He is quick and worthy of confidence. There have never been any complaints against him which suggests that he is a sincere representative of current Government policy.'[11]

As the official responsible for Jewish matters, Papon had to deal with everything from aryanisation of business to ordering the police to carry out *rafles*. About 16,000 documents touching these issues have been discovered at Bordeaux, but the central case surrounding accusations of Crimes against Humanity involved 444 Jews transported to Drancy from Bordeaux on 27 August 1942. Among them were 140 adults and 57 children with French nationality, although original German plans should have excluded the children on grounds of both age and citizenship.

Until the last minute the children were being cared for by Bordeaux foster families, but, after consulting Jean Leguay, Bousquet's aide, Papon ordered a round-up by French police. Over the next twenty-one months, 1690 adults and children were deported from Bordeaux under orders carrying Papon's signature.

He was not asked to account for the deportations when

Bordeaux was liberated and his administrative career continued without interruption, including a period as Paris police chief before being appointed a Cabinet Minister in 1975. After being charged with Crimes against Humanity, Papon dismissed the accusations as 'a political manoeuvre'. He not only denied collaboration, but said that from the beginning of 1943 he had worked for British intelligence.

The determination of families of deported Jews to make Papon answerable for his actions during the war was inspired by Vichy's callous treatment of Jewish children. Research by Jewish organisations has shown that at least 10,147 boys and girls under the age of eighteen were sent to die in Germany between 1942 and 1944. In addition, there was a substantial proportion of boys and girls among other victims whose ages could not be confirmed.'[12]

By including the numbers of children who died in French camps or were executed before arrival in Germany, it has been estimated that about 11,600 Jewish children died as a result of France's racial discrimination between 1942 and 1944.

Identifying the German and French officials responsible for the massacre has proved easier than uncovering the other side of the story – the successful battle to save young people from the gas chambers. There were approximately 84,000 boys and girls among the Jewish community when war broke out. Of these, 72,000 survived, most of them living throughout the Vichy years with their parents.

Families spent the war on the run, protected directly or indirectly by non-Jewish individuals or religious institutions. They were usually helped financially by the Vichy-accredited UGIF movement, officially recognised church aid groups or by international charities, particularly American organisations.

Although many family stories have since been revealed in books or films, it would be impossible to unravel either the extent or motives of the aid given to Jews. Most of it depended on spontaneous humanitarian gestures or a conspiracy of silence in which Christians refused to denounce Jews in hiding or gave them shelter at the risk of arrest or execution.

Often help had to be bought. Usually it was a selfless action by people who will remain unknown. More than fifty years after the war, Israel was still appealing for names of people worthy of the Medal of the Just for helping Jews, but most of the quiet heroes have claimed no merit or compensation.

Running alongside this anonymous chain of solidarity was the highly organised rescue work of Jewish underground movements, usually working closely with Christian groups. They saved between 8000 and 9500 children in secret operations that turned welfare work into an ancillary arm of the Resistance. Before Vénissieux, rescue work had usually been carried out legally under the guidance of UGIF, which was obliged to keep a register of children in foster homes. The drama following the Free Zone round-ups and the deportation of officially protected children at Bordeaux started a general recourse to illegal methods in both zones. The change was swiftly achieved, partly because official and underground welfare groups worked side by side even before the disillusionment in the wake of La Grande Rafle.

The pioneer undercover movement was called the Comité de la rue Amelot, a semi-clandestine movement set up in June 1940 by a veteran Ukrainian refugee worker, David Rapaport, to help Parisian immigrant Jews. The Committee operated from a dispensary in the rue Amelot in the 11th *arrondissement* and, by August 1940, links were formed with the OSE, which had organised rescue work during Russian pogroms. The OSE international president was the scientist Albert Einstein. In France, much of the charity's financial support came from American Jews, and Jewish doctors provided free medical attention at the Committee's clinic. By autumn 1940, the rue Amelot Committee had also attracted young Bundists, Zionists and Trotskyists, and by June the following year the Communist Yiddish section was also involved in welfare work.

Rapaport, who cultivated a resemblance to Leo Tolstoy, was for many months one of the most active members of a Parisian community which had lost most of its leaders since the Fall of France, either because they were in prisoner-of-war camps or because they had emigrated or moved with the Consistory to Lyons. He was on familiar ground, because he had spent a lifetime in welfare work. In 1918, he had created orphanages which sheltered thousands of Jewish children after massacres in the Ukraine, and in 1920 he had run a refugee organisation in Germany. In 1939, he co-ordinated help for Jewish families in France whose fathers had been interned as enemy aliens by the French. He was also one of the first to defy the law at a time when Jews had been persuaded that their safety was better guaranteed by strict obedience to Nazi and Vichy demands.

As early as November 1940, Rapaport's Amelot team looked after some of the first arrested Jews, about 100 illegal immigrants held in a Paris barracks. A few weeks later, the detainees were helped to escape and guided to safety in the Unoccupied Zone. This was probably the first organised action of what was to become known as La Résistance Juive, operations intended primarily to aid the Jewish community as distinct from Jewish participation in the armed Resistance movement.

At about the same time, another element was reorganising that would take part in later secret operations to save children. The Jewish Scouts and Guides movement, Eclaireurs Israélites de France, decided in August 1940 to set up children's homes, establish Scout packs throughout towns in the Free Zone and sponsor rural crafts centres to house young urban Jews. The rural programme was subsidised by Vichy and became part of a Jewish welfare network in the South which, according to official sources, helped 22,500 people outside the concentration camps. Both OSE and the Scouts were affiliated to the ecumenical Committee of Nîmes, which covered both Jewish and non-Jewish charities, like Amitié Chrétienne.

Pressure from the Committee of Nîmes forced Vichy to improve conditions in Free Zone concentration camps and encouraged the increasing use of illegal means to help detained Jews. In the spring of 1941, a Vichy inspector André Jean-Faure confirmed reports of appalling neglect in refugee centres where hunger, overcrowding and brutal treatment had caused an alarming death rate among the 40,000 detainees, of whom about 70 per cent were Jewish. A new-born baby had approximately a 50 per cent chance of survival, as was shown in a report from Rivesaltes camp in the Pyrenees, where, out of 140 babies born in a ten-week period, 60 died.

The inspector's report and the Committee's pressure was largely the cause of Dannecker's disappointment over numbers when he visited the camps during La Grande Rafle. About 13,000 people had been allowed to leave for a form of house arrest after guaranteeing incomes of 1200 francs a month. Of those left in camps, 27,000 were transferred to forced-labour units. Hundreds of others left illegally, among them 450 helped to escape by a Catholic priest and hidden in eighty old people's homes. Welfare workers smuggled out men and women before handing them over to Pyrenean guides for passage to Spain. Daniel Mayer's wife, Claire, smuggled forty-two men out of one camp over several weeks by hiding them under the back seat of her car.

The most intensive activity was devoted to saving children in order to take them to foster homes or refuges. There were already 2000 Jewish children in homes in the South when the 1940 Armistice was signed, and the number of children in concentration camps had grown to nearly 5000 in 1941. After an intense effort by charitable organisations, only 263 Jewish children were still detained in May 1942. Many had been released legally with their parents, and others had been taken in charge by charities, including the Quakers and Amitié Chrétienne. The OSE was responsible for saving about 1000, who were lodged in non-Jewish foster homes.

Illegal activity was intensified in the Occupied Zone, where adults and children were issued with false identity cards or baptismal certificates and guided across the Demarcation Line. Many families scraped up enough money to send their children to the Free Zone when highly efficient smuggling developed. Guides charged about 10,000 francs for a crossing, but at key points like Montceau-les-Mines the system was so well organised that travellers had only to walk a short way after leaving trains in the German zone before they were met by taxis to take them to Lyons.

Many of the forged identity cards were made at the rue Amelot but in November 1942 the Committee lost one of its most important members, Henri Bulawko, who was in charge of forging papers. While walking home near the Père Lachaise cemetery he was stopped by a policeman and accused of trying to hide his yellow star with a newspaper. The policeman was part of a special squad which spent much of its time in the streets trying to catch Jews on any pretext. 'He had spent the whole day looking for someone, without success, and I was his only client,' Bulawko said. 'Even if the charge was ludicrous, there was no way he was going to let me go.'

Bulawko was sent to Auschwitz, but survived. David Rapaport was arrested in a raid on the rue Amelot on 1 June 1943. He died of exhaustion in the Monowitz concentration camp on 2 July 1944.

By the time Bulawko was arrested in November 1942, the impact of the Vénissieux affair had brought its first results. Even before all the boys and girls in the transit camp had been placed in safe hideouts, the consultant doctor to the OSE, Joseph Weill, and a Communist Lyons lawyer, Charles Lederman, had held discussions with Lederman's cousin, Georges Garel, on setting up an illegal operation.

The three Jews had been part of Amitié Chrétienne's sorting committee at Vénissieux. Garel, who had played no part in Jewish welfare work until then, was persuaded to establish an escape organisation that became known as Le Circuit Garel. Within a week the three leaders had gone to Toulouse to meet Saliège to report on the Vénissieux rescue and ask his help. The Archbishop ordered Catholic workers to take immediate responsibility for twenty-four children being cared for by the OSE. They were given aryan identity cards and lodged with non-Jewish families.

Garel, a self-employed civil engineer, used introductions from Saliège to set up a network of non-Jewish aid that included Church leaders and Vichy officials. Within a year, 1600 aryanised young Jews had been placed in safe foster homes spread over four regions based on Toulouse, Valence, Lyons and Limoges. The undertaking involved an enormous amount of paperwork which was necessary to reassure parents who had had to agree not to contact their children while they were in hiding.

As the secret rescue of children became the Jewish community's priority, many welfare workers lived a double life. Among them was Georges Loinger, a sports monitor in the Vichy-sponsored rural organisation, Compagnons de France, who ran an escape route to Switzerland from Aix-les-Bains. The extra risk of smuggling children over the heavily guarded border was necessary because parents of Orthodox Jewish children did not want to see them put into Christian homes.

Children were taken in groups of twenty-five to fifty to the border region near Annemasse where expert smugglers guided them into Switzerland at a cost of 300 francs a head. Towards the end of the German occupation, Loinger had to undertake the work himself because professional smugglers thought it was too dangerous. One of his most successful ruses was to simulate a foot-ball match near the border and send the children across one by one.

Between 1500 and 2000 children were taken to safety in Switzerland, usually in groups escorted by young volunteers. Some of the most successful escorts were Scouts and Guides of the Eclaireurs Israélites de France.

Liliane Klein-Leiber was among many adolescents recruited to look after Jewish children over fifteen years old whom the OSE could not care for any longer. Many were orphans whose parents had died in Germany. The centre of operations was at Moissac, fifty miles from Toulouse, where the Scout movement set up a children's refuge in 1939.

Liliane Klein-Leiber was recruited by the founder of the Jewish Scout movement, Robert Gamzon, when her parents went to live in Grenoble after being expelled from Vichy in 1941. Like many Jews from Alsace, her family had taken refuge there even before Pétain arrived, because the city had a synagogue. Soon afterwards, the Jewish Scout movement was forcibly incorporated into UGIF, which proved to be an invaluable cover for secret rescue work. 'The main activity was finding hideouts for older children, who were often given work as farm labourers with French families,' she recalled. 'We cycled for miles and miles finding safe homes or distributing letters and little presents. The Orthodox children were a special problem. I remember one who was very unhappy. He had been made to cut his hair and look after the pigs.'

Many girls were sheltered by religious movements, particularly the Daughters of Zion, whose nuns were often converted Jews with a mission to proselytise. 'Some of the girls were very excited at going on a pilgrimage to La Salette, the Alpine Lourdes,' said Liliane. 'I forbade that and I tried to make it up by little weekly meetings that ranged from talks on Jewish history to walks in the mountain.'

The most important refuge for Jews was the Cévennes village of Chambon-sur-Lignon in the heart of Vichy territory, south of the industrial city of Saint-Etienne. The beautiful village, set 3000 feet above a river valley, sheltered a Protestant population marked by repeated persecution and massacres by Catholic kings. The Cévennes had been the centre of the eighteenth-century Huguenot Camisard revolt, and there was strong sympathy for the plight of the Jews.

As a model holiday centre for urban children even before the war, Chambon provided perfect cover. The climate was ideal for tuberculosis sufferers, among them the future Nobel prizewinning author, Albert Camus, who began writing his novel *La Peste* in the village in 1942. Chambon could be approached only by a winding road and a twisting picturesque railway. Gendarmerie patrols were spotted long before they arrived, giving time to hide Jewish children lodged in Protestant homes. French informers repeatedly alerted the local Pastor, André Trocmé, by telephone whenever a raid was planned.

New groups of boys and girls under the protection of Le Circuit Garel were taken several times a month by the slow steam train to the village. Because the children had false identity papers, it was claimed that they were poor city children in need of country air, although it was presumed that most of the small farmers who took them as lodgers were aware that they were hunted Jews. The Cévennes was ideal Maquis country and by the end of the war 5000 Jews were hiding in and around Chambon either as refugees or as Resistance fighters.

Pastor Trocmé was taken into temporary detention in 1943 in an attempt to force him to denounce Jews, a police action which underlined the especially courageous attitude of Protestants. Even though leading Protestants held influential positions in Vichy, they were still hated by Charles Maurras and his supporters. Many were suspected of being converted or secret Jews and feared they could be next on the list for mass deportation.

Operations to save children led to several deaths among the organisers and the escorts. Three groups were intercepted while being guided to Switzerland and one case ended in tragedy. The twenty-one-year-old leader, Marianne Kohn, a member of the Zionist Youth Movement, MJS, was jailed in Annemasse with twenty-eight children, of whom seventeen were freed after intervention by the local Mayor. The Resistance wanted to attack the jail to release Marianne, but she refused to abandon the eleven children still in her charge.

On 3 July 1944, members of Barbie's Lyons Gestapo took Marianne away. Seven weeks later, her body was found. She had been executed with a spade.

CHAPTER FIFTEEN

Resistance

THE RESCUE OF children was only one of many facets of resistance by a Jewish community often falsely accused of meekly accepting its fate. Jews were among the first to rally to de Gaulle and other Free French movements and played a dominant role in preparing the Allied landings in North Africa. In France itself, an autonomous Zionist movement was closely linked to British intelligence while actively preparing a Palestinian homeland. Immigrant Jewish Communists led the urban guerrilla campaign against the Nazis and collaborators. Proportionately, they suffered the heaviest casualties of any French fighting unit.

Jewish opposition was used in Vichy propaganda to justify both its police-state policies against active opponents and to explain measures taken against prominent French Jews and a defenceless foreign population. An argument could be made out to suggest that Jewish opposition worsened the community's eventual fate, but this has to be set against Vichy's introduction of legal anti-Semitism before a Jewish revolt was evident. Jews have also been accused of contributing to their own destiny because the official welfare organisation, UGIF, was under the control of leading French Jews who had to work with Vichy officials. This issue still causes tension between Jews of French and foreign origin.

Some Jews made a fortune by collaborating with the Nazis and many others saved their lives by working as informers, but one of the leading historians of this period, Henri Michel, has said that resistance by Jews was far greater than that of any other group, whether judged on racial, political or religious grounds. Michel, a non-Jew, estimated that 25 per cent of the Jewish community was involved in resistance work. 'Often, French of Jewish religion or origin were the creators and leaders of Maquis operations, organising supply drops and sea landings of agents,' he said. 'They commanded resistance networks and represented Free France.'

No attempt has ever been made to produce a full picture of Jewish opposition to Fascism, partly because community leaders felt that this was against the interests of eventual assimilation. The tendency for Jews to change their names in the Resistance or in the Free French forces also diminished post-war recognition of their specific and extraordinarily varied contribution.

Jewish volunteers in General Philippe Leclerc's 2nd Armoured Division, which grew from the first Gaullist fighting units, were advised to cover up their real identities in case of capture. Jews were the Division's largest contingent at the beginning when it seized Chad on an epic march to North Africa, and many took part in the Liberation of Paris in August 1944.

Often *noms de guerre* were retained after the war as a proof of patriotism. The planemaker Marcel Bloch changed his name permanently and became even better known as Marcel Dassault, the country's richest businessman. His elder brother, Paul Bloch, who headed the Fifth Army Corps as a general in 1940, also called himself Dassault after being appointed Military Governor of Paris by de Gaulle in 1944.

Forgotten Jewish origins of wartime heroes were sometimes recalled many years later in surprising circumstances. Raymond Aubrac, one of Klaus Barbie's tortured prisoners who escaped in a daring attack led by his wife, was called as a witness at the Nazi's trial, where it was confirmed that Aubrac's real surname was Samuel.

The three-man military command structure of the Free French FFI, the battle unit of the joint Conseil National de la Résistance, included a Jew, Maurice Kriegel, who was responsible for attacks in the South. After the war he discovered that one of his colleagues, Pierre Villon, who commanded operations in the North, was librarian at the University of Strasbourg. Villon's real name was Roger Guinsburger and his father was a rabbi. Daniel Mayer, who served on the Conseil National de la Résistance set up in 1943 by the national hero, Jean Moulin, said that out of sixteen Council members representing all political factions in the Resistance, four were Jewish.

De Gaulle's London operation was especially attractive to French Jews. One of the first to join was René Cassin, a jurist who was awarded the 1968 Nobel Peace Prize. Despite being crippled by Great War wounds, Cassin played a crucial role in negotiations with the British Prime Minister, Winston Churchill, over support for de Gaulle, as well as ensuring the legitimacy of a provisional French government in the face of American opposition.

On the same boat that took Cassin to England in June 1940, Raymond Aron also escaped, pretending to be a Polish soldier. In recalling the early days, both men mentioned that anti-Semitism at first prevented some Jewish volunteers from being accepted by de Gaulle's entourage. Cassin remembered a later complaint that there were 'too many Israelites on the General Staff', while Aron referred to an unnamed Gaullist future Minister who said he sympathised with Vichy's anti-Jewish legislation.

However, the high number of Jews in de Gaulle's entourage did not lead to any significant campaign to save the French and foreign community in France. The necessity to give patriotism priority over Jewishness ruled out special operations in defence of Jews. No attempt was made to sabotage deportation trains until just before Paris was liberated, although Belgian Resistance carried out an attack on 19 April 1943, helping 231 Jews to escape.

In explaining French Resistance thinking, Daniel Mayer and Raymond Aron, both Jews with a long French ancestry, said independently that efforts could not be diverted to saving Jews without slowing down the war effort in general. Aron, who contributed to the Gaullist London-based journal, *France Libre,* also insisted that Resistance workers had no conception of the consequences of mass deportation. 'Murder on an industrial scale never entered my mind,' he said. 'I couldn't imagine it and, because I couldn't imagine it, I couldn't have known.'

Aron, who died in 1984, was criticised by a younger generation of Jews, particularly the post-colonial Sephardi immigrants from North Africa, who felt that established French Jews simply ignored the threat both before and during the war. Among those to criticise Aron directly in a television programme was Jacques Attali, President François Mitterrand's economic adviser, whose parents suffered under stern anti-Semitic legislation in North Africa which was maintained for months after the Allied invasion in November 1942.

For many other Jews who rallied to Free French fighting units, racial questions were irrelevant. Perhaps the most significant purely military contribution from a French Jew was made by Admiral Louis Kahn, who went to London in 1942, two years after being evicted from the Navy by Vichy. He presented Churchill with new submarine and torpedo techniques that were used in the Battle of the Atlantic. In Algiers he was put in charge of naval construction and was President of the Consistory in Paris from 1963 until he died in 1967.

Because they were excluded en masse from so many professions, intellectual Jews were inevitably hostile to Vichy. Many academics played a leading role as organisers of guerrilla groups, such as the philosopher Jean Cavaillès, in Libération-Nord. Others were propagandists abroad, like the ethnologist Claude Lévi-Strauss, who took refuge in New York along with many Jewish intellectuals such as André Maurois.

The Sorbonne historian Marc Bloch continually defied Vichy by reminding Vichy officials of his Jewish origins before he went underground as part of the Lyons-based Franc-Tireur Resistance movement, itself run by a Jew, Jean-Pierre Levy. Bloch was put in overall command of underground plans for the military liberation of Lyons but was captured by the Gestapo in March 1944 and executed in June.

François Jacob, the future Nobel prize-winner, had not yet finished medical training when he joined the Free French in 1940 and followed Leclerc from Chad to Normandy, seeing most of his close friends killed in battle before he was seriously wounded with the 2nd Armoured Division.

Marcel Bleustein-Blanchet, the young advertising millionaire who worked with Laval's Radio Lyon and *Le Figaro* before the war, was ruined by Vichy sequestration laws and had to live in hiding until he escaped to England in 1943 to join an American bomber squadron. He returned to discover that his pre-war links with Laval had not saved two of his sisters from being gassed in Auschwitz.

The whole Resistance movement owes its anthem to a Jew, the Argentinian-born novelist of Russian origin, Joseph Kessel, who wrote the 'Chant des Partisans' with Maurice Druon. The song, recorded by many performers including Yves Montand, is played at most Resistance gatherings.

One of the most important feats of literary resistance was also achieved by a Jew, Jean Bruller, a Hungarian immigrant, who wrote under the name of Vercors. His book, *Le Silence de la mer*, which romanticised a young Frenchwoman's rejection of a charming Nazi officer, was first produced on Bruller's underground press, Les Editions de Minuit. This secret printing shop produced many clandestine works by Resistance writers, including François Mauriac, but none had the impact of *Le Silence de la mer*, which was reprinted in London. The RAF parachuted hundreds of copies to the Maquis.

Perhaps the most surprising artistic vocation to come out of underground work was that of Marcel Marceau, the mime artist. He adopted an aryan name to disguise his Jewish origins as the son of a Strasbourg kosher butcher. While working as an escort for children being taken to Switzerland, he set up his own travelling theatrical troupe to complete his cover. The stagecraft he learned at the time earned him the accolade as the most popular French stage personality in the United States in an opinion poll taken forty years later.

Most Jews who worked with the Resistance insisted that religious or racial background was irrelevant and that they should be considered only as Fighting French like other opponents of Vichy. But Zionists who belonged to a guerrilla group known as L'Armée Juive were inspired by Judaism. Their autonomous underground combat concentrated on saving Jewish lives, rather than the war effort in general. Most of the Jewish Army's surviving leaders emigrated to Palestine after the war and took part in the creation of Israel. A Russian-born poet, David Knout, sponsored the theory of armed struggle in the cause of a Palestinian homeland while taking refuge in Toulouse in 1940. The Jewish Army did not become a fighting force until 1943 and many of its recruits were young people previously involved in the care of homeless Jews.

Henri Pohoryles, born in Alsace in a Russian emigrant family, was attracted to Zionism when he attended the Ecole Maimonide in Paris, the first Jewish lycée. As a young German teacher, he took refuge in the South before being asked to go to Moissac in the Dordogne as a monitor in a Scout movement children's home. When his parents took refuge in Nice, Pohoryles was incorporated in the Armée Juive. His group's main task was to kill anti-Semitic White Russians serving in the German Army as informers. The Russians were trained physiognomists and among those they pointed out in random street-checks was a schoolgirl, Simone Jacob, the future Simone Veil. 'Our group was never more than a dozen or so people but, after a few killings, the Wehrmacht had to abandon using White Russians,' Pohoryles said. 'Contrary to a common belief, there were very few armed Resistance workers in urban areas at the time, Jewish or not. When I took part in initial talks with Resistance movements preparing the Liberation of Paris, only 300 armed guerrillas could be counted on, unless you included the police.' L'Armée Juive organised other Resistance operations, including the despatch through Spain of volunteers for the British Jewish Brigade.

On one of his missions in the South, where he travelled with false papers accrediting him as a Vichy supply official, Pohoryles was asked to contact an intelligence officer called Charles Porel. The agent was really Karl Rehbein, a German officer in the Abwehr counter-espionage service. When Pohoryles went to Paris, the German agent offered the co-operation of British intelligence in setting up a French–Jewish Legion that would be transferred to Palestine after the Liberation. Nearly all Armée Juive leaders were tricked into coming to Paris to sign an agreement in July 1944. René Kapel, the chaplain who had joined the Zionist Army after witnessing the moving scenes at Noé, arrived secretly from the South and was immediately arrested. Two women and twelve other men, among them Pohoryles, were also caught. They were handed over for torture to the Gestapo's French auxiliaries at their headquarters in rue de la Pompe, in the 16th *arrondissement*.

A few members of the Armée Juive took part in the Liberation of Paris but most armed contingents volunteered for the rural Maquis, mainly in the Cévennes or the Tarn *département*. To distinguish them, Jewish commandos wore blue and white shoulder flashes.

Nearly all the leaders had taken part in operations to rescue children, usually as members of the Israelite Scouts. The Tarn company was named after Marc Hagenau, former Secretary-General of the movement, who was caught by the Gestapo in Grenoble on 18 February 1944, while on an underground mission. After torture, he was killed when he leaped from a window.

Gaullist and Zionist resistance drew primarily on the established French community, but by far the biggest sacrifice was made by the immigrant community. They showed their courage by joining volunteer Foreign Legion brigades before the Fall of France and provided the most effective urban guerrilla units during the Occupation. It was because so many foreign or stateless men had been killed, captured or forced to go into hiding that thousands of mothers and children fell an easy prey to the French police in 1942.

While these urban guerrillas were united first of all by the long history of anti-Semitism in Eastern Europe, they fought for a political ideal: Communism. But the French Party had still not given them full recognition half a century later, after pretending that sabotage carried out by foreign Jews had been the work of Frenchmen.

CHAPTER SIXTEEN

The Resistance Betrayed

O^N 19 NOVEMBER 1988, a group of old men gathered in the Lyons industrial suburb of Vénissieux near the site of the brick-walled barracks that had once been a concentration camp. The building had long since disappeared and the camp did not rate a mention in the Communist Council's official history published the year before. Also absent from the book, with its long extracts on Communist resistance in the city, was an account of the events that brought together the old men, all of them survivors of the FTP–MOI Communist-led guerrilla group made up of immigrants.

It was a significant occasion, all the same. For the first time, a Communist municipality had decided to put up a war memorial to the FTP–MOI, Francs-Tireurs et Partisans–Main d'Oeuvre Immigrée, which contained the most important underground Jewish combat groups. The MOI or immigrant labour movement was divided into four language sections: Italian, Spanish, Hungarian–Roumanian and Yiddish. The last two were specifically Jewish groups and most of the Yiddish speakers were Poles. All language sections included veterans of the Spanish Civil War or foreign volunteer regiments in the Battle of France.

At the Vénissieux ceremony three plaques were unveiled before a Soviet general took part in an international parade to commemorate ninety-four women and men of the Carmagnole-Liberté battalion killed during operations at Lyons and Grenoble. Many of the names were Polish or Roumanian, like Wlacek

Wojcyk, Daniel Karminkel or Stefan Goldberger, who had been buried under French *noms de guerre,* exploited after their deaths to give the impression that they were French Communists. Some of the fighters had so successfully hidden their identity that they were known only by their presumed nationality and an adopted first name.

During the ceremony, five survivors, including Polish-born Albert Goldman, were decorated with the Légion d'Honneur. Hardly a month later, Goldman died at the age of seventy-eight, but not before his son, Jean-Jacques Goldman, the country's favourite popular musician, had dedicated a rock concert at Lyons to his father's old comrades.

Much of the long-suppressed history of Jewish–Communist resistance has been revealed by disillusioned party workers, including Adam Rayski, who co-ordinated Jewish organisations inside the Party during the war. This ranged from Yiddish newspapers to aid committees, as well as immigrant labour.

Rayski had come to France from Poland in 1932 as a seventeen-year-old student and was quickly made a Communist official working as a journalist with *L'Humanité* and then the Yiddish-language *Naïe Presse,* which was linked to the 300-member Jewish sub-section. Throughout the war he was faced with a conflict between the Party's strategy and the aims of many immigrant Jews who were in favour of specific action to save potential deportees. Some had seen their families or friends rounded up in France or remembered racial discrimination in their countries of birth. Rayski summed up their attitude by saying that they knew that the hands on the clock of history advanced more quickly for Jews than for any other population, a sensation that accelerated as the war developed. 'Time showed that the more the war leaned in favour of the Allies, the faster the operations of genocide became,' he said.

Despite the fears of the Jewish community, the Party played

down the dangers of extermination. In the 200 underground wartime editions of the Communist newspaper, *L'Humanité*, attacks on Jews were mentioned only seventeen times. In contrast, *L'Humanité*'s underground Yiddish companion paper, Adam Rayski's *Unzer Wort*, revealed the construction of gas chambers as early as July 1942.

Initial Communist opposition was concentrated against the Vichy Government after the Party had been thrown into confusion by the Stalin–Hitler Pact of 23 August 1939. At the time, twenty-one Communist MPs resigned from the Party in protest, while Communist Jews struggled with the dilemma of being called on to support a German dictator who meant to exterminate them on racial grounds. It was easier to have a clear attitude towards the French Government. The Communist Party had been banned at the outbreak of war and many of its leading French and foreign militants were interned. Repression steadily intensified from the first days of the Vichy regime.

Until mid-1941, when Germany invaded Russia, operations against Communists were carried out only by the French police. For a time, Germany was regarded with benevolence by the Party leadership, which sought its own collaboration deal in an unsuccessful attempt to lift a French ban on the publication of *L'Humanité*. While Vichy was vilified in underground editions of the newspaper, the Party avoided criticism of the Germans for several months. Jewish members who might have wanted to fight both Berlin and Vichy had little choice except to concentrate on welfare work. Meanwhile, the Communist press attacked Léon Blum with the same acrimony as that aimed at Pétain.

In April 1941, when the Stalin–Hitler Pact was wearing thin, Rayski and other officials were ordered to tour the Free Zone to arrange the escape of Communists held in concentration camps as part of a plan to form combat units. At about the same time, a handful of Communists began military training, usually without weapons, or started up the distribution of anti-Nazi tracts.

For most Communists, the invasion of Russia was the beginning of the real war. Foreign and French Jews with suspected Marxist links would quickly pay a heavy price for anti-Nazi activity. Between August 1941 and June 1942, 124 Jews were among the 522 hostages executed by the Germans. In the wake of Pétain's 'ill wind' reforms of August 1941, Vichy made its contribution by guillotining alleged terrorists after summary trials. On 27 August 1941, a special anti-terrorist tribunal condemned to death a Polish Jew, Abraham Trzebrucki, for collecting funds and entering France without a visa, the first of a series of executions specifically intended to convince the Germans that collaboration was working.

This was a signal for concentrated law-and-order programmes against alleged enemies of the state, during which more than 11,000 arrests were carried out by the municipal Paris police force alone over the next year. The Renseignements Généraux, or Special Branch, carried out independent arrests of suspected Resistance workers that led to nearly 700 internments in the same period. Jews caught in these round-ups were usually transferred to Drancy after it had been designated a Jewish internment centre in August 1941.

Just before Trzebrucki was guillotined, the Germans had also executed a young Polish-Jewish Resistance worker, Samuel Tyszelmann, who was known as Titi. He had taken part in the first official Communist sabotage operation, the theft of dynamite by three Jewish Communists in early August 1941. A few days later he was arrested during a Left Bank demonstration and shot on 19 August, with a French demonstrator, Henri Gautherot. This double execution was the signal to start armed Communist resistance two days later. Pierre Georges, a Frenchman who fought as Colonel Fabien, shot dead a German naval ensign, Alfons Moser, on the platform of Barbès-Rochechouart Métro station in northern Paris. As he fired, Fabien told his Jewish accomplice, Gilbert Brustlein: 'Titi is avenged.'

Although many immigrant members of FTP partisan units were not serving Communists, they were all officially recruited by the movement, which supplied 10 per cent of its members to the armed Resistance. Most French volunteers were drafted into the rural Maquis, the underground movement set up in 1943 to be ready for the Liberation.

Transfers from the Party's immigrant Youth Movement in Paris were made on the recommendation of its leader, Henri Krasucki, the future Secretary-General of the Communist-led CGT trade union. Krasucki was eighteen when war broke out and had arrived in France with his family at the age of four. A 1943 French police report drawn up just before his arrest gave a detailed description: '22 years old, 1m70, long nose, Semitic-type face, light-brown hair thrown back and falling on the sides, navy blue overcoat, black trousers, yellow shoes, grey socks.' He was older than most of the men and women he recruited and impressed them by his culture and the way he dressed, usually in plus-fours. Though he was from the poor Belleville area, where he had been brought up as a militant Communist and agnostic, Krasucki had a passion for classical music and literature, marking him out as the intellectual in a group dominated by jobbing tailors.

Among his early recruits for the FTP was Victor Zigelman, a sixteen-year-old typical of the poor Polish immigrant families united more by their isolation than by their politics. Zigelman's pay as a professional Party soldier included a lumber jacket with a sheepskin lining and extra ration cards. Most recruits were foreigners whose accents were a worse burden than any other feature, making them instantly suspect during identity checks even when carrying false papers. Like all immigrants, they tended to group in regional or family clans that provided a loose form of welfare and an early-warning system against police repression. Zigelman's brief period of guerrilla war was also a domestic experience because it was concentrated against Jewish tailors working for the German Army. Every action ended in conspicuous failure.

He was sent to burn down a workshop employing sweated Jewish labour but his bottle of petrol did no significant damage. Once he tried to break into a workshop by taking a mould of the lock with compressed breadcrumbs, and on another occasion attempted to trick his way in by claiming to be a gas inspector, only to be told that the building was not linked to the gas system. An attempt to intimidate another workshop owner by beating him up ended when his home-made cosh broke on the man's head and he was arrested after a chase. A whispered warning of vengeance in Yiddish to the Jewish employer made the man change his mind about identifying Zigelman, who was set free.

Most of the young people's memories of this time reveal a comic-book idea of defying the Germans, including a plan to release cats wearing the tricolour during a big football match, a plan that collapsed because only one cat could be found in a city where pets were usually eaten.

The youth movement was faced with a police force which had pursued immigrant Jews before the war and could use files reinforced by the northern zone census. In June 1943, after a classic tracking operation by the French anti-terrorist squad, Krasucki and about forty other people were arrested, tortured and deported. By then, Krasucki's father had been sent to Auschwitz to be gassed, while reprisals against the Party youth movement led to the arrests of relatives of the underground network.

By that time, many of Krasucki's young followers had been transferred to the FTP–MOI commandos in Paris or had left for the Free Zone, where they were later recruited into urban guerrilla units in Lyons or Toulouse. Those in Paris were involved in a slow war of attrition during daily attacks on German soldiers or sabotage operations, which included the destruction of Jewish tailoring businesses working for the German Army.

For the most part units were made up of men with fighting experience but many volunteers were barely trained. By June 1943 only one mixed commando was still in shape to fight under its

Armenian leader, Missak Manouchian. The others had either been destroyed in combined French and Gestapo operations or had been withdrawn to the Maquis. Repeated requests to the Party leadership to allow Manouchian's unit to join French Communist partisans in rural areas were refused. French detectives had the leaders under close observation from July 1943. During the next few weeks there was a series of round-ups which led to a mass trial of seventy members of the unit. On 19 February 1944, Manouchian and twenty-two other guerrillas were executed. Among them were eleven Jews.

The Germans put up thousands of red wall-posters all over the country announcing the executions. The posters emphasised the group's foreign nationalities and most were named as Jews. Manouchian was said to have killed 150 Germans and wounded 600 others. The posters featured some of the immigrants' photographs, which Simone de Beauvoir remembered seeing in a Left Bank Métro station. 'Despite the roughness of the photos, all the faces shown for our hatred were moving and handsome,' she wrote in her memoirs. 'I looked at them for a long time under the arches of the Métro, thinking with sadness that they would be forgotten.'

Far from being forgotten, the men were at the centre of a running controversy. It reached its peak forty years later when the Communist Party tried to ban a television film which alleged that Manouchian's unit had been deliberately sacrificed because the Party wanted to cover up the fact that most of its urban volunteer fighters were foreigners rather than French.

A more likely explanation, accepted by Rayski among others, was that the unified Comité Français de la Libération Nationale, a provisional government, was being formed in Algeria. Communists had to prove they were a fighting force in order to obtain strong representation on the committee in the face of a hostile de Gaulle. The Party had recently abandoned political isolation to seek an alliance with other Resistance movements and was determined to gain a central role in post-war France. Manouchian's unit was the only fighting force from any Resistance movement that was still regularly carrying out guerrilla attacks in Paris. Its communiqués on derailments, assassinations and bombings were used as part of the bargaining procedure.

Communist strategy was always planned in the perspective of long-term international revolution, which excluded, among other issues, any special interest in the Jewish problem. Members were told at the time that the Second World War had created conditions similar to those before the October Revolution in Russia. The prediction became true in Eastern Europe, starting reverse emigration of Communist Jews from France after the war.

Recriminations in peacetime led to the end of many friendships, not least between Rayski, who left the Party after a stay in Poland as a propaganda official, and Krasucki, who became a member of the French Political Bureau in one of the most hardline Communist Parties in the world.

The destruction of the Manouchian group threw light on the German use of Jewish informers. Some offered help after German promises to release relatives held in concentration camps. The best known was Lucienne Goldfarb, who was eighteen when she was recruited into the Communist Youth Movement by Henri Krasucki after her Polish parents had been seized in La Grande Rafle. She lived in the 11th *arrondissement* among emigrant Jews who had settled in the rue des Immeubles-Industriels, a street in which workshops had been built under flats as an experiment in working-class living. Lucienne was a woman of exceptional beauty with red-blonde hair. She worked closely with the French police from 1942 and they continued to protect her after the war when she built up a fortune as head of a prostitution ring.

Immediately after returning from a German concentration camp, Krasucki told Rayski that Lucienne had to be punished. Apart from betraying his Youth Movement, she was alleged to have given away an underground network involving about 140 adults, as well as the Manouchian group. Rayski persuaded the future trade union leader to swallow his revenge, although the story of a beautiful Jewish traitor still plays an important part in Communist mythology.

There was to be no mercy, though, for another Jew suspected of betraying the Manouchian group. Joseph Davidowicz, a strong, quiet man who was considered one of the most reliable members of the combat unit, was one of the first to be captured and allegedly gave details of his companions without being tortured. After their arrest, he escaped in a chase but was hit in the leg by a German bullet. His story was not believed when he turned up at the group's suburban hideout. The few FTP–MOI survivors tried him and found him guilty of treason. He was strangled to death.

The most spectacular single contribution by Jews to the Allied war effort was accomplished in North Africa where British and American troops landed on 8 November 1942. Operation Torch, which eventually liberated the French territories of Algeria, Morocco and Tunisia, owed its rapid success to a putsch carried out by 400 anti-Vichy underground fighters, of whom more than 250 were Jews.

Although there was no German presence in French North Africa until the Afrika Korps retreated to Tunisia, anti-Semitic legislation was more strict there than in France. One of Pétain's first acts was to abrogate an 1871 law granting automatic citizenship to Algerian Jews. There had been a long history of anti-Semitism in the North African territories, dating back before the Dreyfus Affair. It was reinforced in autumn 1940 when General Maxime Weygand, head of the French Army at the Armistice, was appointed Vichy's Delegate-General in Algiers.

Few people were better suited to impose racial discrimination. Weygand was a dry, vain little man who suffered an inferiority complex arising from his illegitimate birth in Belgium. He claimed to be a royal bastard but recent research has strengthened the theory that he was the natural son of a Jewish trader, David de Léon Cohen, and a gardener's daughter. A naturalised Frenchman with a brilliant Great War record, Weygand never hid his contempt for Jews. The Statut des Juifs was applied with even more rigour in Algeria. The university quota system in force in mainland France was also introduced in Algerian secondary and primary schools. Ten thousand Jewish pupils were forced to leave.

Weygand's administration was also responsible for inhuman detention conditions. Apart from concentration camps, where at least 10,000 Jews were interned, immigrant Jewish former soldiers were forced to work on the Trans-Saharan railway where they were treated little better than slaves. There was no let-up to anti-Jewish feeling after Weygand was recalled to France in 1941 and interned by the Germans. A plan to force Jews to wear yellow stars was dropped only because of the Allied attack.

About 330,000 Jews were spread fairly evenly over the three territories but the strongest Resistance contingent was in Algeria, where academics and teachers were among the most numerous recruits. They worked with a Resistance movement run by a royalist, Henri d'Astier de la Vigérie, and on 8 November seized public buildings, captured Vichy officials or acted as guides for the invading Army. One of the first Vichy personalities to be caught was Admiral François Darlan, who was given administrative control of the whole French African Empire after changing sides. It quickly became evident that the Americans, including President Roosevelt, preferred a Vichy-style provisional government to de Gaulle's multi-faction Resistance movement. They turned to General Henri Giraud, former head of the French Seventh Army, who had escaped from a German prisoner-of-war camp in 1942 and was known for his loyalty to Pétain.

To the surprise of the Jewish population, anti-Semitism continued. Giraud refused to abrogate the Statut des Juifs or restore automatic citizenship. He was encouraged by a meeting between Roosevelt and the anti-Semitic Vichy leader in Casablanca,

General Henri Noguès, the Moroccan Governor-General. According to official American records, Roosevelt gave his support for retaining the Statut des Juifs in Morocco and repeated his opinion to Giraud. It needed weeks of campaigning by the World Jewish Congress, involving Marc Chagall and Edouard de Rothschild, before Giraud gave in to pressure from de Gaulle and repealed the statute in March 1943. It was another eight months before de Gaulle's authority had increased enough to force Giraud to restore the right of citizenship.

Later, Giraud denied accusations that he was a reactionary anti-Semitic, although the man he appointed Algerian Governor-General was Marcel Peyrouton, Vichy Interior Minister in 1940 when anti-Jewish legislation had been introduced. In Algiers, Peyrouton continued to campaign against Jews, blaming them for the defeat and naming both Léon Blum and Georges Mandel, whose lives were in danger after transfer to a German concentration camp.

During the weeks when Giraud, Peyrouton and Noguès continued their anti-Semitic policies, Jews who had conspired in the putsch became involved in opposition to the American-backed Provisional Government. Jewish Resistance workers were the first to volunteer for fighting units but, like all Jews, they were conscripted into non-combatant labour battalions run by non-Jewish officers.

One of the original underground workers, Jacques Zermati, recalled that one Jewish regiment was posted to the high Algerian plateau where conditions were similar to a detention camp. Realising that Jews might never be allowed to take part in the battle to free France, he embarked on a new clandestine career while a member of a pioneer regiment stationed near Algiers. He helped Jewish and other volunteers to escape to join French battalions serving with the British Eighth Army.

About 10,000 men were assembled in a transit camp where they were given false papers making them out to be Free French soldiers on leave. General Giraud suddenly became aware of the drain on his own troops and sent several thousand men to surround the camp. After three days of negotiations, it was agreed that the escapers would not be punished if they returned to their units. The Giraud promise was not kept and they had to desert again. This time, they were sent immediately to British units in Tripolitania.

In the meantime, Jacques Zermati had volunteered with other Jewish Algerians to join a British paratroop battalion which included Jews who had escaped from mainland France. It became a unit of the SAS, fighting behind the German lines in France and Holland.

CHAPTER SEVENTEEN

Barbie Arrives

THE FALL OF North Africa to the Allies precipitated a crisis inside Vichy where officials and some former Ministers seized the opportunity to switch sides. Many of Pétain's supporters believed that the Maréchal should also leave the country and join the Allies. Instead, he preferred the isolation of the Hôtel du Parc and its peaceful grounds along the Allier. His advisers were told that if he left France the Germans would appoint a Gauleiter, and life in Vichy France would become much more unpleasant. This was the same argument he had used in 1940.

Pétain acted as if he was unaware that the opportunity to save France from Nazi domination had been wasted long ago and that the French were beginning to turn to a new military saviour, de Gaulle. The return of Laval and the deportation of Jews were clear signals that the Germans were ready to impose their policies by force if necessary.

Soon, even Pétain's restricted Free Zone kingdom disappeared. By 11 November 1942, the Germans had put into action a longstanding plan codenamed 'Attila' and sent occupation troops into Vichy-controlled France. One of the key targets was the French fleet in Toulon. Vichy threw away what could have been the price of entry into the Allied cause by ordering the Navy to scuttle some of the most powerful warships in the world.

On 17 December 1942, after a brief struggle to maintain Vichy's autonomy, Pétain handed over all legislative powers to Laval, creating a Gauleiter of his own making. The popular post-war view of France dates from this handover: a country torn between the Resistance and collaborationists as the invasion approached. The treachery of the Fascist Milice and the French Gestapo were to ensure Laval's notoriety as a villain who broke the nation in two, thus obscuring Pétain's share of guilt in preparing the repressive legal machinery which made it possible.

The Maréchal had lost the strength to resist by the end of 1942. He was no longer the vigorous leader of July 1940. His power of concentration was seriously limited and his deafness had increased. There was no sign of serious illness but nearly two and a half years in office had taken their toll. The legend of the senile old man, cunningly manipulated by Laval, took root.

Before Pétain declined into the role of a capricious figurehead, he added the final measure to his police state by helping to establish the Milice. The process took a year, starting in January 1942, when an elite Service d'Ordre Legionnaire, SOL, was recruited from ultra-conservative elements of the Pétainist veterans' organisation, the Légion Française des Combattants. In February, the future leader of the Milice, Joseph Darnand, was appointed the SOL's Inspector-General. The movement had its own uniform, khaki shirt and black beret and tie. Members had to make an oath to the Maréchal on their knees after a night's vigil. A list of twenty-one vows was drawn up by SOL members, mostly active supporters of Maurras' Action Française. This was the basis of what was called L'Ordre Nouveau, whose commandments were personally overseen by the Maréchal. All the old hates and passions of royalist and Fascist factions were spelled out. SOL members were against democracy, anarchy, capitalism and the proletariat. They were for the Catholic faith, authority, merit and discipline. The final four oaths in the list of twenty-one concerned 'the enemy': Gaullists, Bolshevists and Freemasons. The twentieth oath read: 'Against Jewish leprosy and for French purity'.

On 30 January 1943, six weeks after Laval took over responsibility for legislation, the Milice was officially formed under

Darnand's command with men chosen from SOL shock troops. The new parallel police force kept the same twenty-one articles of faith drawn up with Pétain's approval as the inspiration of its own law-and-order programmes.

Throughout the turbulent weeks following the North African invasion, the Nazis remained confident that France would co-operate in restarting deportations, which had been suspended in November 1942. In December, while the power struggle inside Vichy was at its height, Colonel Knochen cabled Eichmann in Berlin to say that he could expect trains to start operating again by February.

Gestapo and French police were ordered to carry out arrests in the northern zone and by January there were 3811 internees at Drancy, of whom 2159 were French citizens. On 9 February 1943, the first train for four months left for Auschwitz with nearly 1000 deportees, including 545 women. The Germans planned to despatch the French Jews on 13 February, but Vichy objected and offered to arrest foreign Jews to replace them. During the night of 10–11 February, one of the most cynical *rafles* of the war took place. Foreign children were seized in UGIF refuges, the sick were dragged from hospital and more old people were arrested in the Rothschild Hospice. Two were over ninety years old.

The last pretence that Jews were being rounded up for work in the East had been shattered. Although the brutal action did not cause a protest from either Vichy or the Paris police, the Germans and French were quickly at odds over the next phase. When the final count of 1549 for the latest wave of arrests had been made on 11 February, Knochen sent a note to Berlin saying that despite a French attempt to find substitutes for their own citizens it 'was obvious that both categories would be deported'.

The brief crisis which followed demonstrated the emptiness of Vichy threats. The French refused to provide guards for the 13 February train, but the Germans ignored the protest and there was no incident when the cattle trucks left. Thirty French gendarmes who turned up for duty were told to go home. From then on, the Germans provided their own escorts.

An official French attempt to oppose the deportations was never a serious possibility as far as the Germans were concerned. Just before the *rafle,* French police had shown exceptional co-operation during the destruction of the old port of Marseilles. Since the occupation of the South, the Germans had complained of poor security in the Mediterranean port, which sheltered urban guerrillas, intelligence networks and the criminal underworld. The maze of narrow streets was also a hiding place for Jews. The operation against these various groups meant assembling 12,000 French police from all over the country, a programme that involved several days of joint planning between the French and Germans, who asked Vichy to take the initiative.

On 22 January 1943, the signal was given for a thirty-six-hour police sweep in which 40,000 people underwent identity checks. A special camp had been set up behind the town of Fréjus, but the *rafle* was a flop. There were only thirty arrests of known criminals or suspected Resistance workers. Instead, the camp and Marseilles' Baumettes prison were filled up with 2200 'undesirables', most of them Jews. All were sent to death camps, and Marseilles' old port was reduced to rubble by German engineers.

The French official in charge was René Bousquet. As far as he was concerned, the destruction of old Marseilles was intended as a blow against the Resistance and the underworld, but the mass arrest of Jews had always been part of the plan. Eichmann made a special trip to the port to oversee their transfer to Drancy.

There had been plenty of time for Bousquet to discuss the matter, because the Vichy police chief had travelled overnight to Marseilles in the same compartment as Karl Oberg. It provided the SS-General with an ideal opportunity to assess the strength of French willingness to collaborate in police operations. After Marseilles, the Germans were convinced that an unprecedented level of co-operation had been reached, an assessment stressed in a long article in the German Army propaganda magazine, *Signal.* Soon afterwards, Himmler travelled to Paris to congratulate Bousquet.

The Vichy police chief also impressed the Germans during another southern-zone operation in which about 2000 Jews were forcibly transferred to the Germans from Vichy-run concentration camps. They included many Czechs and Poles who had fought with the French Army as volunteers.

Having proved his good faith, Bousquet received the assurances over future control of police actions which he had sought before La Grande Rafle the year before. In what was known as the second Bousquet–Oberg agreement, signed on 16 April 1943, Article 5 promised that German police involvement would be restricted to protecting German soldiers, while 'all other operations will be generally reserved for the French police'. The agreement accepted that French citizens arrested by Vichy could be judged only by French courts, unless German property was involved. The Germans were given the right to attend interrogations when the occupying Army's interests were threatened.

In outlining the agreement to leading Vichy officials on 16 April 1943, Oberg recalled that he had presented the proposals to Pétain the day before. He added: 'During our interview I was able to verify that his greatest enemy, like ours, was Bolshevism. As he assured me, his greatest personal desire would be to see an understanding between Germany and France achieved after the war in a new Europe.'

The SS-General also made the point of praising Bousquet, but the meeting provided the first implicit recognition that Germany could no longer be absolutely sure of Vichy collaboration at all levels. Oberg noted that 'some highly placed French personalities' preferred to see American troops taking the place of the German Army. In his reply, Bousquet referred to 'feelings of doubt and disquiet in the French police'. 'I recognise that this situation results essentially from the new position in which France finds itself after the Anglo-American aggression in North Africa and the treachery of some important French leaders,' he added.

Bousquet warned Oberg that too much German interference in French law-and-order programmes risked accelerating a process of demoralisation. The police could 'become passive' if they no longer believed they were working in the interests of their own country. Oberg took the hint and sent a memorandum to SS and Gestapo officers in the field stating that they were likely to face difficulties in the future because of reluctance by French police to supply information or hand over suspects.

Over the next few months, co-operation on the Jewish issue would become unreliable, with the initiative passing increasingly into the hands of autonomous Gestapo squads, using French auxiliaries and the Milice. The German occupation of the South ended any restrictions on Nazi activities and they were at last able to investigate the 150,000 Jews who had taken refuge there. Big cities like Lyons, Nice and Marseilles became as dangerous as Paris, while French Jews would soon be as much at risk as immigrants.

The most notorious Nazi unit was led by SS-Lieutenant Klaus Barbie, whose trial in 1987 reopened the debate on Vichy's complicity in racial crimes.

The Palais de Justice in Lyons, where Barbie was tried, stands over a wide stretch of the Saône river where a pedestrian bridge links the left bank with the city centre. Behind the colonnaded building the ancient *quartiers* rise steeply towards the top of the Fourvière hillside where Cardinal Gerlier said his Masses. A funicular railway just behind the courthouse takes visitors to a spectacular observation point near the church, where central Lyons can be seen caught in a compact island of official and residential suburbs between the converging Saône and Rhône rivers.

Despite German occupation for a brief period in 1940 and for twenty-two months from November 1942 to September 1944, no buildings or bridges seen from the observation point suffered damage. Nothing, except for road improvements to cope with increased traffic, would have been unfamiliar to Barbie when he was flown back from his Bolivian hideout to the city in February 1983 and taken to Montluc Fort, the Army prison where he had tortured Resistance workers and Jews.

Other sites also brought home the unique aspects of a trial where a mass murderer faced long-forgotten ghosts at the scene of his crimes more than forty years before. Among the many locations that served as prisons or torture chambers, the most evocative was the Hôtel Terminus, a turn-of-the-century building overlooking the central Gare Perrache where one of the last deportation trains left for Germany on 11 August 1944. The huge hotel accommodated many trial witnesses, forcing them to confront savage memories.

From 1943, the Terminus was the Gestapo headquarters and even the third-floor room where Barbie inflicted the *supplice de baignoire,* immersion in scalding and freezing water, had been left unchanged. In the moments between beatings and other cruelties, his victims had been able to see across the red rooftops to the spire of a small church framed by the tiny bathroom window. As the two-month trial ended in July 1987, workmen moved in to redecorate the former torture chamber, removing the infamous metal bath and installing bright tiling.

After witnesses had put on record the wartime memories that haunted the Hôtel Terminus, other buildings connected with Barbie's reign of terror during Lyons' secretive war were scheduled to disappear. Among them was the damp, abandoned Fort Montluc where the sinister aspect that Barbie rediscovered was not unlike that on 17 August 1944, when, in a last act of pure vengeance, the Gestapo chief lined up sixteen Jews and ordered their deaths by firing squad.

There were fears that the Barbie trial might become an excuse to camouflage other, less tangible souvenirs. The SS-Lieutenant had needed much more than a range of local buildings and French auxiliaries to carry out his mission, which had led to the murder of 4432 men and women and the deportation of 7581 Jews. Among his most useful weapons were Pétain's laws of 12 December 1942, forcing Jews in Vichy-administered territory to have their identity and ration cards stamped 'Juif' or 'Juive'.

Jews were at risk every time they went out shopping or were forced to look for new accommodation. Repressive measures intended to combat the Resistance or round up young French people for obligatory war work in Germany made it almost impossible for anyone to go out without being checked by a French or German police service. A Jewish identity card in the South became as dangerous a sign to carry as the yellow star in the North.

Barbie's task would have been made considerably harder if there had been secret directives to officials to sabotage the Statut des Juifs and other anti-Semitic legislation, but there is no record of any significant action by Pétain. Even attempts by Jews to emigrate were deliberately frustrated, despite the fact that several countries, particularly in Latin America, had issued visas.

Pétain's refusal to reconsider his Government's approach to the Jewish issue, even when it became certain that deportees were being sent to their deaths, was the last link in a process that ended with the fusion of French racist theory and Nazi ideology represented by Barbie. The Gestapo officer's preparation for his mission in France had started about the same time as future Vichy administrators began their calls for anti-Semitic legislation in the early thirties, but the origins of Barbie's racism was a hatred of the French.

The Nazi was infected by revengeful nationalism after the German defeat in 1918 and he blamed the French for the war wound that had turned his schoolteacher father into a tyrannical drunkard. His father died of cancer fifteen years after the Great War and Barbie was probably working for the Nazi secret service from his high-school days in Trier. In late adolescence, he abandoned an association with Catholic youth services and his original intention of becoming a priest, and in 1933 joined the Hitler Youth as a monitor. Two years later he became a full-time member of the SS Security Police, the SD, on Heydrich's recommendation. Barbie's pre-war secret police training was of only marginal significance in relation to his first wartime job in Amsterdam, where he held a post similar to that of Dannecker in Paris until March 1942. Two months later he was sent as a Gestapo agent to the small French town of Gex on the Swiss border, from where he made his first secret visits to Lyons before the Germans occupied the whole of France.

In the dock at Lyons, Barbie was striking only for his non-descript look of a bewildered grandfather caught in the high drama of a tribunal that had been arranged like a huge theatre to accommodate a thousand journalists. Witnesses could not agree on how he looked during the war except to seize on a reporter's descriptions of a mouth like a cruel slash and cold, murderous eyes. The images did not stand comparison with wartime photographs of a small, round-faced man with a well-shaped mouth and dull expression who could have passed for a reliable office worker.

The contradictions between descriptions given by the people he tortured and the evidence shown in photographs could explain why it was never proved beyond doubt that he was present during two of the Crimes against Humanity for which he was nonetheless jailed for life. Barbie owed his power and frightening appearance during interrogations to a hidden personality drawn from his SS uniform and to the indoctrination process that had turned him from the seminary to a bestial ideology. He was a short man who boosted his image by outrageous lies and who shrank to near anonymity without his whip and jackboots. In his cell in Lyons, he turned back to the Catholic religion after refusing to acknowledge that his Nazi crusade was anything more than an honourable battle against the Resistance.

The Lyons trial proved that his most important mission was to contribute to the Final Solution. He had hardly organised his staff in Lyons before the Gestapo raided the UGIF welfare offices in the rue Sainte Catherine. During a day-long operation, eighty-seven staff and visitors were arrested. Most were poor French and foreign Jews desperately seeking help to survive. All were sent to die in Auschwitz or Sobibor.

The raid took place on 9 February 1943, the day the deportation programme restarted. From then on, Barbie's operations would provide thousands of victims among the 33,000 Jews sent to death camps from France between February 1943 and August 1944.

CHAPTER EIGHTEEN

The Italian Example

NEITHER THE OCCUPATION of the Free Zone by the Germans nor the arrival of new Gestapo units in southern cities changed the principle of Vichy control of two-fifths of the national territory. France remained the administrative power as before and had sufficient authority to reject German legislation on imposing the yellow star.

It was a minor defiance in relation to what should have been done to help Jews escape. The last hope of leaving France by legal means had disappeared with the Allied invasion of North Africa. Frontier controls were tightened, making it almost impossible for Jews to leave even when they had visas to foreign countries. Sea links with North Africa, where 10,000 mainland Jews had taken refuge in the previous two years, were cut off. The invasion had also scuttled a Quaker plan to send 5000 orphaned children to the United States.

There was only one escape from the trap: the Italian Zone. From the autumn of 1942 until the Italian surrender to the Allies in September 1943, the Italians defied both Vichy and the Germans in an attempt to save the Jews.

Vichy's indifference to the fate of its Jewish population has been compared unfavourably to action in other European countries, notably Holland and Denmark. In the Dutch case, even Communist trade unionists joined vain protests to stop deportations. In Denmark, King Christian X led opposition to Nazi strategy and nearly all Jews were secretly ferried out of the country to Sweden.

Neither example is as relevant as the Italian attitude. Benito Mussolini became the unlikely protector of Jews on French territory when Germany and France tried to pressure the Italian Army into joining the Final Solution. Official Italian resistance was reinforced by documentary proof showing that Jews were being exterminated in Germany. The evidence was gathered early in 1943, making it likely that other pro-Nazi states were also aware of the destiny of deportees. Italy had its own anti-Semitic laws but these had been administered without resolution. From the start of the Italian occupation of a small section of French territory west of the Alps in 1940, no help was given to the French in the administration of the Statut des Juifs.

Technically, the Italian Zone was subject to Vichy legislation and administered by French officials with the same powers as other Prefects in the North. Disputes were settled at an Armistice Commission, although there were few points of contention until the Germans occupied the Vichy Zone in 1942. The Italians immediately extended their own zone to eight south-eastern *départements* which quickly became a haven for Jews. There was no Demarcation Line and it was easy to settle in cities like Nice and Grenoble.

Tension between the Italians and French over the Jewish issue had been evident in the summer and autumn of 1942 when the Italians had opposed the round-up of refugee Jews whom the French wanted to send north. This did not prevent French police trying again in February 1943, when new *rafles* were started without consulting the Italians. Angry Italian Army reaction was led by General Lazare di Castiglione, who forced Vichy to release detained Jews. In the Alpine city of Annecy, Italian soldiers surrounded a Gendarmerie in a successful rescue operation.

That intervention started a panic in the SS. Knochen warned Berlin that Italian resistance would encourage French defiance. He asked for immediate pressure to be put on the Italians, adding:

'If this demand cannot be imposed, it can be said that from today the Jewish problem in France will be put into question.'

Knochen's anxiety was premature. His warning came just before Bousquet insisted on his loyalty in the wake of the Marseilles operation. But Italian opposition did accidentally upset French co-operation over the deportation of thousands of Jews. France had promised to hand over 50,000 Jews naturalised after 1927 once their citizenship had been removed by decree. Moves to take away their nationality were delayed several times for bureaucratic reasons and were finally dropped in the summer of 1943 when the Allies invaded Sicily. Vichy leaders suddenly became more cautious about betraying their own citizens.

In the beginning, though, Vichy was very much on the German side during a seven-month dispute in which the Italians outmanoeuvred Germany and France through pure courage and tactical cunning. There could be little doubt that if Pétain had copied the Italian example, thousands of more lives would have been saved. Mussolini had even more pressing reasons than the French leader for pleasing Hitler, whose Army was the Duce's only reliable support as the invasion neared. Instead, Mussolini endorsed the obstructive attitude of troops preparing to overthrow him.

On 25 February 1943, following Knochen's irritated report over Italian resistance, the Gestapo chief in Berlin, Heinrich Müller, asked the Foreign Affairs Minister, Joachim von Ribbentrop, to confront Mussolini in Rome and demand an explanation. The Duce dodged the issue by blaming the lack of co-operation on the French, saying they were trying to provoke dissension in the Italian–German axis. He also gave the impression that he would issue clear instructions to his generals to help with the round-up of Jews. According to the official Italian report of the meeting, Mussolini said that his generals 'did not have the correct understanding of the Jewish issue'.

A week later, the Italian representative at Vichy, General Carlo

Avarni di Gualtieri, showed that Mussolini's message was taking its time getting through. Speaking for the Italian Supreme Command, Gualtieri said that Italy would not accept internment measures ordered by French Prefects as this was the exclusive responsibility of the Italian occupiers. All arrests of Jews, whether Italian, French or foreign, had to be dropped, he said.

The Italian attitude accelerated the flight of Jews into the Italian Zone and, by 17 March, German and French anger had reached such a peak that Mussolini suddenly went back on his promise to protect Jews and announced that 'from today, adequate orders will be given which will allow French police an entirely free hand in this enterprise'. At that point, there must have been jubilation in the Nazi camp. Italian co-operation opened the way to an end to France's ambiguous and wavering attitude over the arrest of French Jews.

To the Germans' surprise, Mussolini changed his mind again within forty-eight hours after a dramatic intervention from inside the Italian Government and Army that would remove any excuse for subsequent French collaboration over deportation. In Rome, some of the most committed Fascists in Mussolini's entourage forced the Duce's hand by revealing the truth about Nazi death camps. The lobbying was led by the head of the Italian Foreign Office, Luigi Vidau, and the junior Foreign Minister, Giuseppe Bastianini, who had previously served as Ambassador in London and Governor of Italian-occupied Dalmatia.

According to the Italian Foreign Ministry's own report, a file of photographs was prepared on scenes of massacres perpetrated by the SS in a concentration camp in Poland; to these were added a despatch from the Italian Ambassador in Berlin referring to the gassing of Jews. 'Details in this document were such that they could not fail to arouse a feeling of horror, even among the most cynical,' the official report stated. A note was included for Mussolini which said that 'no country, even allied Germany, can ask Italy, the cradle of Christianity and law, to be associated with these acts for which the Italian people may one day be accountable'.

Bastianini, accompanied by a general, saw Mussolini on 18 March when the damning report was backed up by the junior Minister's own information on the fate of deported Yugoslav Jews. Within twenty-four hours, Mussolini had appointed Guido Lospinoso, police chief in the southern city of Bari, to the post of Italy's Inspector-General for Racial Policy and sent him to Nice. Mussolini also informed Vichy that the Jewish issue would now be the entire responsibility of the Italian police. To offset German anger, Bastianini told Nazi officials that Italian intervention was necessary because the French were not being assiduous enough. The diplomat gained a little more breathing-space by suggesting that Lospinoso would produce his own plan of action within a fortnight.

The new Racial Policy Inspector-General was told by the Army on his arrival in Nice on 20 March that the Jewish move to the Côte d'Azur had reached the proportions of a Biblical exodus and that the priority task was to increase the security of refugees. There could be no doubt that this was Mussolini's personal instruction because the occupying Fourth Army received a note from the Supreme Command on 21 March saying: 'As regards the measure proposed by Il Duce in reference to the Jews: No. 1 priority is to save Jews living on French territory occupied by our troops whatever their nationality, be they Italians, French or foreigners.'

Of the 25,000 Jews known to be in the Italian region, about 2500 were taken by bus to Alpine resorts such as Megève or Saint-Gervais, where they were lodged in hotels, fed adequately and allowed to set up synagogues. A local Vichy administrator complained in an official message that the conditions were too comfortable and that they 'demoralised' the French administration. For the next six weeks, the Italian Army physically protected the Jews, helped them exchange their identity cards, liberated those jailed for transgressing the Statut des Juifs and co-operated closely with UGIF and international refugee organisations.

The central contact was Angelo Donati, an Italian banker, who later became involved in an Allied attempt to transfer all Jews to North Africa. Between them, Donati and Lospinoso enraged both Vichy and Berlin either by active defiance or by cunning action. The SS became so angry with Donati that Heinz Röthke, the Gestapo Jewish bureau chief in Paris, planned to kidnap him. Meanwhile, Lospinoso ignored repeated requests from Knochen for a meeting, although the Italian Racial Policy chief did have talks with René Bousquet on 22 June 1943. Lospinoso announced that he was ready to transfer another 7000 Jews to Megève; Bousquet's response was to suggest that it was time to allow the French a free hand. In a classic delaying tactic, Lospinoso said he would go to Rome to seek instructions.

A month later, Röthke was told by the Sipo–SD in Marseilles that Donati had already negotiated the eventual transfer of Jews to Italy, which had given refuge to 17,000 Jews from Dalmatia. At the same time, there was a local improvement in the French attitude towards Jews. A new Prefect, André Chaigneau, had been appointed in Nice. He co-ordinated policy with the Italian Army and UGIF and removed previous threats to expel foreign or French Jews living illegally in the Italian Zone.

On 25 July 1943, Mussolini was overthrown following the invasion of Sicily. In the chaotic days that followed, the Italians stepped up their protection of Jews. Lospinoso, who had given a false impression of co-operating with the SS, managed to steal a list of Jews in the Italian Zone from the Marseilles Gestapo. He quickly returned to Italy, where he was later to be hunted unsuccessfully by the revengeful SS.

At that point everything was set for a mass rescue operation, but these hopes were dashed by a misunderstanding with the Americans. By 3 September, Donati had negotiated a plan with the British and Americans under which all Jews would be shipped to North Africa. Jews detained in Alpine resorts were repatriated to Nice, while four ships were prepared for the exodus. On 8 September, according to Donati's own recollections, he was in Rome fixing final details. Pick-up points had been allotted and reception centres prepared for between 20,000 and 30,000 Jews. Part of the rescue involved a secret agreement with Washington not to reveal the Italian surrender until the Jews were safe at sea. At 6.30 p.m. on 8 September General Eisenhower's headquarters in Algeria announced the armistice without consulting the Italians.

The Germans attacked their former allies before the Italians had time to prepare a defence plan. The Wehrmacht seized Nice and other big towns in France before rapidly taking control of northern Italy. In the wake of the first shocktroops, the Gestapo took a terrible revenge on Jews who had been so near to safety.

In the violent aftermath of the Italian collapse, nearly 2000 Jews were arrested by a specialist anti-Jewish Gestapo commando led by SS-Captain Aloïs Brünner, a thirty-one-year-old Austrian. He had been sent to France in June 1943 when Heinz Röthke appealed for more help for the next phase of the Final Solution.

Brünner and his nine-man Austrian unit had built up an impeccable reputation for efficiency since before the war, although his background contained nothing to suggest that he was cut out to be an exemplary organiser. He had secretly joined the Austrian Nazi Party in 1931 at the age of nineteen and his only civilian job before recruitment by the SS had been running a café-restaurant. His anti-Semitism quickly led to his appointment as Eichmann's personal secretary.

Later, when head of the Nazi Jewish Affairs office in Vienna, Brünner organised persecution in an attempt to force Jews to emigrate. After war was declared, he was responsible for sending 47,000 to death camps. With that task completed, he returned to Berlin to organise deportations from the German capital and was transferred to Salonika in February 1943. In two months, he cleared the Greek city of all its 43,000 Jews, sending them on a week-long journey to Auschwitz.

His commando's ability to act without outside help made the unit a natural choice for France at a time when collaboration was wavering. Brünner was more cunning than Barbie and took far more risks than Röthke. The Austrian's first action on arrival in France on 10 June was to put Drancy under German command, reducing Gendarmerie responsibility to guarding the perimeter. Drawing on his past experience, Brünner started by calming Jewish fears by involving community leaders in the organisation of deportations and by insisting that Jews were being transferred to a new homeland. To complete this impression, he arranged the exchange of local currency for Polish zlotys and made sure that deportees were well supplied for the train journey. Pro-German newspapers helped by publishing reports of the peaceful resettlement of deported Jews in Silesia, while forged postcards were sent to France from supposedly happy deportees.

At Drancy, the appalling conditions overseen by the dismissed French administration also changed overnight, to reassure internees. The muddy courtyard was paved over, food and accommodation improved and fifteen leading Jews were conscripted to manage the block.

Brünner quickly sorted out internees into two main categories, those covered by exemption and those who could be deported under agreements with Vichy. At the time, he was confident that Laval would denaturalise 50,000 French Jews. Röthke made preparations for their arrest as early as 24 June. When the plan was dropped because of the invasion of Sicily, Brünner decided to reduce co-operation with the French to a minimum and ignore Vichy's objections to the arrest of French citizens. He closed down the French-run concentration camp at Beaune-la-Rolande and arrested the leading UGIF official in the North, Andre Baur, a banker. Baur had complained of Brünner's brutality, but Vichy made no attempt to seek his release and he was sent to Auschwitz with his wife and four children.

Brünner's transfer to Nice on 10 September 1943 was to provide more proof that Pétain's promises to protect French Jews were worthless. Right until the last minute, the retreating Italians had done everything possible to save Jews. The Consul worked twenty-four hours a day to produce hundreds of visas for entry into Italy and then requisitioned trucks to ferry Jews across the frontier. The Consulate was housed in the Hôtel Continental, one of the first buildings seized by the SS unit in the hope of finding files, but these had already been sent to Rome. Livid with rage, Brünner arrested both the Consul and Vice-Consul and had them deported.

SS officers were told that no Jew was to be spared, whatever their nationality. Preparations were made to despatch Jews to Drancy at the rate of a thousand or two thousand a day, while a reward of 100 francs a head was offered to informers. After setting up his headquarters in the Hôtel Excelsior near Nice railway station, Brünner was quickly confronted by failure. The hotel was expected to be a transit centre for about 20,000 Jews hiding along the Côte d'Azur, but they could not be tracked down and the hotel rooms were turned into torture chambers to force Jews to betray their relatives.

The reign of terror had an immediate effect and by 14 September a Vichy Jewish Affairs Commission official reported that Nice had lost its ghetto aspect. 'Jews no longer go out,' he reported. 'The synagogues are closed. On the Promenade des Anglais aryan walkers can use chairs that were occupied by Jews up till now.' The official, a member of the Commission's Section d'Enquête et Contrôle, would probably have phrased his report differently if he had known that the disappearance of Jews had little to do with the number of SS arrests.

Behind the change was a popular revolt by French people, who took over where the Italians had left off. Hundreds of Jews in the

Alpine regions escaped on foot to Italy through the mountains in a three-day trek helped by local guides, although the SS did capture 349 escapers. Most of the Riviera's huge Jewish population went underground with the help of Christian churchmen, Jewish aid organisations and hundreds of volunteers, some of whom were arrested and deported. Police and local government officials either refused to carry out identity checks or helped Resistance workers to hide children or whole families. The Gestapo had to raise the reward for betraying Jews from 100 francs to 1000 francs, and it was reported that White Russian experts were paid as much as 10,000 francs for every Jew they recognised.

By mid-September, Brünner had to face the fact that his methods had failed in France. In all, about 1900 Jews were arrested, 1400 in the Côte d'Azur and the rest in the Alps. Among the internees was one of the most popular pre-war playwrights, Tristan Bernard. He escaped deportation from Drancy after the intervention of the actor–director Sacha Guitry, who was later arrested for collaboration.

In Nice, Brünner never had more than fifteen men at his disposal because the Wehrmacht refused to help. The Nice operation proved what could only be guessed at before: that the Gestapo was incapable of action on a vast scale without the aid of French police.

One Gestapo raid in Nice would have immense consequences in re-establishing the truth of Vichy's responsibility in the Holocaust. Among the men Brünner arrested was Arno Klarsfeld, a Roumanian Jew, whose fate inspired the post-war vocation of his son, Serge Klarsfeld.

With his father, mother and sister, Serge Klarsfeld lived in a flat next to the Gestapo headquarters. Five days after Brünner's arrival, the SS encircled the block of flats at night, lighting up the building with a searchlight. Arno Klarsfeld hid his family behind a false wall he had built in a cupboard. When the Germans approached the flat he gave himself up before they could carry out a search.

From Drancy, Arno Klarsfeld, who had served with the French Army and the Resistance, was taken to Auschwitz and singled out for forced labour. Later, he was transferred to a coalmine after knocking out a kapo (a prisoner in command of a working party) who had struck him. A few months later, Klarsfeld died of exhaustion.

Serge was eight years old when Brünner's men took his father away. Most of the rest of the war he spent in hiding, part of it at a Catholic school. Like so many Jews, Klarsfeld pushed the period to the back of his memory and became an assimilated Frenchman, eventually working for the national radio in Paris where he became an expert on American cinema.

His marriage to Beate Künzel, a Berlin Protestant, did not change his attitude significantly. That happened with the birth of his son in 1965. He was named Arno. A year later, Serge Klarsfeld made a pilgrimage to Auschwitz where he discovered his father's personal file and immatriculation number. On the ramp at Birkenau, where Jews were selected for work or immediate death, his past suddenly reached out to him. 'It seemed that I heard the cry of my people, a cry in proportion to the crime, a cry impossible to interrupt, prolonging itself to infinity,' he said. At that moment, he rediscovered his Jewish identity. His interest in the Holocaust coincided with his wife's courageous campaign against German amnesia. In 1968, she slapped the face of the German Chancellor, Kurt-Georg Kiesinger, after interrupting him in the Bundestag with the shout: 'Kiesinger, Nazi! Kiesinger, Nazi!'

From the early seventies, the Klarsfelds became full-time anti-Nazi activists both as historians and as fieldworkers. They tracked down unpunished SS men in Paris and unmasked Barbie. More recently, they have concentrated on trying to bring to justice French collaborationists like René Bousquet and Maurice Papon, the Bordeaux Prefecture Secretary-General.

One man escaped them: Alois Brünner. The Klarsfelds tracked him down to his hideout in Damascus, Syria, where he had offered his Nazi training to Arab anti-Israéli secret services. In 1989, France officially demanded Brünner's extradition for trial on charges of Crimes against Humanity, a forlorn request repeated unsuccessfully ten years later.

CHAPTER NINETEEN

The Children of Izieu

AFTER THE ITALIAN surrender, France sank into civil war. The Jewish issue was submerged by the battle between Vichy and the Resistance, which was exacerbated by the mass conscription of young people for obligatory war work in Germany. Resistance workers were killed or deported in their thousands. Civilian populations struggled with severe deprivation and suffered appalling casualties in Allied bombing. Family loyalties were still torn between the promises of Pétain and de Gaulle. Vichy maintained support from a large section of the population convinced that the Nazi cause was preferable to a Marxist revolution. Until the Liberation was over, there was no dominant power centre. The fragmented country provided ideal territory for Nazi and Pétainist anti-Semitics to speed up the extermination programme.

The rivalry inside Vichy helped their crusade. The competition for power between Pétain and Laval finally ended in the Prime Minister's favour in December 1943, opening the way to an uncompromisingly Fascist regime. In a last attempt to wreck Laval's growing ascendancy, Pétain tried to introduce constitutional reforms that would have delegated his powers to a reconstituted National Assembly. It was both a disguised message to the Allies that Pétain was repenting for his past choices and an attempt to outmanoeuvre Communists suspected of planning a political takeover. Laval said the reform was 'not a constitution, but an act of contrition'.

When the Germans reacted by stopping Pétain from making a

radio announcement on the changes, the Head of State went on strike for three weeks, cancelling all his engagements as well as his weekly visit to Vichy's Saint Louis church for Mass. The Germans tried to force Pétain's resignation by drawing up a list of diktats which appeared unacceptable. The Ambassador, Otto Abetz, who had been restored to favour, drafted the Maréchal's political obituary, saying he had taken the country to an abyss and that 'the sole and unique guarantor of the maintenance of calm and order in France . . . against revolution and Bolshevik chaos is the German Army.'

The text was intended as a press release, but it was never issued. Pétain accepted the Nazi terms and wrote Hitler an abject letter of apology. After another fortnight of reflection, the Maréchal handed over the last vestiges of his executive power to Laval. To ensure that he could not change his mind, Berlin appointed its own Minister, Cecil von Renthe-Finck, as a personal watchdog in Pétain's entourage. From then on, he was allowed little freedom except walks in the garden accompanied by Ménétrel.

A purge of French officials had also been ordered, which included the dismissal of Darquier de Pellepoix and René Bousquet. The police chiefs place was taken by Joseph Darnand, head of the Milice. Darnand's own career had paralleled the regime's collapse into Nazism. A Great War hero, Darnand had been chosen personally by Pétain as leader of the old soldiers' organisation, La Légion Française des Combattants, the most patriotic of all Vichy organisations. By 1944, after service in the Waffen-SS, he had been promoted to Obersturmführer, the same rank as Klaus Barbie.

With Darnand's appointment to Bousquet's post, the French police and bureaucracy again took a leading role in rounding up Jews. The atmosphere of the *rafles* of 1942 was recreated, particularly in the provinces. On 27 January, hundreds of police were mobilised to clear the central Poitiers region of French Jews on the pretext that they were potential terrorists. With French administrative complicity, the Germans carried out raids in Dijon, Rheims and Troyes before a huge Gestapo sweep in the Nancy region, a traditional Jewish settlement in the Lorraine, when about 800 people were seized.

The area around Toulouse was subjected to repeated operations, while others took place in the Ardennes, the Languedoc and at Orleans. During the first quarter of 1944, 4500 Jews arrived at Drancy from the provinces, compared to about 2000 from Paris. The arrests of French Jews was always covered by the claim that they were probable terrorists, an absurd accusation as a high proportion of those shipped to Auschwitz were old and sick. Among several big families were twelve of the thirteen Schwartzmann children arrested with their parents, Michel and Henriette, near Rheims, on 27 January 1944. Their ages ranged from twenty-two to a one-year-old baby, Marie. The oldest, a boy, escaped because he was serving with the Free French.

While the Germans appeared confident of French co-operation in the provinces, there was more caution in Paris where the municipal police were used only to arrest foreigners. The Nazis had to take into account local hostility. It was reported that during a round-up on 3 and 4 February the police had been ordered to take action against concierges and neighbours who gave false information about Jews' hiding places.

Without French police help, most of the 19,000 Jews who were arrested in the first nine months of 1944 would have escaped. Whenever the Germans operated alone the results were limited. Apart from the failure of Brünner's commando in Nice, the Germans had to admit another setback in Bordeaux. A Gestapo *rafle* on 20 December 1943 ended with 108 arrests. Among them were seventy-nine French citizens, but the total was barely a fifth of the target.

On 10 January 1944, it was decided to ask for French help to round up about 500 French citizens. The regional Prefect,

Maurice Sabatier, asked for time to seek instructions from Vichy, pointing out that the use of French police to arrest French nationals would cause trouble. 'The population will not understand,' he said. The Germans justified their demands by the well-used formula that Jews were carrying out sabotage operations and that it was urgent to arrest the grand rabbi.

After a day of hesitant and equivocal contacts between Vichy and the Nazis, Laval gave the go-ahead, saying that arrests of French citizens by French police had already taken place elsewhere. He was referring to *rafles* in the northern cities of Laon, Saint-Quentin and Amiens on 4 January when the Nazis had not sought Vichy's approval. Half-an-hour later, Joseph Darnand telephoned and likewise gave his assent, ending months of hypocrisy over protection for French Jews.

The last official barrier had been removed, but local administrators were still able to frustrate *rafles* by warning people to disperse or by refusing to hand over files. Instead Sabatier and the man responsible for Jewish Affairs in his Prefecture, Maurice Papon, gave a cowardly example to other civil servants. Papon, who had already supervised the transfer of children to Drancy in 1942, issued orders to French police which resulted in the arrests of 228 of the 473 Jews who were being hunted. After further arrests, 364 Jews, including 50 children, were sent to Paris.

Later, Papon wrote a self-congratulatory note saying that his services had done the maximum 'to attenuate as far as possible the rigours of the fate reserved for this population'. But by 1944 few officials could have had any illusions about the eventual destiny of deported Jews. Well over a year before, both Cardinal Gerlier and the Papal Nuncio at Vichy, Valerio Valeri, had told Pétain that Jews faced probable death. Valeri was also informed of the Italian documents on massacres which had persuaded Mussolini to protect Jews in the Italian Zone.

Attempts to convict Papon and Sabatier of Crimes against Humanity revealed a wartime bureaucratic tangle which could have been used to disperse threatened Jews. Senior SS officers in Bordeaux were absent, while German officials in Paris were unsure of their ground because of repeated warnings by Colonel Knochen that there would be high-level and popular reaction if French police were used to arrest French Jews. In the event, there was no official French obstruction, and Papon's action underlined his belief that few Jews, either foreign or French, were worth saving. While deportees were still being held in Bordeaux, he said that efforts to stop their departure should be restricted to 'interesting' Jews, which he defined as decorated war veterans and war widows. Implicitly, the rest of the Jewish population had become 'uninteresting'.

As the final exemptions disappeared, it was not surprising that by the time the last deportation train left Drancy in July 1944, one of the cattle wagons contained a tiny wooden cot. Inside was a two-week-old French baby boy being sent away to die by slow suffocation.

The lessons of the Bordeaux incident and other French police sweeps were not lost on men like Klaus Barbie, whose excesses would include one of the best-documented war crimes committed against Jews, the arrest and murder of forty-four children in April 1944 at Izieu, near Lyons.

The tiny village provided the most beautiful setting of all the locations linked with the wartime years, a final violation of La Douce France. Set high on a hillside in the thinly populated Ain *département,* the isolated farming community could be approached only by a narrow winding road that led nowhere except to forest and pastureland.

The children lived a few idyllic months in a stone farmhouse set high over an immense valley cut by the Ain river running under spectacular grey cliffs. Their last few weeks were spent surrounded by winter snow turning to a warm spring among fields of mountain flowers. A record of that period has been preserved in dozens of letters and drawings sent by the children to their parents. One of the most descriptive letters was written by Georgy Halpern, aged eight. Writing to his mother, he said:

> I got your letter and the photo which I liked very much. Saturday, there was snow. It's not really cold yet. There's a big terrace where you can see the whole landscape and it's very pretty to see all the mountains covered with snow. Are you feeling well? I'm fine. I'm eating well and having fun and feeling well. Your son loves you very much and sends you 1000000000 kisses. Georgy.

Izieu had been in operation for nearly a year by that time. It was one of the many safe houses set up after the OSE had had to close a big reception centre in the Mediterranean *département* of the Herault following the German invasion of the South. A Polish-born French Red Cross worker, Sabina Zlatin, who had been involved in rescue work since the Fall of France, decided to seek new refuges.

In March 1943, the Izieu farmhouse was located and became the responsibility of Mrs Zlatin and her husband, Miron, a powerfully built Russian-born agronomist. Financed secretly by OSE funds, they were able to create a privileged environment for orphans or children entrusted by their parents. As far as the villagers were concerned, the boys and girls were poor aryan refugees from the Herault, although it was obvious that most people guessed the children's origins.

A Christian assistant, Paulette Paillarès, took many photographs of special occasions when the children were pictured out on hikes in the mountains or celebrating holidays. The air of absolute security evoked in the photographs was not endangered until the Italians pulled out of the war in September 1943, and even then Izieu seemed too remote to be at risk. It was only in March 1944 that Nazi reprisals became a real threat and the

Zlatins decided to disperse the children to even safer areas. As it turned out, the decision was taken days too late.

On Maundy Thursday, 6 April 1944, Sabina Zlatin was in the Montpellier region looking for new hideouts. At nine on a beautiful spring morning while the children were at breakfast, four vehicles drew up outside the farmhouse. Germans threw the children into the back of a lorry and took them to Montluc Fort in Lyons. Barbie proudly sent a telegram to Berlin.

The following day, most of the children were taken to Drancy by passenger train. On 13 April thirty-four were sent to Auschwitz. Two days later they were gassed. All forty-four children eventually died, along with Miron Zlatin and five other adult helpers.

By an extraordinary chance, Léa Feldblum, a twenty-six-year-old aid worker, survived and told her story at Barbie's trial. She could have escaped deportation because she had false papers, but she refused to abandon the children, the youngest of which, Albert Bulka, was only four. She was especially fond of a five-year-old orphan, Emile Zuckerberg, who clung to her during the selection process at Birkenau, the Auschwitz annexe. He was torn from her by a soldier and sent to die with the others.

Twenty-five years later, the Izieu affair became a central motive for the Klarsfeld mission to ensure that Barbie would be tried. In 1971, the Munich Public Prosecutor had decided to close the Barbie inquiry although the Gestapo officer had been identified in Bolivia where he had taken refuge after working for American intelligence in Germany. The Klarsfelds contacted two of the mothers who had lost children at Izieu, Fortunée Benguigui and Ita Halaunbrenner. Three Benguigui children had died in Auschwitz: Jacques, aged twelve, Richard, aged seven, and Jean-Claude, aged five, along with Mina and Claudine Halaunbrenner, aged eight and five. All were French. The Benguigui boys were born in Algeria, and the Halaunbrenner girls in Paris.

The two mothers played a central role in an international

campaign, protesting in Germany, France and Bolivia, before the French Socialist Government negotiated Barbie's expulsion to France in 1983. Both mothers gave evidence at Barbie's trial, where Serge Klarsfeld was one of the prosecution lawyers. It was the first time he had pleaded in an assize court. One of the most dramatic moments came when he read out the names and ages of all the murdered children.

Fortunée Benguigui's desire for justice had begun more than forty years before, a few months after she had been sent to Auschwitz in 1943, where repeated bad treatment crippled her for life. The belief that her children were alive and in a safe hiding place gave her the strength to resist. In the spring of 1944, her hopes were shattered. On a pile of clothing taken from children who had just been gassed she recognised the pullover worn by her son Jacques.

The brutality of Nazi and French *rafles* and the horrors which followed did nothing to shake the zeal of Vichy's pioneer anti-Semites like Charles Maurras, who lived throughout the war in a tiny, disordered Lyons flat, crowded with books. He continued to pour out the anti-Semitic violence that had inspired him for more than half a century. In February 1944, when he was seventy-six, he added one more crime to his long list.

Among his many *Action Française* articles at the time was one headed 'Menaces Juives'. As he had done often before, Maurras denounced a leading Jew living in hiding. Referring to the banker, Roger Worms, who had backed the Popular Front and had been a leading member of the League against Anti-Semitism, Maurras wrote: 'It would be curious to know if the noble family is in a concentration camp or in England or in America or if, by chance, it has maintained the right to let its fine remains of prosperity flower in a favoured corner of the Côte d'Azur.'

Just after the article appeared, the Milice kidnapped Worms at Saint-Jean-Cap-Ferrat and killed him with submachine-gun fire.

It was one of a number of cold-blooded murders of prominent Jews by Darnand's men, who also shot Georges Mandel, Jean Zay and the former chairman of the International Federation of Human Rights, Victor Basch, a lawyer. He was more than eighty years old.

The link between the denunciation of Roger Worms and the murder itself was not proved until eight years later after a long campaign by Roger Worms' son, the author Roger Stéphane, a captain in the Free French forces. There should never have been any doubt about Maurras' role. The Lyons office of *Action Française* was in the same building as the Milice.

Maurras was jailed for life and was first sent to Riom prison. The Provençal poet died in 1952 but his last public statement at his 1945 trial had closed a circle that began with the degradation of a Jewish Army captain in 1896 and ended with the slaughter of thousands of Jews. As he was sentenced, Maurras shouted to the judges: 'C'est la revanche de Dreyfus.'

Another voice from the past also made itself heard in the last days of Vichy. Despite his supposed hatred of the Germans, Xavier Vallat, the first Jewish Affairs Commissioner, volunteered to become Radio Vichy's chief propaganda commentator. His views on the need to isolate Jews were heard again. He had been dismissed as Commissioner in 1942 four months before La Grande Rafle and was able to claim at his trial that he knew nothing about the murder programme.

If leading Vichy officials were still unaware of the fate of Jews in 1944, it was only because they refused to believe the ever-growing pile of evidence. By the time Vallat returned to renew his attacks on Jews, a German extermination camp had been operating on French soil since 1941.

CHAPTER TWENTY

The French Gas Chamber

IN AUGUST 1943, a year before Drancy was liberated by French troops, a deportation train transporting about eighty Jewish men and women left Auschwitz in occupied Poland for France. It crossed the border just east of Strasbourg in Alsace before stopping at a station near the picturesque town of Schirmeck under the blue hills of the Vosges. Nazi guards escorted the prisoners to a concentration camp set in pine forests at an altitude of nearly 3000 feet. Within days, the Jews had been killed in a gas chamber built inside a former dance hall near the holiday village of Natzwiller.

The only Nazi death camp in France is now preserved as a classified historical monument and is reached by a winding road from the village, a centre for long-distance ski-ing. About two miles from Natzwiller, the road reaches a junction where standard French road signs point towards 'Camp de concentration du Struthof' and 'Chambre à gaz du Struthof' – 'Struthof' being the local name for a stretch of pastureland and forest.

A big restaurant stands across the road from the isolated gas chamber, a two-storey building that served as an experimental centre to improve the efficiency of mass killing in Germany and Poland or for tests on the effectiveness of military poison gases. From the restaurant, the view plunges across a valley where the hills of the Vosges stretch out towards the rest of France. Looking westwards, there are no signs of habitation, although on quiet mornings church bells can be heard ringing out from Schirmeck seven miles distant across rolling forest covered by blankets of mist. The bells are recalled by former prisoners as the only reminder they had at the time that Christian civilisation had not been entirely extinguished.

Except for the camp higher up the hill with its crematorium, punishment blocks, watchtowers and surviving barracks, there were few buildings outside the perimeter during the war. When the SS ran the concentration camp under its German name of Natzweiler-Struthof, the Kommandant, Joseph Kramer, lived with his family near the gas chamber in a recently built holiday villa allowing him to walk a few yards to oversee ritual murder in his back garden.

Before Kramer was hanged by the British in 1945 after promotion to Kommandant at Bergen-Belsen, he gave a detailed description of the experimental gassing of Jews in the Alsace camp in mid-August 1943, a description which must have resembled the final unrecorded minutes of life of nearly all Jewish men, women, children and babies deported to Germany from France.

The experiment had been ordered by Dr August Hirt, Professor at Heidelberg Anatomy Institute and the University of Strasbourg, a city renamed Strassburg. Kramer, who had joined the Nazi Party when unemployed and had served in concentration camps since 1934, gave the following account of the Natzweiler-Struthof murders to British interrogators at Belsen in 1945:

> During the month of August 1943, I was given orders to receive eighty deportees coming from Auschwitz and to get in touch immediately with Professor Hirt of the Medical Faculty at Strasbourg. He told me that he had been informed of a trainload of deportees from Auschwitz for Le Struthof. These people had to be killed in the gas chamber at Le Struthof by using asphyxiating gas and their corpses should be put at his disposal. He gave me a container which held about a quarter of a litre of salts which I think were cyanide-based salts. The

Professor told me of the approximate dose which I should use on the internees from Auschwitz.

At the beginning of August 1943, I received the internees and, one evening towards 8 p.m., I started by taking about fifteen women to the gas chamber. I told these women that they were going to a disinfection room and I hid the fact that they were going to be asphyxiated. Helped by some SS, I made them undress completely and pushed them into the gas chamber when they were completely naked. When I closed the door, they started to scream. After closing the door, I put some salt into a funnel underneath and to the right of the observation window. At the same time, I poured some water which, with the salt, fell into a receptacle inside the gas chamber. I lit the interior of the gas chamber with a switch next to the funnel and I watched what happened through the observation window.

Kramer continued:

I noticed that the women continued to breathe for about a half-minute. Then they fell to the ground. When I opened the door after starting the fan in the aeration chimney, I saw that these women were lying lifeless after releasing their fecal matter.

I ordered two SS male nurses to take the corpses to a lorry the following day at about 5.30 a.m. so that they could be taken to the anatomy institute as Professor Hirt had asked.

Some days later, I again took a number of women to the gas chamber and they were suffocated in the same way. Afterwards, I took about fifty men in two or three groups and they were killed, always with the help of the salt I had been given by Hirt.

I felt no emotion in accomplishing these acts because I was bred like that.

The small Natzweiler-Struthof Konzentrationlager, thirty miles from Strasbourg, the city that houses the European Parliament and the European Court of Human Rights, reduced the horrors of the Nazi system to accessible proportions. Auschwitz, with its millions of murders on an industrial scale, or Belsen, which provided the most sensational pictures of savagery as the war ended, both submerged personal human tragedy under unimaginable statistics. In the Vosges hills, where there was a French administration until July 1940, every aspect of the Nazi Nacht und Nebel – Night and Fog – mass murder programme was rehearsed from 1941 on a small scale, while the Vichy regime pretended that it was not aware of the fate of its Jewish or Resistance deportees.

Apparent French ignorance over the atrocities at Natzweiler-Struthof was based on the fact that the French had no administration officials in the frontier province. The three *départements* that formed most of German Alsace-Lorraine between 1870 and 1918 were never officially annexed when they came under exclusive German rule again after the Fall of France. There was no clause in the Armistice handing over the Bas-Rhin, the Haut-Rhin and the Moselle to Germany.

Exclusion of Vichy in an area of traditional Jewish settlement since medieval times was achieved by *force majeure,* when the German Bade region Gauleiter, Robert Wagner, was ordered to administer what was technically French territory. Hitler made his intentions clear to Wagner on 25 September 1940, declaring that Alsace and Lorraine, renamed Oberrhein and Westmark, would be integrated into Germany within ten years through forced resettlement. Customs posts were set up and entry controls instituted while Vichy made only a feeble, private protest.

Wagner, a former primary schoolteacher with a passion for old-fashioned Prussian methods, had been a Jew-baiter since joining the Hitler cause as early as 1920 after heroic service in the Great War. He was proud of the fact that during a Brownshirt parade in Bade he had overturned a café table where a disapproving Jewish family sat, covering them with tea. As a schoolteacher, he had been taught to hand out severe punishments for minor offences before pupils could be tempted into more serious indiscipline. In that spirit, he immediately punished Alsatian Jews by forcing them to sweep the streets, before deporting them en masse to Vichy territory.

There was a bigger pool of potential collaborators in Alsace than the rest of France. Much of the population had been born German and admired Bismarck's pioneering post-1870 reforms in education and social security which made the region the envy of neighbouring French *départements*. Many men who fought with the French Army in 1940 would be drafted into the Wehrmacht and a few survived to serve in the French Liberation forces in 1944. In this atmosphere of split loyalty, nearly 170,000 people in Alsace-Lorraine were given permission to join the Nazi Party but thousands of others remained defiantly French, forcing the Germans to introduce formal bans on French symbols such as the beret.

Inevitably, detention camps had to be set up to intern opponents, whose numbers sharply increased with the forcible conscription of Alsatians into the German Army. The reluctant soldiers were known as *malgré-nous* – despite ourselves – and those who tried to escape conscription were interned. Thousands passed through a forced-labour centre in Schirmeck, which also became an assembly area for prisoners taken to Natzweiler-Struthof.

The camp at Natzweiler-Struthof overlooked a quarry of pink granite. The quarry had attracted a special mission sent by Himmler in September 1940 because there was a shortage of pink granite for Nazi monuments. In April the following year, 200 SS men arrived in a train at nearby Rothau before being taken on a five-mile trip by lorry and car to survey the future camp. A month later the first 150 prisoners arrived to build thirty barrack huts on a sharp slope leading to the granite mine.

For the next three and half years, about 40,000 forced labourers would pass through the camp, where mountain temperatures often fell below 30°C. They included political prisoners from most of Western Europe, French Resistance deportees, gypsies, Allied agents and Jews from nearly every nation under Nazi domination. About half of all internees died in the camp, from exhaustion, malnutrition, exposure, illness, torture, execution or gassing.

Their bodies were burned in a crematorium, where the chimney over the wooden barrack block glowed bright red in the night. For many internees, summary execution was a more merciful fate than the punishment block. Hundreds of men were packed into tiny cells where typhus and malaria killed them slowly if they were not beaten to death by the guards. Others, particularly Jews, were used for medical experiments in laboratories beside the crematorium oven. Survivors were deported to extermination camps in Germany, many of them leaving when Natzweiler was evacuated on 4 September 1944 as the Allies approached. But it was not until two months later that the intact barrack blocks, torture cells, crematorium oven and gas chamber were seized by French troops.

Natzweiler was the first Nazi concentration camp to be liberated, providing definite evidence of gassing and mass execution. The shock was so great that the news was censored. No mention of Natzweiler-Struthof was made until camps like Dachau and Belsen were freed.

Inside France, where the purge of collaborators was at its height, there was an important question to be cleared up before the country could face the truth. Nearly 5000 French internees had been murdered on French territory only miles from Vichy administration in an area of exceptionally strong Resistance and intelligence activity. At Strasbourg, Professor Hirt's Anatomy Institute had also carried out medical experiments on Jews, while a catalogued collection had been made of Jewish skulls as a contribution to racial science.

Even if most of the dead at Natzweiler, including 4500 Polish, were foreigners, could Pétain and his entourage have been unaware that they were sending French citizens and refugees to the cruellest of deaths in France itself? The terrible conditions at Natzweiler were known in detail from January 1943 when an escapee brought the news to London; the camp's existence was revealed by BBC reports in which Natzweiler was called the 'Hell of Alsace'.

Apart from providing another piece of evidence that the French Government knew about the fate of Jewish and Resistance deportees, the escape from Natzweiler-Struthof was one of the most daring adventures of the war.

Even the slightest defiance of Nazi authority was a capital offence, and escapers had to cross an isolated area of well-defended, German-held territory. Five men were involved in the break-out on 4 August 1942, led by a Czech major, Josef Mautner, who was due to be deported to Auschwitz for gassing because he had a Jewish father. His companions were Josef Cichosz, a Pole who had served in the Foreign Legion and the International Brigades, Karl Haas, an Austrian former member of the Brigades, Alfons Christmann, a German political prisoner, and Martin Winterberger, a French Air Force officer born in Alsace.

Christmann was a kapo. Mautner, the Czech, and Cichosz, the Pole, worked outside the camp as surveyors, while Haas, the Austrian, was a mechanic in the SS garage. Winterberger, the Alsatian, had been assigned to the laundry. After weeks of plotting, they stole SS uniforms and a military car, driving away from Natzweiler to the salutes of the Nazi guards.

A month later, Christmann was caught near the Swiss border and taken back to the camp. After torture, he was hanged in November 1942, from a gallows that overlooked the camp. It needed three attempts to kill him as the trap did not work, but before he died he shouted to Kramer that the camp Kommandant would one day be hanged by the British or the Russians.

Mautner and Haas reached Britain in January 1943 after escaping through Spain and Portugal. In London, the Czech Major, a former member of the General Staff, submitted a report on the French concentration camp atrocities to the leader of the exiled Czech Government, Edouard Benes. Promoted to lieutenant-colonel, Mautner led the liberation of Prague in 1945 as commander of a tank regiment. Karl Haas, the Austrian, joined the British 6th Airborne Division, spearheading the Normandy invasion as a glider pilot.

Josef Cichosz, the Pole, joined the Free Polish Army after being imprisoned in Spain, while Winterberger enlisted in the Free French in Tunisia. In November 1944, he was one of the first men to enter the deserted Natzweiler-Struthof camp, where vegetables still grew in Kramer's garden, fertilised with the burned or crushed remains of thousands of men and women.

The atmosphere of terror at Struthof contrasted with the increasing order at Drancy, where Brünner continued with his tactics of deception to allay Jewish fears. He improved the aspect of the central courtyard by adding a lawn where sprinklers worked night and day. German staff also had a vegetable plot, a hen-run and a pigsty. Since his arrival in July 1943, Brünner had a Milice Sémite, an internal police force made up of Jewish volunteers, reinforced to help his SS staff, which was eventually reduced to only five men. Jewish volunteers for the Milice were told that they would be spared deportation, although the risks involved in working for the Germans were high.

Nearly all Jews who co-operated with the Drancy administration were eventually sent to Germany. They were lulled into a feeling of security by an improvement in food and other supplies and by the amount of renovation work in the camp which made dormitories, at last equipped with proper beds, seem almost hospitable. With the removal of all barbed wire in the interior, Drancy looked more like a permanent camp than a transit centre.

Many families spent months there, confidently believing Nazi promises that they would stay in France.

There was so little German surveillance that in November 1943 a 120-feet-long escape tunnel was dug with the intention of evacuating the camp. It was discovered less than ten feet from its projected outlet. Fourteen of the escape team and sixty-five of the Jewish camp's volunteer social staff were arrested and deported. Nineteen cut their way out of cattle wagons in a train that left on 20 November 1943, the biggest group of escapees until a mass break-out in August 1944.

Improvements at Drancy did nothing to lift the spirits of its best-known prisoner, the surrealist French poet Max Jacob, who was taken there suffering from broncho-pneumonia in February 1944. His arrival was the final proof that there were no protected categories left, not even men with an international reputation and the most influential friends in the art and entertainment world.

Jacob had thought he had no reason to hide from either the Nazis or the French. He had converted to Catholicism thirty years before to escape what he called 'Jewish melancholy'. The trap began closing on him in 1942 while he was living near Orleans. He was forced to wear the yellow star and his brother was arrested for walking in a park forbidden to Jews. In August 1943, Jacob tried to dodge showing the yellow star by wearing Indian dress. In the meantime, he made no secret of his hatred for Vichy and for the generals who had led France to disaster, recommending that they should all be shot.

When he was warned that he would inevitably be caught in a *rafle*, he said that he was under the protection of a highly placed French personality. If there was someone at Vichy who valued the life and friendship of one of France's greatest contemporary poets and artists, then he was found wanting on 24 February 1944. Max Jacob was caught in a round-up of the remaining Jews in the Orleans region, a month after his sister had been arrested. The poet was taken to Orleans jail with sixty other people, whom he entertained by singing songs from Offenbach. He was apparently unworried about his fate because he noted in his diary: 'The gendarmes are charming.'

Suddenly, Jacob's will to live collapsed, despite a vigorous campaign to save him by Jean Cocteau and Sacha Guitry, both of whom had many German friends. He was taken to Drancy on 28 February where he said he wanted 'to die on the cross', claiming that he was happy to be with God. The sixty-eight-year-old poet, who had often said that sadness was a sin, died on 5 March 1944 in the camp hospital at Drancy, a block of flats officially commemorated in a memorial to him as 'un haut lieu du martyr juif'.

Pablo Picasso, one of Jacob's closest friends, lived out the war in Paris but did not join the campaign to save the poet, a friend and disciple of Guillaume Apollinaire. When asked to plead with the Germans, Picasso remarked: 'Max is an angel. He does not need us to fly from his prison.'

This image of Max Jacob – a man of 'inimitable grace' in Cocteau's description – flying peacefully to heaven in his own time from a concentration camp has since been put in question. His death might have been accelerated by brutal treatment. There was official embarrassment at his rapid decline. His burial in the local churchyard was kept secret until 22 March when *Je Suis Partout* noted: 'Max Jacob is dead. Jew by race, Breton by birth, Roman by religion and Sodomite by morals, this person represented the most characteristic Parisian one could imagine.'

Several years later, his body was dug up for reburial. It was found that his leg had been broken before his death.

CHAPTER TWENTY-ONE

Le Dernier Wagon

O NLY SIX WEEKS before the Normandy invasion, at a time when repression of Jews and the Resistance was reaching a new level of savagery, Philippe Pétain rediscovered a vocation as national leader. Seizing on public concern over Allied bombings, which killed more than 3000 people between 10 and 25 April the Maréchal went to Paris for a Requiem Mass in Notre-Dame said by Cardinal Emmanuel Suhard.

The reaction of the Parisian population to the first visit by Pétain since the Vichy regime was established in July 1940 convinced him that he had been wrong to stay in the isolated spa town. In a triumphant reception on 26 April 1944, more than a million people acclaimed him at the city hall or during his drive through the capital. The numbers compared favourably to those during de Gaulle's victorious walk through Paris to Notre-Dame only four months later.

Popular support was reinforced throughout May when he toured the northern zone after temporarily moving his base to Rambouillet Château, west of Paris. The Germans encouraged the visit, believing it would contribute to dividing the population before the Allies could land. Wherever he went, Pétain expressed sadness at the pre-invasion bombings and discouraged armed resistance to the Germans.

The enthusiastic welcome in the North, where he had often been criticised by Germans or collaborationist publications, contrasted with his last visit to Saint-Etienne, near Vichy, where he was booed by a population which felt that he had done nothing to save the southern zone from the worst aspects of occupation.

During this period, Pétain again tried to stir up opposition to Laval, even meeting one of the Prime Minister's closest supporters, Marcel Déat, at Rambouillet. Déat had led French opposition to the Maréchal through his Paris-based newspaper, *L'Oeuvre,* but became a privileged confidant when Pétain revealed his regret at not having moved to the North. Déat noted the conversation in his *Mémoires Politiques* published forty-five years after the fall of Vichy. According to his account, Pétain blamed the 'mediocrity' of his advisers for everything that had gone wrong, with an emphasis on Laval. The old soldier believed that he could be confirmed in office after the Allied landing when, according to Déat, Pétain forecast that 'we will be free, free to do what we like'.

Pétain's obsession with unseating Laval and his naive belief that France was ready to plebiscite him in the imminent battle with de Gaulle reflected his failure to take into account his own responsibility in stirring up hatred and division even during the last days of Vichy. There was a direct correlation between the waves of repression by the Milice from the end of April and a solemn statement by Pétain on 28 April 1944, condemning the Resistance and appealing to the country to adopt a 'correct and fair attitude towards the Occupation troops'. After that date, the Vichy leader received hundreds of letters protesting against Milice murders or tortures committed in the former Free Zone, the only territory where they were allowed to operate.

Several correspondents spoke of Milice revenge against Jews, including former soldiers and children. It was not until 5 August, a few days before Vichy collapsed and a month after Georges Mandel had been executed, that Pétain made a formal complaint about the Milice's 'excesses', acknowledging that he had received unfavourable reports over several months. His protest was made directly to Laval, rather than to Darnand, who was responsible for the Milice's discipline but was still well regarded by Pétain. The belated concern appeared to be another attempt to push blame on to his detested Premier.

In the first months of 1944, the battle between the Resistance and the Milice had different consequences for two of the Communist FTP–MOI urban guerrilla units whose Italian, Spanish and Yiddish language groups had merged. In Lyons, after taking part in more than 200 operations, the Communist FTP–MOI Carmagnole-Liberté battalion of immigrants in September 1944 led the armed liberation of the northern Lyons suburb of Villeurbanne, which resulted in the flight of the Germans, including Barbie's Gestapo.

In Toulouse, the predominantly Jewish 35th Brigade, led by a Pole, Jan Gerhaert, had been wiped out by March 1944. Its first leader, Mendel Langer, was guillotined by Vichy in July 1943 just as the Brigade developed its independent policy of concentrating attacks on collaborationists, particularly the Milice, rather than the Germans. The strategy was not approved by the Communist Party, which left the Brigade to its own resources at about the same time as Missak Manouchian's FTP–MOI group was executed in Paris.

The turning point of the Party's attitude was an attack on a Toulouse cinema showing a German anti-Jewish propaganda feature film, *Le Juif Süss*. The film had been circulating from cinema to cinema for four years as part of Nazi and Vichy policy, but it was usually treated with hostility in the southern zone. Two guerrillas and a spectator were killed when a bomb went off too early. Vichy reacted by ordering a new round-up, but Communist Resistance workers in the Toulouse administration neglected to warn the 35th Brigade. Most of the Resistance group was arrested, although Gerhaert survived and returned to Poland. Like many Communist Jews who served in the International Brigades or the French Resistance, he was jailed on his return to his own country after being suspected of political opposition. He was in prison for several years before being murdered in Warsaw.

There were no records kept of the number of Jews in the French Resistance among the 230,000 French deported to Germany for racial, political or Resistance activities; nor has any movement, Communist or Gaullist, suggested that a list should be drawn up. For many, foreign or French, their last words to an execution squad were: 'Vive la France'. Even the children of Izieu left the village which had sheltered them, singing the patriotic song: 'Ils n'auront pas l'Alsace et la Lorraine'.

In the last few weeks before Lyons and Paris were liberated, the French police, the Milice and officials of the Vichy Jewish Affairs Commission's Section d'Enquête et Contrôle, SEC, continued to collaborate in the arrest of Jews. The SEC was intended to be a financial control body but unofficially carried out its own search operations to catch Jews contravening the Statut des Juifs. They were handed over to the Germans along with people hunted down by the Milice or captured in police swoops in Paris which provided 500 deportees for the last big departure from Drancy on 31 July 1944.

This was the seventh overcrowded train to leave since Pétain's triumphal visit to the capital at the end of April. It contained more than 300 children, many of them seized in UGIF homes. The journey in summer heat was one of the worst since deportations began, causing many deaths before the wagons reached Auschwitz.

Among those deported in April were the Jewish poet, Itzhak Katznelson, a refugee from the Warsaw Ghetto who had been granted Honduran citizenship. He had been taken from the camp at Vittel, in the Vosges, where protected categories were held in the spa's grand hotels or in a fortified compound. It was there that he wrote a poem called 'The Song of the Murdered Jewish People' that has served as an epitaph for the Holocaust.

A train which left on 20 May from Drancy was made up largely of Jews from the former Free Zone. Among them were survivors of the camp at Noé. Ruth Altmann, the wife of the camp rabbi who died of grief after she was taken away, was sent to her death on 30 May with her six children. About half the 1150 deportees despatched in another departure a month later had been arrested by French police. There were 162 children, of whom 11 belonged to one family, deported and murdered with their parents, Ernest and Sarah Touitou.

The second-last train to leave Drancy contained 144 wives of Jewish prisoners of war held as hostages. They were sent to Belsen to join 115 other PoW wives. Although many survived, the women received worse treatment than their husbands. All captured French soldiers, whatever their religion, underwent normal PoW internment under Red Cross supervision, but the Swiss charity was excluded from operating in Drancy.

French complicity in the final stages of deportation, even after the Normandy invasion, has been proved beyond doubt, but the last convulsion was entirely Nazi revenge. Klaus Barbie and Aloïs Brünner were both involved.

In the case of Klaus Barbie, his decision to pack 650 Jews and Resistance fighters into a death train that left Lyons on 11 August became the subject of the third charge of Crimes against Humanity at his Lyons trial. A handful of witnesses survived an appalling journey, constantly broken up by the effects of Allied bombing. Among the many delays was a stopover in Alsace to hand over Resistance workers to the SS guards at Natzweiler-Struthof. Survivors later positively identified Barbie as the man in charge of the ultimate departure from the central Gare Perrache under the windows of the Hôtel Terminus.

If Barbie's last victims spoke only of suffering and death, it was a different story for Brünner's final deportees, many of whom survived after a spectacular break-out from the death train.

Brünner, Eichmann's most efficient accomplice, was determined to leave Drancy only after emptying the camp of the last 1467 Jews. The squat, broad SS-Captain with a taste for cleanliness and order, was undeterred despite a high risk of capture as General Philippe Leclerc's tanks rushed towards Paris after the Allied victory at the Falaise Gap in Normandy. Brünner even defied his own retreating Army in a desperate attempt to fulfil his anti-Semitic mission before returning to Berlin.

Every Jew being held in prison or known to be in Jewish refuges was brought to Drancy for a planned departure on 13 August 1944. Despite the need for trains to stem the invasion or repatriate wounded Germans, Brünner managed to assemble forty-eight wagons at Bobigny station, which the SS-Captain preferred to Le Bourget because it was nearer. Many of the new internees were experienced Resistance fighters and there was a risk of rebellion until thirty-one German Army police, known as Schupos, were drafted into Drancy to help Brünner's five SS men and his Milice Sémite. The Schupos quickly quelled indiscipline by throwing grenades and firing at buildings with submachine guns.

Whether there would have been enough of them to force Jews to leave the camp without French help was never proved. On the eve of the intended departure, Brünner learned that the Wehrmacht had seized his train. Not even his SS rank had any effect on the Wehrmacht Colonel whom he confronted on the platform at Bobigny. Brünner's demand that Jewish deportations had a higher priority than military defence was brushed aside. Knowingly or unknowingly, the Colonel's defiance saved more than 1400 lives.

Stubbornly, Brünner set about arranging another train for 15 August. The wagons he expected did not turn up at Bobigny. There were seventeen derailments reported near the station on the previous night and it has been presumed that the Resistance, soon to be backed by a Parisian police uprising, deliberately sabotaged Brünner's plans.

After the 15 August disappointment, Brünner prepared to pull out, ordering his men to burn camp documents while he made one last effort to find a train. He was only partly successful, commandeering two coaches for his soldiers and a cattle wagon for the Jews. He decided to leave with fifty-one prisoners, perhaps the most representative group of French and foreign Jews subjected to a common fate since the war began.

Of the fifty-one deportees, twenty-six were Resistance workers. They belonged to the Communist FTP–MOI, the Gaullist Secret Army or Zionist movements like the Armée Juive. Some had opposed Nazism since long before the war. With them were the most protected category of rich French Jews who had lived out the Occupation believing they could come to no harm because of Pétain's stature. To these groups were added influential Jewish hostages being taken to Germany as a possible bargaining counter.

There were also devout Orthodox Jews resigned to joining the inevitable sacrifice of thousands of their innocent coreligionists at Auschwitz. Finally there was a child, a twelve-year-old French boy, destined for a martyrdom as cruel and as sad as any child has ever suffered. The entire history and consequences of France's wartime anti-Semitism seemed to have been assembled in what was to become known as 'the Last Wagon'.

The Resistance fighters included Rabbi Rene Kapel. His Army service, his role in warning Archbishop Saliège of the cruelty at Noé and his capture as an agent of the Armée Juive by an Abwehr agent posing as a British intelligence officer had made him determined to survive to make the truth about Vichy's persecution known. With him was Henri Pohoryles, the Armée Juive urban guerrilla who had killed informers in Nice and who had been caught in the same Abwehr trap in Paris.

Despite his military experience, Kapel agreed that escape plans should be the responsibility of Maurice Margulies, a thirty-five-year-old Austrian brought to Drancy from the prison at Fresnes. Margulies had opposed the Nazis since the early thirties, first in street marches in Vienna and then as an urban guerrilla. One of his opponents in Austria and Paris was Brünner's assistant, an SS-Sergeant-Major who had been put in charge of the detachment guarding the SS coaches and deportees' wagon. Their long duel ended soon after the war when Margulies, working for the Austrian police, gave evidence that helped to hang the Sergeant-Major.

Margulies was taken to the deportation train after saying goodbye to his wife Ida, whom he had just seen for the first time in a year. She had also been brought to Drancy from prison after being repeatedly beaten and tortured. Another veteran Nazi opponent from Vienna, she had been caught spying under a false name as a secretary in the Kriegsmarine office on the Place de la Concorde.

There was, though, only one woman Resistance worker in the Last Wagon, which had been attached to a retreating artillery regiment's train. Paula Kauffman represented what were known as 'the Dutch', mainly German and Austrian Jews who had come to France after anti-Nazi work in Holland or Germany. Among them was Ernest Appenzeller, alias Leboucher, one of the victims of Brünner's round-ups in Nice. Appenzeller had been officially listed as an aryan after a meeting with Georges Montandon, a Swiss-born ethnologist at the Jewish Affairs Commission.

Montandon claimed that no Jew could escape his racial-identity methods, which depended on identifying a range of supposedly unique anatomical features. Because of his theories, he was the final arbiter in claims for pure aryan certificates, measuring claimants with special instruments and analysing their skin and blood. It was an ideal position for blackmail and corruption. Montandon often put aside his anti-Semitism and charged up to 10,000 francs for certificates of convenience. The owner of the Paris Lido was said to have bought his freedom with three cases of champagne.

After being accused of breaking anti-Jewish laws, Appenzeller claimed to be a Frenchman and was awarded his clearance by sheer bluff, even convincing Montandon that his circumcision was a medical operation. After a long examination with forceps and magnifying glass, the racial theorist accepted the explanation and dismissed the naked Appenzeller as 'an interesting case'. Later, the Austrian was caught again after taking part in urban guerrilla operations and turned down a chance of another meeting with Montandon. The Resistance shot the racial expert dead in July 1944 before he could spend his illegally accumulated fortune.

Resistance workers in the Last Wagon included established French Jews. One of the youngest was Jean Frydman, eighteen, a future director of the country's biggest commercial radio station, Europe 1. He had made desperate attempts to reach the Free French through Spain, but his brief experience was less colourful than that of another Frenchman, César Chamay, perhaps the only Resistance worker to use the Ritz as his headquarters. A banker, Chamay had been turned out of his Paris flat to make way for the German Navy and moved to a suite at the Ritz in the Place Vendôme. Well known to the staff before the war, he was tipped off about imminent arrest and escaped across the roofs of Paris. Chamay had also got away from a deportation train on the way to Drancy following a French police operation in the Free Zone where he was picked up as 'a dangerous Jew'. He was finally taken to the transit camp at Drancy after being arrested on a mission in Paris.

Despite Chamay's past as a rich and respected member of the French-Jewish community, this was not enough to bridge the gap between the Resistance and the other half of the deportees, collectively known as 'Les Bourgeois' and led by Armand Kohn, a banker and administrator of the Rothschild Hospital. Kohn represented a section of the established Jewish population which lived out the war believing that they were safe from anti-Semitism. He was related to the Rothschilds through his mother and had been warned by Philippe de Rothschild in 1940 that he should leave the country. Kohn rejected the advice, pointing out that he was a Great War invalid who would be protected by Pétain. While most of his friends left Paris, Kohn continued to live openly at his

16th *arrondissement* flat, surrounded by his family and obeying laws that forced them to wear yellow stars. He refused to let his four children leave, saying that nothing could harm them if they stayed together.

Unfortunately, Brünner considered him an implacable enemy. Kohn had courageously tried to resist police raids on the Rothschild Hospital when nursing mothers, among other patients, were seized for deportation. After several rows, the hospital administrator himself was arrested and taken to Drancy on 17 July 1944. With Armand Kohn were his adolescent daughters, Antoinette and Marie-Rose, and his sons, Philippe and Georges-André and their grandmother.

The banker was anti-Communist and, before the war, had supported the view that the political activities of immigrants would rebound against the Jewish community in general. He had been proved right, as the Nazi and Vichy propaganda linking Communist urban guerrillas with their Jewish backgrounds had increased the suspicion in which all Parisian Jews were held.

His resentment of the Resistance was the cause of a division between the two groups of deportees when the Last Wagon left Bobigny at 5.30 p.m. on 17 August. The Resistance workers grouped at one end of the cattle truck and Les Bourgeois clung together at the other end. Apart from the Kohn family, Les Bourgeois included Princess Olga Galitzine, widow of the founder of the Printemps department store, and other rich or religious Jews taken as hostages. One man stood silently apart. This was the plane-maker Marcel Bloch, later known as Dassault. He was being deported for consistently refusing German offers to work for them.

Two days later, on 19 August 1944, when the locomotive had been immobilised by attacking Spitfires, the gap between these two hostile communities had partially closed. Philippe Kohn decided to join an escape plan and defied his father's orders discouraging any friendship with Resistance workers. Only a few miles had been covered in those first two days but the occupants of the Last Wagon enjoyed a relatively comfortable journey compared to Jews despatched in previous overcrowded trains. Despite the sign 'Juden Terroristen' painted on the side of the truck, the Nazi guards had made only a cursory search before the train left Bobigny and had not seized generous supplies of food and clothing given by UGIF representatives intent on getting rid of all remaining stock. The deportees were lucky that Brünner had decided to return to Germany by car, leaving the train in charge of less assiduous SS NCOs and Oscar Reich, head of the camp's Milice Sémite.

Treatment was almost humane. The deportees were allowed to wash and to renew drinking water when the train was stopped by bombing. Repeated Allied attacks finally played into the escapers' hands. The artillery regiment's wagons were detached after the Spitfire raid and the train continued its journey with another requisitioned locomotive. In the original train, the deportees' wagon had been located behind the engine. In the new arrangement, the SS coaches were placed behind the locomotive and the deportees' truck literally became the Last Wagon.

Left unguarded by their careless escort, twenty-seven people escaped at one o'clock in the morning on 21 August 1944, after cutting their way through the truck's small barred window. Among the women were Paula Kauffman, Antoinette Kohn and the Princess Galitzine. Philippe Kohn disobeyed his father's orders to stay with the family and jumped clear of the wagon with his sister, not far from the northern city of Saint-Quentin.

Most of the other escapers were Resistance workers. Kapel, Pohoryles, Margulies, Appenzeller, Frydman and most of their companions safely crossed the German lines, arriving in Paris during the Liberation. The escapers had vainly tried to persuade Marcel Bloch-Dassault to join them but he stoically refused, saying he wanted to 'follow France's calvary to its bitter end'.

The figure of twenty-seven escapers was contained in the official SS report. Although eight remained untraced when an investigation was carried out more than thirty years later, it was presumed that they had all survived the war. Of the twenty-four other deportees in the Last Wagon, fifteen returned from concentration camps. Marcel Bloch survived because the Germans were sure that they would finally tempt him into joining their aircraft designers. Another survivor was the banker Armand Kohn, whose value as a hostage saved him from execution.

The Orthodox Jews, who had spent the journey praying, were gassed almost immediately. Marie-Rose Kohn, a pupil at the Paris Conservatoire, died with her grandmother. Staying together as a family had not saved the Kohns. To this day, Philippe Kohn, who later headed a hotel chain, has to live with the regret that he did not persuade his twelve-year-old brother, Georges-André, to jump to safety.

In 1979, when a French journalist, Jean-François Chaigneau, was researching a book called *Le Dernier Wagon,* Philippe Kohn finally heard of his little brother's cruel death. Georges-André survived for several months as a child labourer before being transferred to a camp at Neuengamme, near Hamburg. For the first time since leaving France, he was well fed and looked after along with nineteen other children aged from five to twelve under the care of two French doctors. There was another French child in the group, Jacqueline Morgenstern, a twelve-year-old Parisienne. Like Georges-André, her health and well-being were important because the children were being used by the camp's Nazi doctor, Kurt Heissmeyer, for experiments on tuberculosis. The children received regular injections of TB germs and experimental remedies. They were still alive and well when they were given their last injection on 20 April 1945, fifteen days before Germany surrendered.

That night, British infantry fought their way into the Hamburg suburbs. On 21 April they entered the medical laboratories at Neuengamme. The French doctors and the twenty children were dead. All of them, including Jacqueline Morgenstern and Georges André Kohn, had been hanged.

CHAPTER TWENTY-TWO

Retribution

OUTSIDE THE FORMER Drancy concentration camp, only a half-hour train ride from central Paris, there is an impressive concrete monument commemorating the internment of 'nearly 100,000 Jewish men, women and children' and recording that only 1518 survived. The figures are wildly inaccurate, but they provide an indication of bureaucratic and political indifference to the aftermath of deportation, the first stage of a process intended to bury the issue as quickly possible. No census was made of missing Jews and many families had to wait thirty years before private investigations by Jewish organisations traced their relatives' final journeys.

Most local authorities simply forgot that there had been deportation centres or blamed French-organised atrocities on Nazi barbarity. La Grande Rafle all but disappeared from public memory until a book was published in 1967. Apart from a plaque, again giving misleading statistics, near the demolished Vélodrome d'Hiver in Paris, it was not until 1992 that officialdom corrected the mistakes after consulting the astonishing census carried out by Serge Klarsfeld's association, Fils et Filles des Déportés de France, which named every deportee sent to Germany, ending with a count of 75,721 of whom about 2500 came back.

The inauguration of a monument on the site of the former bicycle stadium to commemorate the fiftieth anniversary of the 1942 round-ups preceded a rush of belated measures by President Jacques Chirac and his Prime Minister, Lionel Jospin, to seek a pardon from a tortured minority. But, by neglect and official obstruction, France had made its Jewish community suffer for more than half a century before trying to clear its conscience as the millennium ended. Nearly every year since the Vichy regime disappeared in September 1944, with the arrest of Philippe Pétain by the Germans, was marked by acts of official indifference in which blame has to be shared by every post-war president, including the first four heads of the Fifth Republic, Charles de Gaulle, Georges Pompidou, Valéry Giscard d'Estaing and, most of all, François Mitterrand.

History is unlikely to find any valid reason why these men, who had lived through the war as adults, extended the tragic consequences of persecution of thousands of broken families. A trail of negligence, deliberate evasion and bureaucratic cowardice can be traced back to the day the Maréchal was arrested at the Hotel du Parc on 20 August by an SS commando. Two weeks later, the last dregs of his authority disappeared when he was taken to Sigmaringen in Germany where 30,000 collaborators were given refuge until Germany surrendered in May 1945. In a long farewell address, he told the people that he had sacrificed himself for France and added: 'While it is true that de Gaulle has bravely raised France's sword, history will not forget that I patiently held the French people's shield.'

It was not a claim that impressed the provisional Government that succeeded the Vichy regime. De Gaulle's retribution had begun six months earlier in Algeria with the execution of Pierre Pucheu, Darlan's former Interior Minister, whose repressive legislation paved the way for mass deportations. Pucheu had taken refuge in North Africa in 1943 during the Vichyist anti-Semitic administration of General Geraud. When de Gaulle gained the ascendancy, France's new military saviour used Pucheu's trial and death sentence to destroy the myth of benevolent collaboration.

The treatment of Jews was barely touched on during Pucheu's trial and was also subordinated during 'L'Epuration' – the purge

– of the mainland Vichy administration and the punishment of collaborators. The first phase was uncontrolled vengeance by the Resistance during which 9673 collaborators were summarily executed. The second phase was a drawn-out official process in which nearly 7000 pro-Germans were sentenced to death although only 767 were executed. Another 146,000 people were accused of helping the Nazis of which about 40,000 were sent to prison.

Of the few revelations of cruelty to Jews, the two most important cases were more criminally than racially based. Hundreds had been robbed and tortured by an independent French Gestapo group, which operated from the rue Lauriston in Paris's 16th *arrondissement*. All were members of the criminal underworld to whom violence and theft were a way of life. Aryanisation laws, including the confiscation of property, played into their hands, as well as those of unscrupulous lawyers, Jewish Commission officials and art dealers who made fortunes from sequestered goods, some of which financed post-war political careers. None, though, acted from more sinister motives than a GP, Marcel Petiot, who promised to smuggle Jews out of the country and told them to come to his surgery with their most precious belongings. Soon after the Liberation, the remains of twenty-seven corpses were identified. They had been burned in his kitchen stove. The doctor was guillotined in 1946.

Pétain's own trial started two months after the war and was the first real occasion for a calm examination of the Jewish persecution. A special Parliamentary High Court treated the issue as little more than an aside and it was for high treason and aiding the enemy that the Maréchal was sentenced to death on 15 August. Three days later, he was reprieved by de Gaulle and transferred to the Ile d'Yeu where he died in 1954 at the age of ninety-five. The reprieve contributed to a persistent belief that Pétain had been playing a double game with the Nazis and had been unwittingly drawn into criminal actions only because of his growing senility.

Within weeks of Pétain's transfer to the Atlantic island, the ideal villain was put on trial. Pierre Laval had returned to France from Spain on 23 July in time to give evidence against Pétain. Three months later, he was shot by a firing squad a few hours after a failed suicide attempt. Five days earlier, the Milice chief, Joseph Darnand, was also executed.

The purge was intended to discredit the most shameful period in French history. Instead, it gave Pétainists the chance to re-establish themselves in positions of power. For many years after the Liberation, revenge on Vichy was represented as an episode worse than the Revolutionary Terror. Allegedly, a million people were arrested by the Resistance and 120,000 were said to have been executed without trial. Exhausted by five years of defeat, treachery and civil war, France lost its taste for vengeance. Most of the 11,000 civil servants dismissed or suspended for collaboration were given back their posts. Suspect behaviour, such as that of Maurice Papon in Bordeaux, was overlooked. Only a few of the most notorious killers or traitors were condemned to death including Lucien Déhan who was blamed for the murder of 406 Jews while working with Vichy's anti-Semitic Section d'Enquête de Contrôle in Bordeaux.

The surviving Jews who could talk about the deportations were too few in number to press for an investigation and, because France was on the winning side in 1945, none of her allies pressed for an explanation even when the issue was raised at the Nuremberg hearings. Inside the country, forgetfulness was increased by a hopeless lack of political coherence. De Gaulle resigned and withdrew from politics until his recall in 1958. Léon Blum, who might have raised the Jewish issue, was recalled as Prime Minister in 1945, but his personal attempt to establish the Socialists as parliamentary leaders lasted only six weeks.

The Fourth Republic proved as unmanageable as the Third Republic and none of the most influential Jewish politicians between 1945 and 1958, including Pierre Mendès France and

Jules Moch, had either the time or inclination to investigate the past and open up old wounds.

A consensus was impossible after the political left recreated the divisions of the pre-war years within months of de Gaulle's departure. The ideals of Resistance leaders collapsed in fratricidal quarrels, opening the way to a revival of the right. A destructive left-wing battle with the Communists ended in an electoral disaster in 1951 and Parliament was again controlled by right-wing MPs, many of whom had collaborated or voted full powers for Pétain. Both the President and the Prime Minister were chosen from ultra-conservative groups tainted by the Vichy years. Among the police, civil service and professions the same faces had reappeared, confirming a study by a Communist journalist, Pierre Hervé, as early as 1946. In a book called *La Libération trahie*, he named Government officials, employers, writers and entertainers who had served Pétain who were gradually filling their wartime posts.

Rehabilitation of the compromised right had been helped by fears that Communists would start a rebellion after the beginning of the Cold War in 1947. Detectives and secret servicemen who had spent the war penetrating Marxist movements used the same Vichy and Gestapo files that had proved so successful in rounding up guerrilla movements. No one demanded the destruction of Special Branch archives, which included the Jewish censuses that often provided clues to Communist sympathies.

Inevitably the return of the right contributed to official silence on the fate of missing Jews. The few hundred men and women who survived the concentration camps returned to a country indifferent to their suffering. In contrast, a hero's welcome was reserved for Resistance deportees. They were taken to the Hôtel Lutétia, one of the former German command centres, where a Resistance chief, Henri Frenay, was in charge of repatriation procedures. 'Neither I nor anyone who was there will forget the arrival of the first trainload of repatriated women,' he wrote in his recollections, *La Nuit Finira*.

'We will never forget these fleshless faces at the windows of each compartment; sometimes lifeless, sometimes full of frenetic joy. On the railway platform, we stood motionless, throats tightening, eyes full of tears as we made contact with the sinister reality of deportation.'

Jews were among the last to arrive. They were taken to the same hotel where relatives often waited in vain for weeks before it became clear that 97 per cent of racial deportees had died. Among the repatriated victims was Simone Veil, who quickly learnt that Vichy's anti-Semitism had left its legacy and that there was little hope of reparation. During her medical examination, she was treated with contempt by the French woman doctor, who called her a 'sale Juive'.

'If Jews returned from camps it was assumed that they had done something dishonourable to save their lives,' she said. 'For years, I have had to deny the most degrading accusations. It was common to suggest that Jewish women had served in brothels or that the men were informers or kapos.'

Sensing a persistent hostility, thousands of Jews, whether they had survived camps or lived out the war in France, aryanised their names or emigrated to Britain, Palestine or the US. They had been outcasts during the Vichy years and a Jewish identity was a complication in finding jobs and housing. Popular hostility was widespread. A 1946 opinion poll showed that 37 per cent of the French population still felt that Jews could never become loyal French citizens.

French administrators simply forgot the role the Paris police played in La Grande Rafle and rewarded the whole force with the honour of wearing a red shoulder strap for having taken to the streets in the Liberation. The Gendarmerie was treated with the same indulgence, even over its running of the Drancy concentration camp. As the press also quickly pushed the round-up of Jews into the background, the true conditions at Drancy remained sketchy until a 1991 investigation by Maurice Rajsfus, whose family's arrest at Vincennes was recalled at the beginning of this book. Haunted by the memories of his lost parents, he has written a dozen books on French complicity in the Holocaust including the only account of the transit camp in the Paris suburbs.

Evidence such as Georges Wellers's descriptions of the terrible condition of children arriving from French camps near Orleans in 1942 were confirmed by a search of long-forgotten Jewish archives such as those of the semi-clandestine Comité de la rue Amelot. They left no doubt that the moral poison of anti-Jewish laws percolated down from the remote Vichy bureaucracy to the lower levels of the uniformed guardians of the law. An anonymous former detainee told the rue Amelot committee in November 1941: 'Their mentality had been forged to see us as habitual criminals, thieves and rogues. They came down hard on us. They didn't stop kicking us if we didn't move quickly enough. They acted the same towards detainees decorated with the Croix-de-Guerre, Médaille Militaire and the Legion d'Honneur.'

The report was made only five months after the camp was opened when Vichy, which administered the Gendarmerie throughout the country, was proclaiming protection for Jewish war veterans. After Government propaganda was stepped up in preparation for La Grande Rafle, cruelty intensified. The violence, corruption and other criminal activities of the police, which continued even while they escorted trains to Germany, finally became public and it was decided to prosecute fifteen gendarmes in 1947.

Judges were told by an interned lawyer, Henri Blaustin, that the police's attitude from the first days was odious and that 'they were animated towards us with the same hate that the Nazis felt'. Other detainees filed into the witness box to give evidence of savagery towards children, of public beatings and summary punishments ranging from solitary confinement to immediate deportation. Gendarmes stole internees' rations, money and jewellery, ran the camp black market and charged exorbitant sums to smuggle letters in and out.

In comparing the French police's behaviour with the viciousness of the last days of Brünner's administration, witnesses described the gendarmerie captain, Marcellin Vieux, as 'an abominable brute', hitting detainees with a riding crop and ordering his men to use batons and revolvers to keep discipline. Two of his lieutenants, Paul Barral and Ange Pietri, were known as 'notorious anti-Semites'. The description was used in a BBC broadcast in 1943 when Captain Vieux and his two worst accomplices were warned that they would be executed after the war.

But the trial was a farce. Vieux, aided by insiders, jumped bail and was never punished. Five other gendarmes escaped judgement for various reasons and, like most of their colleagues, were reintegrated into the force. Barral received the heaviest sentence: two years in jail before being pardoned a year later.

Indulgence for the French camp guards contrasted with severity towards foreigners. The head of Brünner's Milice Sémite at Drancy, the Austrian Jewish refugee Oscar Reich, a former international footballer, was brought back from Vienna and executed.

The same disproportionate sentencing was reflected at all levels once the fury of the Liberation purges had subsided. Compromised French officials either received no punishment or were promoted while their SS negotiating partners, including Karl Oberg and Helmut Knochen, were jailed for life in 1954 and served seventeen years in prison. The two French Jewish Affairs Commissioners, Xavier Vallat and Darquier de Pellepoix, got off lightly. Although condemned to death in his absence, Darquier died in Spain forty years later – still preaching violent anti-Semitism. No attempt was made to extradite him. Vallat was equally unrepentant and justified Vichy's policies in press and newsreel interviews when released from jail in 1949. His arguments had been refreshed by daily meetings with another prisoner, Charles Maurras, who served seven years and helped

Vallat to write a book. Raphaël Alibert, who oversaw the first Statut des Juifs, took refuge in a monastery and was sentenced to death in his absence. His successor as Minister of Justice, Joseph Barthelémy, author of the second statute, had died a few days after the war ended.

Judgement on the established Jewish community's attitude during the persecution will probably remain an open question for ever. Many Jews from immigrant families remember with bitterness the unsympathetic reception they were given before the war and remain suspicious of the motives of the Union Générale des Israélites de France, UGIF, whose records were transferred to New York. The Vichy-created organisation was dominated by established families, some of whom were drawn into close co-operation with Pétain's policies. After the war, a jury of honour twice cleared UGIF officials of collaboration with the enemy but doubts remained over whether some organisers betrayed poor immigrant Jews to protect the French community.

If this did happen, the most important UGIF officials gained no advantage in the end. The Germans believed that the organisation encouraged passive resistance and took their revenge on leading members including the first President, Raymond-Raoul Lambert, who headed UGIF in the South after working inside a refugee welfare committee. He was sent to be gassed with his wife and four children in December 1943 after protesting to Pétain about Gestapo cruelty.

The Germans forced Jewish leaders to co-ordinate welfare and supplies in concentration camps so that Jews themselves would be blamed for poor hygiene and food. The union's vice-president, André Baur, responsible for the northern zone, was booed and jeered when he visited the Vélodrome d'Hiver during La Grande Rafle and later publicly reproached Brünner for brutality at Drancy. Baur, his wife and four children were sent to a death camp by another train on the same day as Lambert's departure.

Their sacrifice did little to remove hostility as UGIF was also responsible for raising special taxes from the Jewish community equivalent to 120 francs a month in the Free Zone and 320 francs in the North. The organisation became so unpopular among foreign Jews that FTP–MOI commandos attacked their offices in Lyons and Marseilles and destroyed their registers.

The main accusation against UGIF was a refusal to defy the Germans. The union was officially responsible for children whose parents had been sent to die. Just before the Liberation, Barbie used UGIF files in Lyons to arrest hundreds of boys and girls. Despite the raid, UGIF did not disperse those under its protection in Paris. On 30 July, Brünner forced his way into eleven hostels in the capital and its suburbs and seized 250 children. Most were forced into a train for Germany on 31 July, a month before Drancy was freed.

The murder of the two UGIF officials, Baur and Lambert, showed the enormous risks taken by leaders whose welfare work was essential to the survival of thousands of people. At the end of the war, 30,000 Jews in Paris depended on UGIF funds. Financial and material help continued to circulate despite a Nazi tactic of closing offices one by one and sending the most important officials to Auschwitz. The offices in the 8th *arrondissement* were entered in July 1943 and fifty staff were arrested. This did not stop replacements taking over the work, ignoring what amounted to a suspended death sentence.

In 1951, on the initiative of the Interior Minister, François Mitterrand, Parliament voted an amnesty for collaborators, a measure reinforced by another law in 1953 that brought a halt to most prosecutions. Within ten years, most war crimes were covered by a statute of limitations and a convention on Crimes against Humanity, with no prescription, was not approved until 1970. The legal hurdles appeared to remove the last hope of pursuing Vichy officials on the run, even those condemned to death in their absence. From the early fifties, police willingly dropped their inquiries as France entered into a period in which historians and journalists rewrote wartime history by insisting on a theme of France Résistante, where the majority had opposed the Nazi occupation.

This heroic version suited both the Gaullist and Communist movements whose credibility depended on their wartime anti-Nazi activities. The darker side of the Vichy years disappeared under a deluge of patriotic films and media coverage. Pétainists exploited the Maréchal's claim to being the national shield to step up the pace of their own rehabilitation. Facts and locations linked to racial murders slipped rapidly from memory. More than forty years later, Vénissieux, centre of such dramatic events in 1942, did not even mention the Jewish detention centre in its official history and even the town of Drancy made only a brief account of its notorious camp in its brochure while devoting pages to the sacrifice of its Communist working-class population.

German guilt was insisted on by commemoration of atrocities like the massacres at Oradour-sur-Glane, where 642 villagers were murdered by an SS tank division, and by the preservation as a national monument of the Natzweiler-Struthof concentration camp. Meanwhile, families who made pilgrimages to sites like Gurs in the Pyrenees, where thousands of Jews were interned, found little except an overgrown site where thick vegetation covered all but the surfaced paths between the long-demolished barrack blocks and a graveyard with 1100 tombs. At Rivesaltes, another Free Zone camp in the Languedoc, vandalised and roofless brick buildings stood on a desolate zone, forgotten by all except a few survivors.

Another camp in the south-west at Le Vernet, where Arthur Koestler experienced conditions worse than Dachau, lost its link with Jewish persecution over the years. After housing Republican Spanish, suspected enemy aliens, refugee Jews and collaborators, the camp near the Spanish border was reopened in 1961, to accommodate Algerian militia, known as Harkis, who fought for France in the independence war, and was still in use forty years later.

A general attempt to forget wartime treachery soon became official policy leading to deliberate and voluntary censorship by historians and Government. The most striking action was taken against a 1954 documentary on the Holocaust, *Nuit et Brouillard*, by the director, Alain Resnais. He was forced to cut a scene in which the képi of a French gendarme was visible among German troops during the loading of a deportation train. The message was quickly understood by all sections of the media, leaving the only serious attempt to maintain records and collect memoirs to an understaffed Centre de Documentation Juive Contemporaine in Paris's Marais district. Hardly surprisingly, after years of near-silence, the French were taken aback in 1971 by a film documentary, *Le Chagrin et la Pitié*, which showed both the level of collaboration and the lack of true Resistance in the Vichy-controlled city of Clermont-Ferrand. Two years later they were even more astonished when a young American historian, Robert O. Paxton, wrote a stark account of high-level wartime treachery in *La France de Vichy*, which destroyed the illusion of unwilling collaboration.

Reluctance to face up to this period had, by then, served institutions who had no intention of giving in either to remorse or reparation. French museums were gorged with paintings stolen by the Germans or confiscated by Vichy, and never returned to their Jewish owners. The judiciary, where only one judge had defied orders to take an oath of fidelity to Pétain, made no distinction between collaborators and Resistance workers. Its official record of war dead listed both without reference to their loyalty. As for the civil service, functionaries who had served Vichy, like Papon, climbed steadily up the promotion ladder where they could obstruct independent research into official archives.

The most disturbing case involved the Catholic Church, which felt obliged to make a public apology to Jews only in the dying years of the twentieth century. Not only did Church leaders refuse to acknowledge their collaboration with Pétain, but they protected suspects after 1945, Alibert among them, helping them to leave the country, giving them refuge until the amnesty took effect and even lobbying for pardons.

As a secretive institution, with friends throughout the bureaucracy, the post-war activities of the Catholic Church in favour of collaborators might have never become public without the arrest in May 1989 of Paul Touvier in a monastery in Nice. As the Lyons Milice leader, his name had been at the centre of the Klaus Barbie trial two years before. The former SS officer had told prosecutors of the invaluable help given by Touvier's Milice unit, which operated its own torture chambers and Jewish extermination squads. On the run since 1944, Touvier had twice been sentenced to death in his absence and was rumoured to be under the protection of priests.

After Barbie was jailed for life, pressure to try a Vichy militiaman became irresistible, although Touvier was considered a minor figure in comparison to executives like René Bousquet, Jean Leguay and Maurice Papon. A scapegoat was needed and Touvier fitted the role. French police reluctance to arrest him ended when an investigative newspaper, *Le Canard Enchaîné*, revealed that he was living in a Nice monastery under the protection of Les Chevaliers de Nôtre Dame, a Catholic order with links to Vichy. The reluctant arrest confirmed suspicions of a conspiracy stretching back forty-five years.

During that time, when officials said Touvier was impossible to track down, he had given press interviews on three occasions at locations which were passed on to detectives. In talks to the press, he recalled that he was taken into custody in 1944 and, despite accusations of racial murders, was set free without being judged. He met Cardinal Gerlier, the Archbishop of Lyons, and was assured that he would be kept in safety till the end of his life, allegedly because he had spared Jews awaiting execution although there was a persistent view that he knew too much about the illegal activities of local dignitaries to be handed over for trial. Although Touvier was condemned to death three times in his absence for war crimes, the French secret service discreetly employed him to keep track of Communists by exploiting Milice and Gestapo files.

In 1971, a high-level Catholic delegation convinced President Georges Pompidou that Touvier had repented and was devoutly religious. He received a secret pardon but one of the first actions of the 1981 Socialist Government was to overturn the presidential act of mercy and issue an arrest warrant that took another eight years to put into effect. Delays before he was put on trial at the age of seventy-seven were explained by the difficulty of framing accusations covered by Crimes against Humanity which contain a specific vocation of genocide.

The hearing, in a specially equipped court in Versailles, which ended in March 1994, amounted more to a judgement of the Catholic Church than of the supposedly repentant Touvier. After he received a life sentence, historians were given limited access to confidential Church files of the wartime years in Lyons, which confirmed Gerlier's obedience to Pétain. An inquiry commission produced only a complacent condemnation of the Church's attitude but their report unlocked a long-closed door. Irresistible pressure grew for a general opening of records, including police archives, which was finally accorded by the Socialist Prime Minister, Lionel Jospin, in 1998.

As for Touvier, it was evident that he was a pathetic figure, hardly worth the fuss that surrounded the first show trial of a Vichy official for Crimes against Humanity. He was neither an Eichmann nor a Brünner, just a small-time uniformed psychopathic militia intelligence officer and crook, exploited by Barbie because of his visceral anti-Semitism and his greed. Had Touvier been tried straight after the war, he would have been quickly executed and quickly forgotten. Instead he was raised to a unique place in French history, a merit undeserved by an indoctrinated former railway despatch clerk.

Impressed by the authority of his right-wing Catholic father, a follower of Charles Maurras, Paul Touvier first studied to be a priest before being called up in 1939. After demobilisation in 1940, he joined Pétain's Service d'Ordre Légionnaire (SOL) which became the Milice in 1943. Although he had been involved in the murder of Jews, including the assassination of Victor Basch, aged eighty, and his wife, Hélène (Basch, a former chairman of the League of Human Rights, had campaigned for Dreyfus), some of his acts were covered by a double-jeopardy rule because they formed part of earlier war crimes' sentences in his absence.

The prosecution's search for conformity with the Nuremberg ruling on what consituted a crime against humanity eventually restricted charges to the execution of seven Jewish hostages at Rilleux-sur-Pape, near Lyons, in August 1944. His defence was based on the often-used Vichy excuse that if he had not carried out the murders, the Nazis would have intervened and killed more Jews. Two years later at the age of seventy-nine he died in solitary confinement of cancer, a disease evident as he sat behind a bullet-proof screen at Versailles assizes looking blankly at the nine-member jury as if he had already lost the will to live.

The Touvier trial had at last shown that Vichy officials were not untouchable despite the widespread suspicion that President Mitterrand was ready to do everything in his power to stop public examination of their guilt. The militiaman· had slipped through the net of obstruction because his trial had taken place during a brief period of Gaullist Government but fundamental questions remained unanswered. The evil comportment of an armed, ill-educated militiaman, with limited authority, had thrown only an oblique light on the excessive obedience to Vichy that led rational and cultured functionaries to condemn thousands to their deaths through written orders issued after civilised meetings.

Evidence heard at the Touvier hearing of the zeal and efficiency of men like Bousquet and Papon made it impossible for them to be exempted from punishment just because they had never operated a gas chamber like Kramer at Struthof or tortured children as Barbie did at the Hôtel Terminus. Serge Klarsfeld and other lawyers who had been pressing for public prosecutions without success since 1979 had an even more convincing reason to believe that the law could at last be persuaded to take their side.

In autumn 1989, a Paris tribunal ruled that Jean Leguay, the senior Vichy police representative in the northern zone, was guilty of Crimes against Humanity. In an historic decision, the judges said that Leguay, a central figure in La Grande Rafle, had participated in 'Crimes against Humanity committed in July, August and September 1942 . . . consisting of illegal arrests, arbitrary sequestration, barbaric acts and the kidnapping and bad treatment of children.' This long-awaited recognition of active complicity by the Vichy administration in the Holocaust had one serious drawback. Leguay had died in July 1989 before a date for a hearing could be fixed. Ten years of legal proceedings that included appeals and presidential disapproval had frustrated a public trial even though Leguay had been charged in 1979, five years before Barbie was brought back from Bolivia.

To the independent legal team led by Klarsfeld, the judgement remained a highly significant step forward. The documents and evidence used against Leguay were the same as those assembled to prosecute René Bousquet. It seemed only a matter of time before the organiser of La Grande Rafle and the arrests in the Free Zone would appear before the assizes, even when Klarsfeld's view that obstruction came from the Elysée Palace was confirmed. Presidential aides let it be known that the President saw such hearings as a 'threat to civil peace', a formula close to the Vichy idea that order was more important than justice.

As it turned out, the real threat to civil peace was the high-level cover-up itself. On 8 June 1993, Didier Christian, a middle-aged unpublished writer, rang the door bell of Bousquet's flat in Paris's Avenue Raphaël. Despite innumerable death threats and demonstrations outside his home by militant Jews, Bousquet opened the door himself and was hit by four bullets from a revolver. Before police could arrest him, Didier, who had once tried to kill Barbie, gave a televised press conference, denying any suggestion of a conspiracy. Satisfied that it was a gesture by an unbalanced lone avenger, a court punished the killing with a ten-year jail sentence.

Didier's bullets did more than kill the former chief of police, already condemned by lung cancer. A long, often embarrassed silence over an association between Bousquet and François Mitterrand, President of the Republic, finally broke into public scandal.

CHAPTER TWENTY-THREE

A Presidential Scandal

On 28 October 1978, the weekly magazine *L'Express* published an interview with Darquier de Pellepoix, the second Commissioner-General for Jewish Affairs, who had been hiding in a village in Andalusia since fleeing France at the end of the war. Bedridden, the old man had lost none of his hate for Jews or his attachment to Nazi ideology. The interview caused a shock of revulsion in France, relaunching moves to bring Bousquet to justice. 'Only lice were gassed at Auschwitz,' Darquier said. Then, in an explosion of hatred against the Vichy police chief, he added: 'La Grande Rafle – it was Bousquet who organised it from A to Z. He did everything.'

For Klarsfeld's team of investigators, the interview was perfectly timed. Most of their recent efforts had concentrated on prosecuting three German officers involved in the anti-Semitic persecution in France, Herbert Hagen, Kurt Lischka and Ernst Heinrichsohn. In 1980, they were jailed in Cologne for up to ten years. The shock of Darquier's words, and the fact that he had lived untroubled in Spain despite a death sentence in his absence, mobilised public opinion, provoking what became known as L'Affaire Bousquet.

Although a detailed investigation into the 1942 Paris round-up had been published in 1967, with a preface by the Jewish writer Joseph Kessel, the revelations were quickly obscured by the student rebellion in May '68 and de Gaulle's resignation a year later. Bousquet had been named in the book as the main figure in

La Grande Rafle but the significance was ignored or missed by business colleagues and politicians who had helped him build a post-war career as a banker and company director. Superficially, the rehabilitation seemed justified despite Bousquet's four years in custody after the war.

A specially convened Parliamentary High Court acquitted him in 1949 of helping the Germans, convicting him only of 'unworthy behaviour' after a three-day hearing. A token sentence of five years' national disgrace was immediately annulled on the grounds that he had given secret information to the Allies. Details of the twenty-eight judicial interrogations he underwent were then locked away in confidential archives.

Bousquet's rapid return to respectability and influence was managed by a network of pre-war Radical Party friends and associates from the Vichy days. Within weeks of his acquittal, Bousquet was appointed technical adviser to the Banque de l'Indochine and quickly became secretary-general, travelling widely to administer the bank's interest in colonial territories. After de Gaulle's return to power in 1958, he unsuccessfully ran as an anti-Gaullist parliamentary candidate in the Marne before concentrating his political activities on behind-the-scenes financing of anti-Gaullist movements. Bousquet's appointment as an administrator of *La Dépêche du Midi* in Toulouse provided him with another platform in his unchallenged acceptance as a respectable member of the business establishment.

In 1968, Bousquet's entry in the French *Who's Who* noted that he was a board member of the Banque de l'Indochine and the UTA private airline, but reference to his wartime past cited only 'special service for the Interior Ministry', while his detention in Germany was described as 'on detachment'. Once the truth was out after the Pellepoix interview, his business career crumbled. On the airline board, he had sat next to Antoine Veil, Simone Veil's husband, who was the first to turn his back on Bousquet and demand his resignation. Within days, the only post left to him was an association with the Baccarat crystal firm run by Pierre Laval's son-in-law, René de Chambrun. The job was a reward for devotion to the executed Prime Minister during his trial, even writing the notes for his defence.

In the wake of the *L'Express* interview, accounts of the 1949 Bousquet trial resurfaced. Little interest had been taken in the Jewish issue during a hearing which revolved mainly around his attitude towards the Resistance. The police role in the administration of the Jewish Statute merited only five lines in the national newspaper *Le Monde* which reported: 'Referring to the Jewish question, René Bousquet defended himself by saying he had tried with all his strength to limit action by the Commissioner-General, Darquier de Pellepoix, while appearing to support it.'

The former police chief – whom the Vichy Justice Minister, Joseph Barthélémy, described as an ambitious, handsome and elegant arriviste who took joy in boasting about arrests – maintained a reputation for cool arrogance in the dock. Confronted by a fifteen-member jury of MPs, Bousquet 'sure of himself and impeccably dressed', according to one newspaper, poured scorn on accusations of pursuing Jews. 'I am supposed to have served the policy of racial persecution,' he said. 'Eh, bien, messieurs, if I supported this policy, it was like a hanged man supports the rope and if we can talk about collaboration in this area, it would be better to think of collaboration between a lightning conductor and the lightning.'

His claims were backed from the witness box by Jean Leguay, who was never prosecuted, and no questions were asked by the judge or jury. The state prosecutor provided his own explanation for not pursuing Bousquet for the Jewish murders by saying that Laval and the former police chief 'could not prevent the deportation of foreigners from the southern zone because of the German threat to arrest all French Jews in the Paris region; but Bousquet ensured that it was done only by French police'.

Because Bousquet had never been judged for racial war crimes, a rereading of the 1949 evidence after the 1978 *L'Express* interview opened the way to charges of Crimes against Humanity but another thirteen years went by before the judicial system started making arrangements for a trial. During that period he was confident of high-level protection, taunting Klarsfeld's private prosecution team while living in comfortable retirement in the Avenue Raphaël in Paris's 16th *arrondissement*. The former Vichy police chief, which a collaborationist paper once described as a 'cut price Don Juan', was the Jewish lawyer's near neighbour. As chances of a court case diminished through high-level obstruction, Bousquet could hardly retain a triumphant smile when he crossed Klarsfeld in the street.

The assassination occurred only days before Bousquet was due to be summoned to the Palais de Justice in the first stage of an assize court trial, but attempts to prove a conspiracy theory to cover up high-level interference in the judicial procedure have never been proved. His death, though, left only one final thin chance of trying an important Vichy figure, Maurice Papon, a man in robust health despite his advanced age. Since being forced to resign as a Gaullist minister in 1981 (the consequences contributed to President Giscard's defeat), he had led the life of an untroubled pensioner, surrounded by his family and grandchildren in the country mansion where he was born near Paris. He was so confident of never being tried that he successfully sued a magazine in 1990 which accused him of deporting Jews from Bordeaux. His certainty that death would overtake him before justice could be done only fed suspicion of a much greater scandal: was François Mitterrand, President of the Republic since 1981, a hypocritical accomplice in sabotaging Jewish-led prosecutions?

No President had been so overt in showing friendship to the Jewish community. He was so close to the Nobel prizewinner Elie Wiesel that the two men wrote a book together. At his inauguration ceremony in 1981, Mitterrand had made a point of embracing Mendès France and telling him that the left owed its victory to the Fourth Republic Prime Minister and war hero. Jacques Attali, a Sephardi from North Africa, became the President's most intimate political adviser, and the first minister to receive presidential favour was Robert Badinter, son of a murdered Russian immigrant, who was given the honour of seeing the abolition of capital punishment through Parliament. In 1984, the President chose Laurent Fabius, the son of an established Jewish family, as the youngest Prime Minister of the century, indicating that he had the character to succeed him at the Elysée.

To these men and the Jewish community as a whole it was unbelievable that the President could be playing a double game by preventing the trial of men at the centre of mass deportation and death. Eventually, after a number of inexplicable judicial delays, Klarsfeld openly accused Mitterrand of engineering obstacles, alluding to the President's own political rise sponsored by an inner circle of former Vichy administrators. In 1992, when Mitterrand inaugurated a specially commissioned monument on the site of the Vélodrome d'Hiver, the President was whistled and jeered by a hostile crowd because he turned down a request from Jewish activists to condemn Vichy. He justified his refusal by saying that the French Republic could not be held responsible for the actions of Pétain's French state.

'Don't ask for any action by the Republic, it has done what it should do,' he added, brushing aside the fact that the same officials who had served the Third Republic worked for Vichy and then for the two post-war republics. A denial of a continuity in the responsibility of successive regimes was not taken into account when, only four months after the fiftieth anniversary of La Grande Rafle, Mitterrand sent a wreath to Pétain's tomb on the Ile d'Yeu to mark the 1918 Armistice. In the ensuing row, the Elysée claimed that honouring the tomb of First World War leaders was a tradition which previous presidents had respected.

This proved untrue and it was discovered that Mitterrand had sent flowers every year since 1984. The gesture contributed to a rapid disillusionment among the Jewish community during the President's last months at the Elysée palace.

By the time he died in January 1996, two years after completing fourteen years in office, Mitterrand's Jewish friends, including Wiesel, Attali and Fabius, had publicly marked their distance, shocked by Mitterrand's belated admission of a fifty-year association with Bousquet – 'a man of action, passionately interested in politics and very sympathetic'. Reaction to such praise eventually led Mitterrand to turn on what he called the 'Jewish lobby' just before he retired in 1995, already dying of prostate cancer.

Like much of France's wartime history, the President's past had disappeared from public memory during a turbulent half-century. Even the Communists, who had revealed all the details of Mitterrand's Vichy years during violent political campaigns in 1946, buried the issue when he became the left's most credible leader from the mid-sixties onwards. Eventually, when details resurfaced in the mid-90s they appeared like revelations, feeding conspiracy theories that suggested he had never broken away from the ultra-conservative background that drove his early post-war political career.

As a child of a south-western provincial Catholic family, Mitterrand was predestined to sympathise with militant right-wing movements. The beginnings of his long political journey were chronicled in detail by Pierre Péan in *Une Jeunesse Française*, in which the President was persuaded to reveal facts he had covered up during interviews with leading political commentators during his presidential campaigns.

While studying law in Paris in the thirties, Mitterrand joined an anti-republican movement as a Volontaire Nationale in Colonel de la Rocque's nationalistic Croix-de-Feu, an association often described as Fascist-like at the time and which provided much of Pétain's wartime support from its ranks of First War veterans.

The future President also developed a friendship with the anti-Semitic Eugene Schueller, financier of the Fascist and violent Cagoulard movement. They shared a fascination for the monarchy and went to visit the French pretender, the Comte de Paris, exiled in Belgium. Schueller and Mitterrand, along with several other mutual friends from the thirties, would become associates after the war when the former headed the L'Oréal cosmetics business. Mitterrand was given the editorship of the firm's popular women's magazine *La Beauté*, where he also ran the agony aunt column.

In 1941, Mitterrand had escaped from a prisoner-of-war camp and was given a junior post in the documentation centre of Vallat's Légion Française des Combattants where he was reunited with friends from the Croix-de-Feu movement. His later work for repatriated prisoners of war earned him one of only 2500 Francisque medals given by Philippe Pétain personally for loyal service.

An article in an Pétainist anti-Semitic magazine, *France*, in which he blamed the country's defeat on 150 years of errors since the Revolution and a photograph of him talking to the wartime Head of State, resurfaced in the last year of his presidency when rows over the protection of Vichy officials were at their height. He claimed that the medal and his attachment to Vichy philosophy were covers for Resistance activity.

Mitterrand's liking for secrecy had been evident from 1943 when he ran his own anti-German intelligence network among prisoners of war while opposing General de Gaulle's Free French. A lifelong antipathy developed which helped Mitterrand in the immediate post-war period when his political career was sponsored by Vichy sympathisers combating both Gaullism and Communism.

Personal links with Bousquet only became apparent after the

police chief's murder when photographs showed that nearly all the personal staff surrounding Mitterrand when he was Fourth Republic Interior Minister in 1949 were wartime familiars of the Vichy police chief and had served in his entourage during the war. The same officials remained central and recognisable figures throughout Mitterrand's Fourth Republic career when he held eleven different ministries. Several were close to him during four presidential campaigns.

As the decline in Jewish sympathy for Mitterrand set in during his last months, evidence accumulated of links with Bousquet going back to 1942, although their difference in bureaucratic rank ruled out friendship at the time. Contacts were more open from 1949, three years after Mitterrand was nominated as a militant anti-Communist parliamentary candidate for the Nièvre, a central département, which became his political fief for the next half-century. The move had been prepared for him by Edmond Barrachin of the Parti Republican de la Liberté, political heir to the Croix-de-Feu movement, and sponsorship was provided by a network of aristocratic and Catholic backers, some of whom had been compromised during the war.

In the years that followed, Bousquet's longest-standing friend, Yves Cazaux, was appointed préfet or governor of the département, a crucial position during elections, while Mitterrand took as his chief regional political aide Pierre Saury, who had served with Bousquet as a Renseignements Généraux officer in the Marne before being transferred to Paris just before La Grande Rafle.

Under suspicion at the Liberation, Saury found a job with the occupying forces in Germany and eventually became Mitterrand's parliamentary nominated successor while managing a network of supporters in la Nièvre and representing Mitterrand on the board of the influential local newspaper, *Le Journal du Centre*. Even after Mitterrand became the left's most credible leader, Saury was chiefly responsible for maintaining exchanges between Mitterrand and Bousquet.

The relationship had been cemented by mutual debts. On the second day of Bousquet's 1949 trial, Mitterrand had persuaded the Cabinet to introduce an amnesty for all except capital offences under Vichy. In 1959, Bousquet was officially nominated by Mitterrand's own political party as an anti-Gaullist parliamentary candidate in the Marne, where he gathered only 9 per cent of the votes. From then on, he concentrated on the role of a political broker.

After Schueller and former Croix-de-Feu supporters had helped Mitterrand's early political campaigns, the rising politician was among many right-wing candidates to draw on funds from Bousquet's bank, which supported several anti-Gaullist movements. In 1965, Toulouse's *La Dépêche du Midi*, where editorial policy was in Bousquet's control, was the only newspaper to support Mitterrand's anti-de Gaulle presidential campaign, which gave him the national credibility he needed for future triumphs as leader of the left. The paper, which had historical links with Vichy, printed all the candidate's brochures and posters for nothing, before rallying the extreme right to support what was implicitly a left-wing campaign.

Bousquet arranged for a full-page petition to be signed by prominent Pétainists, including Jacques Isorni, the Maréchal's counsel in 1945, and Georges Blond, who wrote for *Je suis Partout*. Mitterrand was credited with supporting promises proposed by an extreme right-wing candidate, Jean-Louis Tixier-Vignancourt, an active anti-Semite propagandist at Vichy, whose followers included Jean-Marie Le Pen, future founder of the racist National Front.

Despite his description of the Vichy police chief as 'sympathetic', Mitterrand's later denials that Bousquet was a close friend were probably true; they were more like business and political associates whose only way of maintaining influence was to be surrounded by a caste of like-minded activists. Immediately after the war, Vichy's bureaucrats were often treated like pariahs, forcing them to gather in a loose, reciprocal self-help society. But Mitterrand's claims that he had rarely met Bousquet outside official meetings were contradicted by a number of witnesses. On at least two occasions, Bousquet and Mitterrand were the only leading personalities in a tiny group of former Vichyists who attended the funerals of mutual friends. Bousquet was also photographed by chance at an informal luncheon with Mitterrand at his country home during the 1974 presidential campaign. Even after Mitterrand's presidential win in 1981, Bousquet was seen at the Elysée several times, in the words of one confidant, 'talking politics'.

François de Grossouvre, the President's secret service adviser, said that Bousquet was far too proud to ask for favours such as exemption from prosecution, but if Mitterrand had made a promise to protect the Vichy police chief sometime in the past, he would have honoured it. Loyalty brought its rewards. Before the 1981 election, Bousquet helped to arrange a secret meeting between Mitterrand and the editors of all France's extremist and Pétainist publications. Among promises in exchange for their support was a pledge to pardon the four generals who had led an uprising in Algeria against de Gaulle in 1961. Despite left-wing protest, the measure was passed soon after Mitterrand entered the presidential palace.

The President also fulfilled a pledge to remove broadcasting censorship from the National Front, allowing Le Pen to take part in influential television political debates that contributed to a ten-fold increase in the racist movement's vote and brought it close to partnership with a Gaullist-led Government in the mid-nineties.

The late President still had many defenders ready to argue that he had acted only from loyalty towards friends and in the interests of political stability. In his favour, they pointed out that he was the first Head of State to attend a ceremony for the Vélodrome victims and that the 16 July day of national mourning was instituted during his period in office. He had also admitted before a visit to Israel in December 1992 that the 'probleme sensible' de Vichy needed to be re-examined.

'At that time, many people were not aware of an event like the *Vél d'Hiv*,' he said. 'Today the part taken by the administration of Pétain's State seems particularly heavy.'

This partial recognition of Pétain's responsibility did not satisfy Jewish community leaders. The phrase 'seems particularly heavy' was badly received and after long hesitation, Mitterrand finally conceded that France had taken part in 'one of the most abominable crimes in history'.

When he gave in to repeated demands and decided to institute 16 July as a national day of commemoration, the move was seen as electoral as it was decided just before the 1993 general elections. Other matters, such as the trial of Vichy civil servants and the wreath laid on Pétain's tomb, were left hanging in the air. The President's failure to face up to history and his own past remains the best example of France's reticence and confusion over Philippe Pétain's crimes. No one was better qualified to judge the regime or had better access to official evidence than this former Vichy representative who became a Resistance leader, lawyer, writer, and politician of the greatest influence.

This multiple career did not prevent him from claiming that he was unaware of the numerous books and media programmes which had left no doubt about Vichy's complicity in the Holocaust. Sadly, there was no shortage of functionaries and judges to use the President's examples to obstruct the prosecution of war criminals. The most astonishing example was given in the run up to the Touvier trial.

In April 1992 the three judges of the Chambre d'accusations ruled that the Milice officer could not be tried for Crimes against Humanity because Vichy was not an anti-Semite state.

'It appears that the crime was not committed in the execution of a concerted plan accomplished in the name of a state practising ideological political hegemony to bring about the extermination of civilian populations or any other inhuman act or persecution for political, racial or religious motives' – a judgement that ignored the Jewish statutes, more than 1700 anti-Semitic laws, sequestration of property and the mass deportations that followed.

Faced with a torrent of criticism, twelve judges of the Cour de cassation, changed the decision eight months later through another ambiguous ruling. Touvier's trial was considered just, not because of Vichy's policies, but because he had collaborated with the Nazis' genocide programme.

Circumstantial proof of the effectiveness of Mitterrand's commitment to his Pétainist friends, and his determination to obstruct reparation for Vichy's anti-Semitic legislation, emerged immediately after he finished his second seven-year presidential mandate in May 1995. On 16 July that year, the official newly instituted day of mourning for murdered Jews, his successor, Jacques Chirac, spoke at the Jewish memorial in front of the demolished Vélodrome d'Hiver and declared Vichy a criminal regime.

> On this day [in 1942], France, the country of light and the rights of man, land of welcome and refuge, carried out an irreparable act. Abandoning its word, it delivered its protected people to their torturers.
>
> These dark hours have sullied our history for ever and are an insult to our past and our traditions. Yes, the criminal madness of the occupying force was seconded by the French people and the French State. We must recognise the faults of the past and the faults committed by the State.

In a national awakening of conscience that followed, the Catholic Church made a public apology at an ecumenical service at Drancy in 1997. A declaration was read out by the Bishop of Saint-Denis, Olivier de Berranger, in front of a cattle wagon representing the last form of transport for thousands of Jewish families. After a half-century of dissimulation, the Church admitted that it had remained silent 'in the face of violations against human rights and left the way open to a lethal process'.

> This failure by the French Church in its responsibility towards the Jewish people is part of our history. We confess our sins and we implore God's pardon and we ask the Jewish people to listen to this word of repentance.
>
> In their majority, spiritual authorities, trapped by loyalty and docility which went far beyond traditional obedience towards the established power, remained enclosed in an attitude of conformity, caution and abstention. This act of memory includes the need for greater vigilance in favour of the rights of mankind both today and in the future.

Simone Veil, who was in the crowd, said she felt as if 'a great weight had been lifted from me', fifty-one years after she had been sent to Auschwitz.

More practical measures were taken when a left-wing Government, led by a Protestant Prime Minister, Lionel Jospin, was elected in 1997. Historians were given permission to examine all archives, including closed police records, and a commission completed three years' work by drawing up the first itemised list of property confiscated by Vichy. In 2000, compensation was at last authorised for Holocaust survivors and relatives of murdered deportees. The building of a memorial listing all the Jewish dead was approved for central Paris along with the establishment of a permanent study centre to house the notorious Jewish census. Millions of francs' worth of unclaimed money confiscated during the war was allocated to permanent research work.

Some progress was already evident. The house at Izieu where Barbie arrested the forty-four children had been turned into a permanent museum and Paris had created a Place Léon Blum around a bronze statue in one of the busiest parts of the city. The army made its contribution by inaugurating a plaque in memory of Alfred Dreyfus at the entrance of the Ecole de Guerre where he was wrongly disgraced. The introduction of compulsory teaching on the Holocaust and French participation in racial crimes concluded the rapid change in France's perception of the Vichy years as the new millennium dawned, but it was not achieved without one painful last judicial action: the judgement of Maurice Papon.

With Mitterrand out of office, reluctant judges had little hesitation in formally charging Papon with Crimes against Humanity, overruling de Gaulle's own patronage of the former bureaucrat as well as emotional appeals that it was inhumane to put a man of eighty-seven on trial for actions committed when he was a young official. The resulting show trial at Bordeaux was chaotic, bringing out all the contradictions and ambiguity of France's relationship to its troubled past that helped to explain why it had taken so long to examine the guilt in public.

Papon's life story was not unlike that of Bousquet and Mitterrand. Brought up with memories of Pétain's own glory in the First World War, his middle-class Catholic background – his father was a notaire and industrialist – prepared Papon for the civil service after graduating with political science and literary degrees. His career sponsors, like those of Bousquet, were Radicals, the most adaptable political movement that later provided much of Vichy's administration. After pre-war service with various Government departments, Papon was attached to the Interior Ministry at Vichy and transferred to occupied Bordeaux in April 1942, where his duties included running the Jewish Affairs section.

An assiduous bureaucrat with the title of Secretary-General for the Gironde Département, he was in office during the deportation of 1690 Jews – three-quarters of the community – and left behind a pile of signed documents ordering arrests and transfers to Drancy. In 1944, he began helping the Resistance, a precaution which convinced de Gaulle that he was trustworthy after the war.

After postings in the North African colonies, Papon became de Gaulle's police chief in Paris in 1958, and for seven years was at the centre of repressive machinery, notably during the Algerian war of independence.

At the Bordeaux hearing, the nine-member jury was told that he had ordered police action against a peaceful Algerian march in October 1961 in which as many as 200 people were drowned or fatally beaten, although the official version counted only three deaths. After being awarded the Légion d'Honneur for his repressive actions, he was elected a Gaullist MP in 1968.

His distinguished bureaucratic and political careers appeared to be heading for peaceful retirement when he was chosen as Budget Minister by Valéry Giscard d'Estaing in 1978. During the 1981 presidential elections, his reputation crashed and he was forced to resign. Revelations by Jewish survivors in Bordeaux linked him to the round-ups and murders and opened the way to private prosecution by surviving families. During a sixteen-year-long rearguard action to avoid a court appearance for complicity in Crimes against Humanity, Papon presented himself as a modern Dreyfus and, when finally cornered, he associated himself with Jesus Christ as 'a victim of the Jews'.

The six-month Bordeaux trial that ended in February 1998 after several interruptions covered every facet of the long-running controversy over France's responsibility in the Holocaust. Historians were called in to relate the evolution of Vichy or to defend its record. Resistance workers either supported or condemned Papon. Few judicial traditions were respected. Most of the witnesses took part in public meetings outside the court and in radio and television interviews before giving evidence. Lawyers on both sides held running press conferences to refute or confirm testimony or harangue the presiding judge.

The team of Jewish lawyers representing survivors' families, including Arno Klarsfeld, Serge's son, could not agree on Papon's personal level of guilt. Rows continued in public over the amount of freedom of action at Papon's disposal, reviving the fundamental Pétainist claim that if he had disobeyed the Nazis the consequences would have been worse for the Jews.

There were accusations that the court had more sympathy for Papon than his victims when he was treated with greater humanity than Barbie. Having complained that he could not support prison conditions because of heart trouble, Papon was allowed to live freely, attending the case only when he felt necessary. The Vichy official also gained sympathy when his wife died during the case but lost as much by his cold unrepentance when he frequently interrupted his defence counsel to claim that he had 'done my duty at the peril of my life'.

His dry, military bearing added to the shock of an admission that he knew that deported Jews faced 'a cruel fate' and 'probable death', but he compared the situation with 'the unhappy side of war such as food and fuel rationing'.

The judgement, based on the conviction that Papon was an accomplice in the deportation and deaths of 1484 Jews despatched in ten trains, included the damning phrase that 'from the first operations against Jews [in July 1942] Papon came to the conviction that their arrest, detention and deportation led them inescapably to their deaths' – a summing-up implicitly aimed at Pétain's entire regime. The conclusion had to be drawn that if a middle-level executive, far removed from the seat of power in Vichy, knew that death awaited deportees, it would have been impossible for Pétain to have remained ignorant.

Perhaps because the court felt it impossible to hand down a life sentence to a medium-ranking functionary when so many more important figures had gone free, the jury settled for a ten-year jail term and allowed the defendant to go home while awaiting an appeal. Certain that high-level protection would come to his aid, Papon left the assizes believing that the appeal hearing would never take place and, even if it did, he would be acquitted.

Instead, in October 1999 he was summoned to Bordeaux after

being told that he would be held in prison like a common criminal during the appeal hearing. Before he could be arrested, he took refuge in Switzerland while rumours circulated that he had been hidden by a powerful network of pro-Nazis, like those who had arranged a 'rat run' for war criminals at the Liberation. His rapid arrest in Switzerland and his incarceration in La Santé prison in Paris to serve a ten-year sentence at the age of eighty-nine provided one of the most convincing proofs that the Vichy era had at last been officially discredited.

As it turned out, there were no powerful friends, no rat run and in trying to escape punishment Papon had given additional support to the simplest explanation of the spineless collaboration of the French civil service in the murder of thousands of defenceless families. In his case, considerations of doctrine and loyalty to Pétain were far outweighed by moral cowardice on an inhuman scale.

The eventual collapse of a quasi-benign view of Vichy, from the date of Chirac's condemnation to Papon's undignified flight and arrest in his hotel bedroom, covered the same period of time as the brief birth and death of Vichy itself. There had been no civil disorder, as Mitterrand predicted, only a sentiment of shame and sadness. Majority opinion in France, once it had been given proper access to the truth, now uses the word 'crime' in relation to Vichy reflexively, although the description was considered provocative when this book was written in 1990. The impression has been left that half a century has been wasted in a sterile argument, contributing to a loss of faith in France's human rights commitment by all its minority religious and racial communities.

At the heart of this damage was a persistent, relentless attempt to rehabilitate Philippe Pétain and isolate him from responsibility in the Jewish deportations. In his defence, it was often pointed out that he never mentioned Jews directly in his speeches or broadcasts nor did he make any recorded anti-Semitic remarks. This discretion conveniently covered over his personal choice of Raphaël Alibert to draw up the Statut des Juifs. In August 1940, at the height of his powers, the Maréchal could have objected to discriminatory projects as the initiative was an open secret from the moment the regime was created. Within six weeks of Pétain's assumption of power, the official Vichy news agency prepared the public for reforms instituted two months later. A document emanating from the Justice Department was published in all newspapers, announcing the intention to introduce fast-track discriminatory legislation even before the Nazis had drawn up their own programme.

Extracts of the statement in *Les Temps*, Pétain's daily reading, stated:

> Inter-France, attached to the Vichy government, has demanded in an article the promulgation of a special statute for Jews in France. The Jewish question is said to be a burning one since Jews were not only tolerated but promised a role in the state. The article points to the growing control of Jews in the medical and judicial professions, in the radio and in cinema.
>
> It protests against the Popular Front Government which allowed Jews from Germany, Austria, Poland and central Europe to enter France by their thousands. This is why the French people feel more and more rancour against Jews. The question must be resolved in its totality by a special statute and the introduction of quotas. In cancelling the 21 April 1939 decree which protected Jews under the pretext of a threat to national unity, the press must be given the freedom to denounce the pernicious activities of Jews.

All the laws that isolated and identified Jews before the big round-ups dated back to the two years when Pétain's authority was unchallenged, even by Germany. The personal oath of loyalty from all high-level functionaries after the 'ill wind' speech of 1941, and endorsement of the Milice's 'Jewish leprosy' oath of 1943, bound him intimately to the savage treatment of the vulnerable minority.

De Gaulle himself, in describing Pétain's old age as a 'shipwreck', contributed to the belief that the Maréchal was near-senile and easily manipulated. His medical records disappeared with the death of Ménétrel, but there is ample visual contemporary evidence of a vigorous leader in Vichy newsreels showing an alert and physically active Head of State undertaking marathon trips among ecstatically loyal crowds as late as summer 1944. A personal view of the Maréchal's state of health, at least until the German occupation of the Free Zone in November 1942, was given to me by Jean Borotra, the vice-president of the Association to Defend the Honour of Pétain. The pre-war tennis champion was Commissioner-General for Sport under Darlan.

> Pétain had personal control over his ministers and interviewed them alone when he appointed them. He was impressively fit and his faculties were sharp but it was his attention to minor details that surprised me the most. Pétain took a close interest in the athletes' oath which I had been asked to draw up as part of the National Revolution. This was the basis of a physical education programme which I believed was intended to prepare French youth for a new army in defiance of German orders. In a private interview he read through the oath with me and told me what changes had to be made. He took advice from nobody.

On the question of whether Pétain was kept in ignorance of the fate of the Jews, Borotra supported a theory that it was possible to be at the centre of Vichy and have no idea of the severity of policies outside the spa town – an argument also put forward by François Mitterrand. Until he was arrested and deported in 1942 for trying to join the Resistance, Borotra spent his leave in his flat in Paris's Avenue Foch, next door to the SS Jewish Affairs section run by Dannecker and Röthke. Despite being in Paris during La Grande Rafle and the Free Zone deportations, Borotra was taken aback fifty years later when told that Pétain had approved the arrests and the transfer of Jews into German hands. 'I have learned something for the first time,' he said.

If Pétain had protected France's most vulnerable minority at the risk of his life and freedom, he would have been thought of today as an even greater hero than the soldier who triumphed at Verdun. Instead, in a country that revered its leader, millions were persuaded that Jews were a lesser species who merited the callous laws. From a soldier of such stature, a word of disapproval would have brought Bousquet's cold and efficient deportation programme to a full stop; a gesture of disgust would have halted the violence in French concentration camps; a military order or the effacement of the anti-Semitic clause in the personal oath would have shown the Milice a nobler meaning of patriotism. A secret command passed through the provincial administration might have made zealous civil servants like Papon delay carrying out instructions instead of seeking approval from the Nazis for their bureaucratic efficiency.

When giving evidence at Pétain's trial, the 1940 Prime Minister, Paul Reynaud, said that the French people had been deceived by the Vichy leader and that the whole country had become a victim of his pride. 'In this affair, we are all guilty – we worked to make him divine,' he said. Others struggled to come to terms with the monumental betrayal, but predicted that there would never be a consensus on the Vichy leader's responsibility and that the argument would go on from century to century. François Mauriac, the Nobel literary prizewinner, wrote: 'Whatever happens, for everyone, admirers or opponents, he will remain a tragic figure, halfway between treason and sacrifice.'

After the changes in French policy during the last decade of the twentieth century, it would be impossible to make such an ambiguous judgement today and it was never shared by Jews. In preparing this book, it became clear that there was no statute of limitations for grief, that the pain of the Jewish community, worsened by post-war hypocrisy, would be passed on from generation to generation until infinity. There was no sympathy among Jews for the argument that it was revengeful to punish old men for distant cruelty while many of his victims, some of them far older than Pétain, still suffered in their bodies and minds. Half a century had passed and parents still wept for their murdered children. Sons and daughters still felt the agonising loss of fathers and mothers who died by gassing. The old, the poor, the crippled and insane still underwent daily anguish from the relics of torture, starvation and humiliation inflicted by a Christian country they thought would protect them. Their descendants will weep and remember at memorial services for decades to come.

For Jews, there is no need to find evidence on who to blame for this great crime against humanity. They only have to consult the two Statuts des Juifs which begin with the words: 'Nous, Maréchal de France, chef de l'Etat français', and end with the signature: Philippe Pétain.

Chronology of Vichy's Jewish Persecution

1940

16 July: Review of Jewish naturalisation.

27 August: Act forbidding racial insults abrogated.

27 September: All Jews in northern zone submitted to a census. Jewish shops forced to announce 'entreprise Juive' in their windows.

3 October: Cabinet approves first Statut des Juifs.

4 October: Law authorises internment of foreign and stateless Jews.

18 October: All Jewish businesses obliged to employ an aryan administrator.

1941

29 March: Creation of Commissariat-Général aux Questions Juives.

26 April: Administrators given right to sell Jewish property to aryans.

14 May: 3747 men rounded up in Paris's first mass arrests.

2 June: Second Statut des Juifs.

20–23 August: 4230 Jews, including French, arrested and sent to the newly opened Drancy camp.

2 June: Jews in Free Zone submitted to a census.

22 July: All Jewish influence in national economy removed.

13 August: Jews banned from owning radios.

17 December: Jewish community fined a billion francs for anti-German activities.

1942

7 February: Curfew on all Jews from 8 p.m. to 6 a.m.

10 February: Jews denied right to change their names.

12 March: First deportation train leaves for Germany.

8 July: Jews denied access to all entertainment. Shopping hours restricted to between 3 p.m. and 4 p.m. Forced to ride in last wagon in Paris Métro.

16–17 July: La Grande Rafle.

19 July: First French deportees gassed at Auschwitz.

11 November: All identity cards stamped with 'Juif' or 'Juive' after Germans occupy Free Zone. Last of forty-five deportation trains for the year leaves from Drancy. The year's total of deportees reaches 41,951.

1943

February–December: Seventeen deportation trains, with 17,069 Jews, leave Drancy.

1944

January–August: Twelve more trains, with 14,830 deportees, leave Drancy and Lyons, bringing the total to 73,853. The final figure of 75,721 recorded by Serge Klarsfeld includes 1868 Jews sent to Germany by other means.

Jewish Statute: 3 October 1940

Article 1: Will be regarded as Jewish for the purposes of this law anyone born of three grandparents of the Jewish race or of two grandparents if the spouse is also Jewish.

Article 2: The access to or the exercise of public functions and mandates enumerated below are forbidden to Jews:
1. Head of State, member of the Government, State Council, Council of the national order of the Légion d'honneur, supreme appeal court, accounts court, mining corps, bridges and roads corps, appeal courts, tribunals, justices of the peace, and all elected professional bodies and assemblies.
2. Officials dependant on the foreign affairs department, secretaries general of ministerial departments, directors general of ministerial central administrations, prefects, under-prefects, secretaries general of préfectures, inspectors general of administrative services in the interior ministry, civil servants of all ranks attached to all police services.
3. Residents general, governors general, governors and secretaries general, inspectors of colonies.
4. Members of the teaching corps.
5. Army, navy and air officers.
6. Administrators, directors, secretaries general in businesses benefiting from concessions and subsidies granted by a public body, posts nominated by Government in general interest enterprises.

Article 3: The access and exercise of all public functions other than those listed in Article 2 are closed to Jews who cannot claim one of the following conditions:

a. Holder of the 1914–18 veterans' card or having been decorated during the 1914–18 campaign;

b. Having been decorated during the 1939–40 campaign;

3. Having been decorated with the military Légion d'honneur or the Médaille militaire.

Article 4: Access to and exercise of liberal professions and independent professions, functions dependent on ministries and judicial auxiliary jobs are open to Jews as long as public administration regulations on their proportion have not been fixed. In this case, the regulations will determine the condition on which surplus Jews will be eliminated.

Article 5: Jews will not be allowed to exercise the following professions:

Directors, managers, editors of newspapers, magazines and news agencies with the exception of strictly scientific publications.

Directors, administrators, managers of businesses related to the fabrication, printing, distribution and presentation of films; film directors, artistic directors, scriptwriters . . . theatre, cinema and entertainment . . . and radio managers.

Article 6: Jewish functionaries mentioned in Articles 2 and 3 will cease working in the two months following the promulgation of this law.

Second Jewish Statute:
2 June 1941

Article 1: Will be considered as Jews:

1. Anyone, belonging to whatever religion, who is born of three grandparents of the Jewish race, or of two only if the person is born of two grandparents of the Jewish race. Will be regarded as of the Jewish race if the grandparent belonged to the Jewish religion.

2. Anyone who belongs to the Jewish religion, or who belonged before 25 June 1940 . . .

After listing the same banned professions as in the first statute, the new law continues:

Article 4: Jews cannot exercise a liberal profession, or a commercial, industrial or craftsman's profession . . .

Article 5: Jews are banned from the following professions: banker, change agent . . . advertising agent, estate agent, commercial negotiator . . . forest manager, casino operator, publisher . . .

Article 9: Without prejudice to the prefect's right to intern in a special camp, even if the person is French, (contraventions) will be punished by:

1. Six months to two years in jail and fines of 1000 francs to 10,000 francs . . . for any Jew who exercises a forbidden activity . . .

2. A year to five years in jail and fines of 1000 francs to 20,000 francs for any Jew who evades or tries to evade the present law by untrue declarations or fraudulent manoeuvres.

NOTES

1. The Dreyfus Affair was considered politically dangerous until 1975 when a ban on film and TV documentaries was lifted.
2. There was no pre-war census of Jews. Estimates for those in wartime are based on Vichy and Nazi censuses of 1940 and 1941. Several thousand Jews with aryan names did not register or used false papers.
3. Mendès France's premiership lasted from June 1954 to February 1955.
4. In 1934, Pétain told a defence inquiry that the Ardennes sector could be left lightly defended as German tanks could not penetrate the very forest through which they broke in 1940. In 1939, he praised a book called *Une Invasion – est elle encore possible?* which declared that it was impossible to pierce the French defence system.
5. Quoted by Pétain's aide, Henri du Moulin de Labarthète.
6. From André Halimi's *Délation sous l'Occupation* (see Bibliography).
7. Quotations are from Gestapo documents held in the Jewish Contemporary Documentation Centre (CJDC) in Paris. The documents were abandoned in the avenue Foch offices at the Liberation but were not fully sorted and numbered until more than thirty years later.
8. Quoted from Lucien Steinberg's *Les Allemands en France* (see Bibliography).
9. Interview in *Historia*, 1972.
10. See Marrus and Paxton, *Vichy France and the Jews* (see Bibliography).
11. Evidence gathered by Michael Slitinsky in Bordeaux for the private prosecution of Maurice Papon.
12. The names of every Jew sent to Germany are contained in *The Memorial to the Jews Deported from France*, a 660-page book published by the Beate Klarsfeld Foundation, New York.

BIBLIOGRAPHY

Abitbol, Michel, *Les Juifs d'Afrique du Nord sous Vichy,* Maisonneuve et Larose, Paris, 1983

Amouroux, Henri, *La Vie des Français sous l'Occupation,* Fayard, Paris, 1961

——, *Quarante Millions de Pétainistes,* Robert Laffont, Paris, 1977

Aron, Raymond, *Memoires: 50 ans de reflexion politique,* Julliard, Paris, 1983

Aron, Robert, *Histoire de Vichy,* Arthème Fayard, Paris, 1954

Azéma, Jean-Pierre, *De Munich à la Libération,* Seuil, Paris, 1979

——, *Le Parti Communiste français des années sombres,* Seuil, Paris, 1986

——, Jean-Pierre and Wieviorka, Olivier, *Vichy,* Perrin, 2000

Badinter, Robert, *Libres et Equax,* Fayard, Paris, 1989

Bleustein-Blanchet, Marcel, *Mémoires d'un lion,* Perrin, Paris, 1988

Boegner, Marc, *L'Exigence oecumenique,* Albin Michel, Paris, 1968

Boegner, Philippe, *Ici on a aimé les Juifs,* J.C. Lattes, Paris, 1982

Bourdet, Claude, *L'Aventure incertaine de la Resistance,* Stock, Paris, 1975

Bulawko, Henry, *Les Jeux de la mort et de l'espoir,* Encres, Paris, 1980

——, *Les Juifs face au Nazisme,* CRTF, Paris, 1985

Burrin, Philippe, *La Dérive fasciste,* Seuil, Paris, 1986

Calef, Henri, *Le Sabordage de la IIIe République,* Perrin, Paris, 1988

Chauvy, Gerard, *Lyon des années bleues,* Plon, Paris, 1987

——, *Lyon 40–44,* Plon, Paris, 1985

Coutau-Begarie, Hervé and Huan, Claude, *Darlan,* Fayard, Paris, 1989

Déat, Marcel, *Memoires politiques,* Denoël, Paris, 1989

Duquesne, Jacques, *Les Catholiques françaises sous l'Occupation,* Grasset, Paris, 1988

Duroselle, J.B., *L'Abîme 1939–1945,* Imprimerie Nationale, Paris, 1982

Ferro, Marc, *Pétain,* Fayard, Paris, 1987

Girard, Patrick, *La Revolution Française et les Juifs,* Laffont, Paris, 1989

Graetz, Michel, *Les Juifs en France au XIXe siècle,* Seuil, Paris, 1982

Halimi, André, *La Délation sous l'Occupation,* Alain Moreau, Paris, 1984

Hyman, Paula, *De Dreyfus à Vichy,* Fayard, Paris, 1985

Jacob, François, *La Statue intérieure,* Seuil, Paris, 1987

Johnson, Paul, *A History of the Jews,* Weidenfeld & Nicolson, London, 1987

Klarsfeld, Serge, *Vichy–Auschwitz 1 & 2,* Fayard, Paris, 1983, 1985

Kupferman, Fred, *Laval, 1883–1945,* Balland, Paris, 1989

Lacouture, Jean, *Léon Blum,* Seuil, Paris, 1977

Lazare, Lucien, *La Résistance juive en France,* Stock, Paris, 1987

Lottman, Herbert, *L'Epuration,* Fayard, Paris, 1986

Lustiger, Jean-Marie, *Le Choix de Dieu*, De Fallois, Paris, 1987

Marrus, Michael and Paxton, Robert, *Vichy France and the Jews*, Schocken, New York, 1983

Ory, Pascal, *Les Collaborateurs 1940–1945*, Seuil, Paris, 1976

Paxton, Robert, *La France de Vichy*, Seuil, Paris, 1973

Péan, Pierre, *Une jeunesse française: François Mitterrand, 1934–1947*, Fayard, 1994

Rajsfus, Maprice, *Jeudi Noir*, L'Harmattan, Paris, 1988

——, *Drancy*, Manya, Paris 1991

Rayski, Adam, *Nos Illusions perdues*, Balland, Paris, 1985

Rimbaud, Christiane, *L'Affaire du Massilia*, Seuil, Paris, 1984

Shirer, William, *The Collapse of the Third Republic*, Pan, London, 1969

Steinberg, Lucien, *Les Allemands en France*, Albin Michel, Paris, 1980

Sternhell, Zeev, *Ni droite, ni gauche*, Seuil, Paris, 1983

Veillon, Dominique, *La Collaboration*, Livre de Poche, Paris, 1984

Webster, Paul, *Mitterand*, Félin, 1995

Wieviorka, Annette, *Ils étaient Juifs, résistants, communistes*, Denoël, Paris, 1986

INDEX

PICTURE ACKNOWLEDGEMENTS

Bundesarchiv page 5 above. CDJC pages 3 above, 6 below left and right, 7 above. Dild archiv page 5 below, 6 above. Documentation Française page 7 below. Hulton-Deutsch page 1. Musée de la Guerre, Paris page 2 above. All other pictures are from the author's own collection.

GITTA SERENY ·

Albert Speer: His Battle with Truth

Papermac £12.00

After twelve years of research and writing after Speer's death, *Albert Speer: His Battle with Truth* is one of the most intimate and best-informed books on Hitler and the Third Reich.

Albert Speer was Hitler's architect before the Second World War. Through Hitler's great trust in him, and Speer's own genius for organization, he effectively became the second most powerful man in the Third Reich. Sentenced to twenty years' imprisonment in Spandau Prison at the Nuremberg Trials, Speer attempted to progress from moral extinction to moral self-education. How he came to terms with his own acts and his real culpability in Nazi war crimes are the questions at the centre of this book.

'This is a book not to be missed by anyone interested in Nazi Germany or, for that matter, in the complexity of human behaviour.'
Alan Bullock

RON ROSENBAUM

Explaining Hitler:
The Search for the Origin of his Evil

Papermac £12.00

Ron Rosenbaum spent most of a decade investigating the attempts of historians, psychologists, philosophers, artists and theologians to understand the man who stands at the dark heart of the twentieth century.

Through face-to-face encounters with brilliant and controversial explainers such as Hugh Trevor-Roper and Daniel Goldhagen he shows how the meanings we attach to Hitler reveal hidden beliefs about human nature and the notion of evil.

In a brilliant and controversial study, the author illuminates the surprising and revealing ways in which the quest to explain Hitler has become the quest to understand ourselves.

'A truly brilliant book.'
Frank McLynn, *Irish Times*

'Intriguing, thought provoking and intelligent.'
Guardian

'Professor Rosenbaum . . . has produced a work of
importance and fascination.'
George Steiner

ROBERT SERVICE

Lenin

Papermac £12.00

Lenin is a colossal figure whose influence on twentieth-century history cannot be underestimated. Robert Service has written a calmly authoritative biography on this seemingly unknowable figure.

Making use of recently opened archives, he has been able to piece together the private as well as the public life, giving the first complete picture of Lenin. This biography simultaneously provides an account of one of the greatest turning points in modern history. Through the prism of Lenin's career, Service examines the origins of the USSR and casts new light on the nature of the state and society which Lenin left behind.

'Vivid and readable. This is a splendid book, much the best that I have ever read about Lenin . . . I was overwhelmed by the power and vividness of this portrait.'
Dominic Lieven, *Sunday Telegraph*

'Lenin's life was politics, but Service has succeeded in keeping Lenin the man in focus throughout . . . This book deserves a place among the best studies of one of the most fascinating figures in modern history.'
Harold Shukman, *The Times*